D1300561

ECONOMIC POLICY
AND PROJECTS

ECONOMIC POLICY AND PROJECTS

The Development of a Consumer Society in Early Modern England

by

JOAN THIRSK
*Reader in Economic History
in the University of Oxford*

1978

CLARENDON PRESS · OXFORD

Oxford University Press, Walton Street, Oxford OX2 6DP

OXFORD LONDON GLASGOW NEW YORK
TORONTO MELBOURNE WELLINGTON CAPE TOWN
IBADAN NAIROBI DAR ES SALAAM LUSAKA
KUALA LUMPUR SINGAPORE JAKARTA HONG KONG TOKYO
DELHI BOMBAY CALCUTTA MADRAS KARACHI

ISBN 0 19 828274 5

*Set by Hope Services, Wantage
and Printed in Great Britain by
Billing & Sons Ltd., London,
Guildford and Worcester*

PREFACE

If brevity be the soul of wit, it is also the essence of the Ford
Lectures. And having pruned my text to compress a large
subject into a small compass, I have resisted the temptation
to expand it again in print. I therefore offer these lectures
much as they were given, with the addition of one concluding
chapter, setting my subject in a wider economic context.

I am deeply grateful to the Electors for having invited me
to give the Ford Lectures at Oxford in Hilary term, 1975. I
did not have a ready-made subject to hand, but I was
developing an interest in the new industries and new kinds of
employment that came into existence in the late sixteenth
and seventeenth centuries. I had already explored stocking
knitting and tobacco growing, and I was beginning to assemble
a list of other occupations. Moreover, I had recently indexed
a volume of *Seventeenth-Century Economic Documents*, and
this dull task had given me unexpected insights. I was struck
by the frequency of references to consumer goods like brass
cooking pans, cambric, gold and silver thread, hats, knives,
lace, poldavis, ribbons, ruffs, soap, and tape. Instead of
allowing my eye to slide over these trifling items, the task of
indexing made me note them and ponder their significance in
the seventeenth-century economy. I recognized some of them
as consumer goods which had been roundly condemned in
1547 as foreign fripperies that robbed this kingdom of its
bullion. Yet here they were in everyday use in the seventeenth
century, and, what is more, being manufactured in England. I
decided to pursue their origins. In the end, as these chapters
show, I found a deliberate government policy to foster the
native manufacture of consumer goods. It succeeded and had
many unforeseen consequences. Not only did the new occupations offer much employment, they added a new dimension
to the home market by diversifying its wares and expanding
consumption. Ultimately, they taught lessons that under-
mined and transformed the old political economy. When
Adam Smith in the middle of the eighteenth century wrote

that 'consumption is the sole end and purpose of all production', and chose the pin industry as the best example of
the division of labour, he was distilling into a theory the
essence of seventeenth-century experience.

In tracing in these pages economic policy, the emergence
of new industrial and agricultural occupations, and the
evolution of new theories of political economy, I have touched
lightly on many seventeenth-century employments that
plainly deserve more detailed investigation. I would like to
write more about woad growing, starch making, and pin
making, but I hope that others will catch my enthusiasm, and
will think it worth while to investigate numerous other
consumer industries that so far have been almost totally
neglected.

I owe warm thanks to many people who have shared my
interest in this subject as its full dimensions unfolded. My
graduate students, Paul Brassley, Peter Edwards, Peter Large,
Mary Prior, Adrienne Rosen, Malcolm Thick, Barbara Todd,
and Roger Vaughan, were especially alert in collecting
illustrative material. Other colleagues too numerous to name
individually helped me, sometimes unwittingly, to see things
in perspective. But for some of my most telling references I
would like to express particular thanks to Professor Maurice
Beresford, Dr. Maxine Berg, Dr. John Chartres, Mr. J.P.
Cooper, the late Mr. J.W. Gough, Mr. Negley Harte, Mrs.
Carolina Lane, Professor Peter Mathias, Dr. Roger Richardson,
Dr. Paul Slack, and Mrs. Marion Stowell. Last, but most of
all, I thank Dr. Christopher Hill, whose encouragement
induced me to persist with this subject.

JOAN THIRSK

Oxford, March 1977.

CONTENTS

ABBREVIATIONS

AHEW	*The Agrarian History of England and Wales, IV: 1500–1640*, ed. Joan Thirsk (Cambridge, 1967)
APC	Acts of the Privy Council
BL	British Library
CSPD	*Calendar of State Papers Domestic*
DNB	*Dictionary of National Biography*
EcHR	*Economic History Review*
Eng. Hist. Rev.	*English Historical Review*
HMC	Historical Manuscripts Commission
LQR	*Law Quarterly Review*
Oxf. Rec. Soc.	Oxfordshire Record Society
PRO	Public Record Office
RO	Record Office
TED	R.H. Tawney and E. Power, *Tudor Economic Documents* (London, 1924)
Thirsk and Cooper	Joan Thirsk and J.P. Cooper (eds.), *Seventeenth-Century Economic Documents* (Oxford, 1972)
VCH	Victoria County History

I. INTRODUCTION

It is an entertaining, but also an instructive, exercise to identify words that occur frequently in the literature of an age and that seem to evoke its mood and preoccupations. In the sermons and pamphlets of the 1530s and 1540s the two words 'covetousness' and 'commonweal' constantly recur. They are antitheses which illuminate the anxieties and sympathies of their time. The covetousness of rich men obtruded itself and offended thinking men with a social conscience; 'the commonweal' summed up the aspirations of those who sought a new kind of society to replace the old. These men came together to form a sufficiently cohesive group to earn, on one occasion, the name of a Commonwealth party.[1] Their influence upon government was strong under Protector Somerset, and appeared to collapse at his fall. Yet the ideas of the Commonwealthmen retained their hold in governing circles and imposed a deep impress on the economic policies and social legislation of the second half of the sixteenth century.[2] The word illuminates economic and social thought and policy for another sixty years.

Towards the end of the sixteenth century, however, concern for this abstract ideal, the commonweal, switched to more material concerns, and in the seventeenth century two of the key words that characterized the new era were 'project' and 'projector'. Everyone with a scheme, whether to make money, to employ the poor, or to explore the far corners of the earth had a 'project'. The concrete noun is significant. A project was a practical scheme for exploiting material things; it was capable of being realized through industry and ingenuity. It was not an unattainable dream like the commonweal. Yet in effect it did much to promote the commonweal, by creating employment, and dispersing more cash through all

[1] CSPD *1547–80*, 22.
[2] For a discussion of the idea of the Commonweal and its practical implications, see A.B. Ferguson, *The Articulate Citizen and the English Renaissance* (Durham, N.C., 1965), 363 ff. *et passim*.

classes of society. As the projects of the seventeenth century
worked themselves into the economy, they transformed its
structure. They effected a redistribution of wealth: geographically—as new industries and new crops in agriculture
introduced fresh employment and new commercial attitudes
into dark, neglected corners of the kingdom—and socially—as
cash flowed in new channels to reach more of the labouring
classes at the very bottom of the social scale.

At a relatively late stage the success of projects was reflected,
if dimly, in the changing pattern of foreign trade. By the end
of the seventeenth century many projects had become
established industries, making goods that left their mark
upon overseas trade accounts. Whereas cloth had dominated
exports in the sixteenth century, it had to share a place in
the seventeenth century not only with re-exports from the
colonies, but with miscellaneous home-produced wares,
originally designed for the home market, such as knitted
woollen stockings, knitted caps, felt hats, iron cooking pots,
iron frying pans, knives, sword blades, daggers, nails, pins,
glass bottles, gloves, earthen pots, and copper wares, not to
mention some of the specialized products of farms and
market gardens, such as saffron and hops. These articles
represented occupations which had blossomed in the later
sixteenth and seventeenth centuries as projects, sometimes
very humble projects, but were now finding a sale abroad
as well. Between 1660 and 1700 the rate of increase in the
exports of these miscellaneous goods, writes Professor Ralph
Davis, was 'hardly less rapid than the growth of re-exports'.[3]

Overseas trade figures, however, are not a reliable measure
of the importance of projects in the economy, and we shall
diminish their stature if we judge them by that yardstick.
Foreign trade handled a very small part of the nation's total
industrial and agricultural production. In 1688 Gregory King
estimated total production at £48 million, of which exports
represented only £3.4 million, or 7 per cent of the total.[4]
Most of the projects to be investigated here feature among

---

[3] R. Davis, 'English Foreign Trade, 1660—1700', in *Essays in Economic
History*, ed. E.M. Carus-Wilson (London, 1962), ii.261.
[4] B.R. Mitchell and P. Deane, *Abstract of British Historical Statistics* (Cambridge, 1962), 366, 279.

that much larger selection of wares produced for home consumption, worth £44.6 million altogether, and constituting 93 per cent of total production.

The projects under discussion, then, were schemes to manufacture, or produce on the farm, goods for consumption at home. Since they served the domestic market first and foremost, they were distributed through the kingdom without pomp or ceremony, and without leaving any statistical account. Such articles were hawked around the countryside on the backs of pedlars, or stowed by chapmen into pack-saddles, or stacked in bales and loaded on barges that passed down river, or they were stuffed into sacks, pokes, and boxes and consigned to carriers who maintained a regular service on the road with carts and wagons, using the inns as bus-stops. We can never measure the scale of this trade for very few towns have preserved any toll or brokage books. Chapmen, trowmen, higglers, and others distributed these wares more silently and stealthily than the smuggler by moonlight.

Hence although projects supplied an impressive range of goods entering into the ever-expanding network of English internal trade, we have no trade figures by which to measure their significance to the economy. They can be measured only by the amount of work they created. In many cases they did not at the outset provide full-time jobs, but offered a by-employment, especially in rural areas where they afforded an additional source of cash to supplement what people got from their land and rights of common. But that extra bit of cash could turn a mere pittance into a tolerable living. Woad growing, for example, could raise the income of a household from the husband's bare wages of 3s. 4d. a week to 5s. or 6s., by employing his wife and two children, 'to their great comfort', as one contemporary expressed it.[5] A new project in a village could thus transform a miserable collection of beggarly poor into a self-respecting community.

We can perceive the scale of the new employment by looking more closely at the labour demands of two projects. One is woad growing. A great interest in woad growing

[5] R.S. Smith, 'A Woad growing Project at Wollaton in the 1580's', *Trans. Thoroton Soc.* lxv (1961), 41.

developed in the early 1580s, and the crop spread with astonishing rapidity through the southern half of England. To cultivate an acre of woad, it was reckoned that four women and children were needed for one-third of the year.[6] One country gentleman in north Oxfordshire—admittedly the grower of an unusually large acreage—had 100 acres of woad under cultivation in 1586.[7] Thus he gave work to 400 women and children. Yet the parish in which he lived contained only 8 taxpayers in 1523, and 28 householders in 1665.[8] In 1586 the parish cannot have had more than 100 inhabitants of all ages. This woad grower must have been an employer of labour not just from his own village but from the whole neighbourhood.

In the counties of Hampshire, Sussex, and Surrey it was not at all unusual in the 1580s to find growers who had 20, 30, 40, or even 60 or 70 acres under woad, while others in the same village had small plots of one or two acres.[9] Here was work for anything from 100 to 300 people in a single parish, in other words work for far more hands than many parishes could supply. Fifteen acres would probably have been enough to employ most of the idle people in the average township.[10]

We can examine woad growing over a much larger territory. Altogether in twelve southern counties, 4,910 acres were sown with woad in 1586.[11] If we call this 5,000 acres, we can identify work for 20,000 people, earning 4d. a day for four months of the year. This is equivalent to the *total* population of 25 modest market towns of 800 inhabitants apiece, or 100 villages of 200 inhabitants each.[12]

If these calculations begin to sound too theoretical and remote from reality, we can turn to two detailed accounts of woad growing. One relates to an undertaking at Wollaton in Nottinghamshire in 1591 and 1592. Woad occupied 40 acres

    [6] Ibid.
    [7] BL Lansdowne MS. 49, no. 59.
    [8] VCH *Oxon*. ix, 189, 112; *Hearth Tax Returns, Oxfordshire, 1665*, ed. M.B. Weinstock, Oxf. Rec. Soc. xxi (1940), 143.
    [9] PRO E 163/15/1; St. Ch. 5, A 35, 21.
    [10] That is, if we accept Richard Haines's reckoning in 1674 that every parish had about 60 idle people (Thirsk and Cooper, 91.)
    [11] BL Lansdowne MS. 49, no. 54.
    [12] A. Everitt, in AHEW iv. 478.

of Wollaton's fields, and, as was the usual practice, the leaves were picked two or three times in the course of each summer. On the second of these occasions in 1591, the wage bill for two days in August (assuming a wage rate of 4*d*. a day) represented payment to 775 people altogether, i.e. 387 people per day. The bill for the third picking represented the wages of 832 people, while the first picking of the woad leaves in the following year, June 1592, occupied 1,000 people. It is thus not surprising to learn from the same account that the woad gatherers in 1592 were recruited not only from Wollaton, but from Nottingham and five other neighbouring townships, Lenton, Beeston, Chilwell, Radford, and Basford. The three or four hundred people called to work on one day represented three or four times the total population of the average Midland village. The second account of woad growing concerns an enterprise of Lionel Cranfield at Milcote in Warwickshire, where he grew 41 acres of woad in 1626. The name of every labourer was recorded each day. When weeding began on 15 May 158 people were hired; by 19 May the numbers had risen to 231. The average number of workers employed daily in the second half of the month was 224. In June, when weeding and picking went hand in hand, an average of 249 workers worked in the fields each day; in August the average was 145, and in September 136. Nine different townships supplied hands, but the majority came from neighbouring Welford and from Stratford-upon-Avon, with some reinforcements from 'travellers'—migrant labourers, some of whom perhaps arrived for the woad season, while others were vagrants picking up casual work along the road.[13]

Another new occupation that appeared on the scene in the later sixteenth century was stocking knitting. By the beginning of the seventeenth century knitted stockings had become standard articles of clothing, and, if we reckon that the average person wore out two pairs a year (and that is surely a modest estimate), somewhere around 10 million pairs of stockings were needed to dress the whole population. The merchants reckoned that one knitter completed two

[13] Nottingham Univ. Archives, Middleton MSS., Mi A70; Kent Archives Office, U269, A 415.

pairs of stockings per week—a reasonable estimate, for knitting was commonly a by-employment. On this basis the domestic market could have employed about 100,000 people for 50 weeks of the year. Counting one knitter per household, 13 per cent of Gregory King's class of labourers and paupers in 1695 could have supplemented their living by knitting.[14]

Stocking knitting and woad growing are but two of the numerous new occupations that came into existence between 1560 and 1630. To call them 'new' occupations, however, is to use a convenient, shorthand term; it is necessary to define more exactly in what sense they were 'new'. Some were, indeed, entirely novel occupations in England, but others had existed, though hardly more than that, before Elizabeth's reign. Workers, formerly engaged in them, had supplied local needs, but their wares had not reached further afield, often because they were of poor quality. In Elizabeth's reign, however, many of these old occupations took on a new lease of life, producing articles in far greater quantity than ever before. Many factors contributed to their success, but one of the most important was an improvement in the techniques of manufacture or methods of cultivation. This statement will be elaborated below; here it is sufficient to make clear that projects whose economic significance is being measured were of two kinds: some were entirely new; some, through technical advances, were enjoying a new success.

Among these 'new' projects on the industrial side were stocking knitting, button making, pin and nail making, salt making, starch making, soap making, knife and tool making, tobacco-pipe making, pot and oven making, alum mining, ribbon and lace making, linen weaving, the brewing of alegar and beeregar, and the distilling of *aqua vitae*. On the

[14] Thirsk and Cooper, 587, 781. Gregory King made two very different estimates of the number of labouring, cottager, and pauper households in the kingdom. In an earlier article on the stocking knitting industry. ('The Fantastical Folly of Fashion: the English Stocking-Knitting Industry, 1500—1700' in N.B. Harte and K.G. Ponting (eds.), *Textile History and Economic History* (Manchester, 1973), 64) I accepted the figure of 100,000, given in the first draft of King's calculations (see Thirsk and Cooper, 768). I have here adopted the later figure, given in King's final draft, namely 764,000 households (ibid. 781). Gregory King in 1688 also reckoned the 'annual consumption' of stockings at about two pairs per person, i.e. 10 million altogether. See Greater London Council Record Office, Burns Journal, fo. 203. I owe this reference to Mr. Negley Harte.

agricultural side, they included the growing of rape for the sake of the oil; flax and hemp growing, partly for the oil, but more for the making of thread, linen, and canvas; woad, madder, and weld growing for dyes; tobacco growing, flower and vegetable growing, vine growing, and mulberry growing for the feeding of silkworms. Not all these projects were destined to succeed: mulberries and vines, for example, did not live up to their projectors' hopes. But equal enthusiasm and hard work were put into them all, for, in anticipation, all seemed equally capable of achieving success.

Great economic significance must be attached to projects in creating employment in certain rural areas and in certain towns. But their significance does not end there. The combination of all these projects stimulated economic energies that filtered through to the very heart of the national economy, making it beat faster and more strongly. We shall find no clue to their invigorating power so long as we concentrate attention on the well-established economic activities of the sixteenth and seventeenth centuries—wool cloth making, coal mining, iron and lead mining, corn growing, dairying, and meat production. To focus attention here, however, is like viewing England through a telescope stationed half-way to the moon. Only the most conspicuous landmarks are visible. While the principal elements in the national economy stand out clearly, none of the subtle changes within the structure of innumerable local economies can be discerned. Yet it was in scattered and undistinguished communities that new projects first made their quiet entry. Before their appearance in the sixteenth century husbandmen and labourers—two-thirds of village populations at the least—had produced no more than the staple necessities of life: corn, meat, butter, cheese, cloth, and fuel, and then often only in quantities sufficient to meet their own needs. Only the gentry and yeomen of the average parish produced a substantial and regular surplus, not the husbandmen, and certainly not the cottagers and labourers. In short, the majority of the population in many local communities did not begin to accumulate much cash in hand until they began to produce commodities other than the staple necessities of life. When they did so, such commodities might be toys, buttons, pins, or lace, items which politicians labelled as frivolities, as indeed they were. But the truth is that they were the source of that extra cash which made all the difference between a precarious existence and a modicum of comfort.

In broader terms these industrial by-employments heralded the development of a consumer society that embraced not only the nobility and gentry and the substantial English yeomen, but included humble peasants, labourers, and servants as well. It gave them cash and something to spend the cash on, whether it was a brass pot for the kitchen shelf, a colourful pair of striped stockings, or a knitted Monmouth cap. And as these new occupations in bewildering variety appeared in so many townships in the kingdom in the sixteenth and seventeenth centuries, they set the wheels of domestic trade turning faster, encouraging the making of yet more consumer goods, spinning an ever more elaborate web of inland commerce, and increasing the speed with which money circulated. From modest beginnings projects in the end diversified industry and agriculture to an unprecedented degree.

Finally, the truth of the matter dawned upon the political economists, and their essays in the second half of the seventeenth century, discussing ways of promoting the prosperity of the nation, took on a fresh look. They no longer bestowed all their eloquence on overseas trade and the balance of payments. Instead they emphasized the potential benefits of production at home, in manufacturing industry and in systems of farming that employed labour intensively. Their attitude to middlemen also underwent a radical change. Whereas it had been one of the principal maxims of the sixteenth century that middlemen were undesirable and contemptible profiteers, caterpillars that came between the bark and the tree, while another maxim had insisted that entry into many crafts and trading companies must be regulated and restricted if they were to flourish, by the end of the seventeenth century propagandists favoured occupations that employed as many people as possible and promoted trade that passed 'through the hands of a multitude'.

Thus the success of projects taught new attitudes towards labour and labour-intensive enterprises. The examples of the new industries sprang readily to the pens of seventeenth-century political economists, who expatiated upon their merits in employing labour and increasing the wealth of the nation. By the eighteenth century they were commonplaces, and recur frequently as illustrations of Adam Smith's propositions in the *Wealth of Nations*. First of these, of course, was the pin industry, used by Smith to exemplify the economic benefits of the division of labour. But many of Smith's other propositions about industrial organization and his analysis of domestic economic policy can only be fully understood in the light of the lessons taught by successful sixteenth- and seventeenth-century projects, now firmly established as domestic industries and functioning continuously before Smith's own eyes.

But at what date do projects begin? Contemporaries observed the projecting mania and commented upon it at various times in the course of the seventeenth century. No one, however, had a sufficiently wide view, or long enough memory, to trace it back to its beginnings. Daniel Defoe, writing his *Essay on Projects* in 1692–3, placed the beginning of the 'Age of Projects' in 1680, though he admitted that 'it had indeed something of life in the time of the late Civil War'. Like so many of Defoe's confident generalizations, he saw too much novelty in his own day. He was born in 1661. 'The Projecting Age', as he called it, started from the time when he reached nineteen years of age and saw life around him with a new perception. His explanation fastened on the immediate and obvious: it was the losses and casualties inflicted by the war against France that set merchants and traders in search of projects and ingenuities to repair their damaged fortunes. Necessity had been the mother of invention and had induced 'the general projecting humour of the nation'. Merchants, *and* their insurers, he added (for moneyed interests were prominent in Defoe's world of projectors), feeling 'a sensible ebb of their fortunes', racked their wits 'for new contrivances, new inventions, new trades, stocks, projects, and anything to retrieve the desperate credit of their fortunes'.[15]

Defoe glimpsed a small part of the projecting mania and

---

[15] D. Defoe, *An Essay upon Projects* (London, 1887), 31, 19, 11–12, 21.

generalized from it. His view was restricted because his experience at this point in his career was limited. He had started as a hose factor in London. He became embroiled in Monmouth's Rising, and, when it failed, he found it diplomatic to disappear to Spain, where he sold diverse, unspecified wares—'civet cats' according to one unkind contemporary. In 1692 he was back in England, bankrupt, and in prison. Thence he fled to Bristol to escape his creditors, and it was there that he wrote his *Essay on Projects*. In short, Defoe's career so far had taught him something of the intricacies of foreign trade, and this had persuaded him that the world of overseas commerce and negotiation was the best school of training in 'all project, contrivance, and invention'.[16] As he wrote of the golden years since 1680, Defoe fixed his attention on financial and trading projects. And in a sense he was shrewdly percipient: carried along on the rising tide, financial and trading projects increased in number and recklessness, only to be shattered with the South Sea Bubble in 1720.

But there were other kinds of projects, 'in arts, and mysteries, of manufacturing goods or improvement of land', and these are the ones to receive attention here. Defoe mentioned them only cursorily. The example he selected for special praise was the knitting frame, found, he said, 'in every stocking weaver's garret'. The illustration came readily to the mind of this former hose factor, but the date he gave to it was wildly wrong. It was 'contrived in our time', he declared.[17] In fact, it was contrived in 1588, and improved for silk knitting in 1598, nearly a century before Defoe wrote. Plainly, we must dismiss the chronology of Defoe's 'Age of Projects', and look for another beginning well before Defoe was born.

A projector viewing an earlier span of time was Sir Richard Weston. He stood athwart the first half of the seventeenth century, having been born in 1591, and dying in 1652. Some of his projects were agricultural, others were concerned with the improvement of rivers to promote inland trade. Writing a treatise of advice and exhortation to his sons in 1645, he

[16] Ibid. 6–9, 22. A sixteenth-century list (undated) of goods imported from Spain names civet skins. (BL Lansdowne MS. 110/51.)
[17] Defoe, op.cit. 25, 31.

claimed that 'ingenuities first began to flourish in England' fifty years before.[18] This takes us back to 1595. A roughly similar view was advanced by Sir Roger Wilbraham, who noticed correctly an abundance of projects being canvassed at the beginning of James I's reign. His attributed it to the accession of the new king. 'It is the manner, after the death of a long-reigning prince, that by discontented minds or wits starved for want of employment, many new projects, suits, inventions, and infinite complaints are brought to the successor instantly. . .so it happened at this time.'[19]

James I's reign certainly produced plenty of projects, but was it so singularly inventive? Probably not more than Elizabeth's. But it was much more scandalous. In Elizabeth's reign projects became entangled with patents and monopolies. In James's reign the abuses mounted and the parliamentary struggle against them reached its climax, leaving a memory indelibly stamped on the minds of those who survived the Civil War. Charles II was told after the Restoration that patent disputes had cost his father his head.[20] Thus James I was given the credit for inaugurating the age of ingenuities; in fact he was responsible for the worst of the scandals.

Scandals about projects, however, were but the scum on the surface of a healthy current of water that flowed strongly underneath, and it is this current which we must follow. There will be times when it becomes almost indiscernible beneath the mud, froth, and other debris floating on the surface—almost indiscernible, but not totally. Fortunately, the sources of our evidence do not all rise under Westminster Bridge, and no one with the slightest acquaintance with sixteenth-century England would seriously seek the beginning of projects in 1603. The stream of invention and experimentation had been flowing strongly for fifty years before, so much so that even sober courtiers and ministers of the Crown under Elizabeth had been mesmerized by promises of a golden fortune and had joined together—Lord Burghley, Lord Leicester, and Sir Thomas Smith among them—to form the Society of the New Art, promoting a dreamlike project for

---

[18] S. Hartlib, *His Legacie* (2nd edn., London, 1652), 8.
[19] R. Ashton (ed.), *James I by his Contemporaries* (London, 1969), 63.
[20] C. Wilson, *England's Apprenticeship, 1603–1763* (London, 1965), 101.

transmuting iron, lead, and other mineral ores into copper and quicksilver.[21] Projects had so captured the imagination that they even turned the heads of wise men in the 1570s.

Elizabeth's reign, however, produced more solid and enduring schemes than this. Some of them attracted the attention of historians so long ago that they have already earned more than one monograph. There exist good accounts of the government-inspired projects for establishing iron foundries, making glass, mining copper, and making brassware. Other private enterprises, such as nail making and the manufacture of gold and silver thread, have also received the attention of historians. More recently Mr. J. W. Gough in his book on *The Rise of the Entrepreneur* has brought together, in one attractive account, a much larger selection of projects than any earlier writer. But even he does not encompass the full range. How then does one arrive at a full list, and reach back to the first beginnings? If James I's reign bears the stigma of the monopoly scandal, it also deserves credit for showing a more alert, self-conscious interest in the constructive achievements of sober, honest projects. We owe to Edmund Howes, the modest writer who continued John Stow's *Annals of England* into the seventeenth century, but of whom next to nothing is known, our first authoritative list of successful projects.[22] With great care Howes listed as many new crafts and skills as he could discover which were then bearing fruit. He confessed himself unable to identify them all; plainly he knew London best, and fastened on occupations that were based in London or were supported by London merchants and courtiers. Even so the list is impressive.

Spinning on the distaff had been introduced in Henry VII's reign and this had led to the first making of Devonshire kerseys and Coggeshall cloths. The manufacture of Spanish felt hats had been introduced into England in Henry VIII's reign; also the perfecting of gunfounding and making of iron

[21] BL Lansdowne MS. 14/15 gives a summary of the privileges conferred on this company. See also M. Dewar, *Sir Thomas Smith: a Tudor Intellectual in Office* (London, 1964), Ch. 13.

[22] John Stow published his first edition of the *Annals* in 1580, continuing with fresh editions until his death in 1605. When Edmund Howes, thereafter, continued and supplemented Stow's *Annals*, he showed a special interest, not revealed by Stow, in innovations.

ordnance (this last was the one and only innovation mentioned by Stow in his original editions). Howes next listed some of the New Draperies: bays, tufted taffeties, cloth of tissue, wrought velvets, braunched satins, and silk cloth of many kinds. The use of coaches was introduced in 1564, followed by the building of coaches. At much the same time, new ways of making starch and new starching techniques were introduced. The hand knitting of worsted, jersey, and silk stockings followed, along with the introduction of the manufacture of pins, of needles in the Spanish style, of earthen pots and portable ovens on the Spanish model, of fine knives and knife handles, the digging for alum and copperas, and the making of innumerable fashion goods for women such as ruffs, masks, busks, muffs, fans, periwigs, bodkins, and embroidered gloves. Among new crops and foodstuffs introduced in the sixteenth century he named hops, apricots, and pippin apples, the rearing of carp and turkeys, and finally the planting of liquorice and tobacco.

Not all the inventions named by Edmund Howes had started in his lifetime. His information reached back to the early years of the sixteenth century, but the great majority had originated since the beginning of Elizabeth's reign.[23] As we shall see, it was not a complete list, but it was a brave attempt. It will serve as a preliminary guide. If we search for lists at an earlier date in the sixteenth century we find lists of aspirations rather than lists of achievements. We meet the planners, and realize that we are now getting near to the beginnings of projects: many were planned in Elizabeth's reign, none certainly originated in Mary's reign, three or four started in Edward VI's reign, and one or two in Henry VIII's reign. We seem to have reached the source of the stream.

One of the most informative and early drafts of a programme for projects was written in 1549. It is the *Discourse of the Common Weal of this Realm of England*. This treatise, written in the form of a dialogue, discussed the condition of the English economy in a period of financial crisis. Its arguments concerning the causes of inflation have attracted most

[23] John Stow, *The Annales of England...until...1605* (London, 1605), 983–4; *idem, The Annales of England...unto 1614* (London, 1615 edn.), continued by Edmund Howes, 866 ff.

attention from historians in the last forty years, for inflation was the root cause of the 'manifold complaints of men touching the decay of this commonwealth and realm of England'.[24] But we also see the ideas for projects maturing here. Indeed, they may be deemed to have been something of an obsession with their author, Sir Thomas Smith, occupying many pages in all three sections of his *Discourse*.

In Smith's view, England was a producer and exporter of sensible, durable goods such as wool, cloth, fells, leather, tallow, tin, pewter vessels, lead, beer, butter, and cheese. These represented occupations 'requiring the industry of a few persons'. At the same time, England was importing from foreign countries a large range of goods not made at home, or not produced in sufficient quantity. About some there was no dispute: they were essential to the economy, like iron, steel, salt, tar, rosin, pitch, wax, oil, hemp, and flax. Others were arguably essential for civilized life, but were not in the same class as the first group: wines, spices, dyes, linen and silk, fustians, worsteds, coverlets, carpets, arras, tapestry, painted cloths, oranges, pippins, and cherries. Finally, there were haberdashers' wares that might be 'clean spared'—white and brown paper, drinking and looking glasses, window glass, pins, needles, knives, daggers, pouches, hats, caps, brooches, aglets, silk and silver buttons, laces, points, perfumed gloves, dials, tables, cards, balls, puppets, penhorns, inkhorns, toothpicks, earthen pots (elsewhere called gallie pots), and hawks' bells.[25] The list descended from luxuries to frivolities. But why the intense prejudice against them? Of course they wasted treasure but so did all imports. What roused burning indignation was that these frippery things were made from materials cheaply bought in their country of origin, and cost their producers almost nothing but their labour. A deep prejudice lurked against goods that held value only by virtue of the labour applied to them. Gloves, for example, were made up from otherwise valueless offcuts of leather. Fruit grew naturally on the trees, and was there for the taking; it

---

[24] *A Discourse of the Common Weal of this Realm of England* ed. E. Lamond (Cambridge, 1954), 10.

[25] Ibid. 16–17. Aglets are the metal tags of laces. They were at first purely functional, and then became ornamental.

would be eaten and gone in less than a week. Employing the idle to pick the fruit or to sew the small leather scraps to make gloves did not somehow redeem these goods from their original sin—the fact that the raw materials could be had for nothing. An anecdote told by the doctor in the *Discourse* suggests that this prejudice was widely held. An English vessel had once put into Caernarvon with a cargo of apples. The townsmen were so outraged at being offered apples where they had looked for good corn that the town council forbade the inhabitants to buy them, and the cargo lay in the harbour untouched until the apples rotted. The Welsh bailiff lectured the English shipowner thus: his vessel had come to fetch their best Welsh wares: friezes, broadcloth, and wool. How dare he bring them in return goods that 'should be spent and wasted in less than a week'.[26]

Such value-judgements, setting a price upon goods whose raw materials were recognized as having a substantial value, while despising those whose value lay principally in the labour conferred upon them, bring to light concepts that we no longer understand. It was part of a world that was passing away even as Smith wrote his *Discourse*, in which people spared cash only for the purchase of substantial goods that were essential to maintain life and to facilitate work. Now it was becoming possible to indulge in a few luxuries to delight the eye. Elegant clothes and ornaments about the house were catching on rapidly as money circulated more freely. Indeed, the taste for these foreign fashions had taken such a hold within the last twenty years that the streets of central London had been turned into a kind of Carnaby Street of the sixteenth century.

I have seen within these twenty years, when there were not of these haberdashers that sell French or Milan caps, glasses, daggers, swords, girdles, and such things not a dozen in all London. And now, from the Tower to Westminster along, every street is full of them. And their shops glisters and shine of glasses, as well looking as drinking, yea, all manner [of] vessels of the same stuff; painted cruses, gay daggers, knives, swords, and girdles, that is able to make any temperate man to gaze on them, and to buy somewhat, though it serve to no purpose necessary...What grossness be we of, that see it, and suffer such a continual spoil to be made of our goods and treasure by such means?

[26] Ibid. 44–5, 63–9.

And specially that will suffer our own commodities to go and set
strangers on work, and then to buy them again at their hands; as of our
wool, they make and dye kersies, frisadoes, broad cloths, and caps
beyond the seas, and bring them hither to be sold again.[27]

Worse than this was another complaint: London fashions
were not confined to foolish, light-headed Londoners. The
craze had spread to the provinces; the country bumpkin was
no longer satisfied with the goods he could buy in the nearest
market town; he wanted a Spanish girdle or a Spanish knife.
The gentleman insisted on buying his cap, his hose, his shirt,
'his gear', as Sir Thomas Smith trendily expressed it, from
London.[28] All this contributed to the decay of towns and
had to be put right. And the solution? There was but one. If
people would not live without these fripperies, they must be
manufactured within the realm.

The Discourse of the Commonweal expressed the ideas not
of one eccentric man, but of many intelligent and influential
thinkers, preachers, and politicians, who called themselves
Commonwealthmen. The *Discourse* was in some sense a party
programme. Hence the remedies that were suggested in the
third part of the *Discourse*, and which take us to the origin of
projects, also reveal their connection with the Commonwealthmen. If these foreign manufactured goods were made at
home, it was argued,

twenty thousand persons might be set awork within this realm. . .I
think these things might be wrought here, not only sufficient to set so
many awork and serve the realm but also to serve other parts, as all
kind of cloth, kerseys, worsted and coverlets, and carpets of tapestry,
knit sleeves, hosen, and petticoats, hats, caps; then paper, both white
and brown; parchments, vellum, and all kind of leather ware, as gloves,
points, girdles, skins for jerkins; and so of our tin, all manner of vessel;
and also all kind of glasses, earthen pots, tennis balls, tables, cards,
chests (since we will needs have such kind of things); and daggers,
knives, hammers, saws, chisels, axes, and such things made of iron.'[29]

The lists begin to repeat each other. The same articles will
reappear in the lists of skills demanded of foreigners who
were invited to live in England in Elizabeth's reign. As a
result, many foreigners founded projects that later became
established industries. But Englishmen too were just as

---

[27] Ibid. 64–5.   [28] Ibid. 125–6.   [29] Ibid. 126–7.

responsive. Most Elizabethan projectors took their cues from these planners of the 1540s.

In 1549 the list of artificers in England already making the wares listed above, or capable of making them, was short. England had its clothiers, cappers, and worsted makers (though the worsted makers were only recent comers to Norwich), pewterers, and tanners. The other industries, writers agreed, would have to be newly set up 'as making of glasses, making of swords, daggers, knives, and all tools of iron and steel; also making of pins, points, laces, thread, and all manner of paper and parchments'. But it did not mean in all cases a start from scratch. Coventry had once had a flourishing industry, making blue thread, and 'then the town was rich even upon that trade only'. But now all our thread came from overseas, 'wherefore that trade of Coventry is decayed and thereby the town likewise'. Bristol once had a great trade by making points but now no more.[30] Foreigners had stolen a march on the English by perfecting a more satisfactory article. Perhaps it was of finer quality, perhaps it was more attractive to the eye, perhaps it was cheaper—we are not told. But plainly it would not be so difficult to revive the manufacture of some of these goods in places where there were already craftsmen with some skill or memory of the trade.

The following chapters trace the first steps by which the manufacture at home of many of these foreign wares was put in hand. But plans for economic development should not be separated from the social ideals which underlay them, and which forged strong links between the Commonwealthmen and projectors. It is not usual to allow projectors any ideals. The very name became a dirty word in the early seventeenth century, synonymous with rogue and speculator. Fuller, looking back on the age of James I, described projectors then as 'such necessary evils then much countenanced'. Recalling the 1650s John Houghton remembered how 'scarce anyone durst offer for improvements lest he should be called a Projector, as if he came from the fens to borrow 5s. to purchase £5,000 a year'. Projector, wrote Defoe, was a

---

[30] Ibid. 127–8.

'despicable title'. Such men always had 'their mouths full of millions'. Yet projects did not start with this evil reputation.[31]

We have seen how the Commonwealthmen, in the years of Edward VI's reign when their influence was at its height, were advocating the setting up of many new industries. At the same time, they also gained a reputation as friends and helpers of the poor. Earlier, in 1535, we find a compiler of a scheme of public works to provide jobs for paupers, William Marshall.[32] Men were genuinely concerned to find constructive solutions to the problem of poverty. Moreover, as Sir Thomas Smith recognized in his *Discourse*, the foreign goods that found such a ready sale in England, and created so much work, used raw materials that cost next to nothing. In short, they offered a tailor-made solution to the problem of finding work for the poor. Projectors became the strongest allies of the Commonwealthmen in their endeavours to help the poor. We do not have to believe that they were all pure philanthropists. Rather, in the words of those who have described colonial ventures in Africa and India in the nineteenth century,[33] Englishmen found that they did well by doing good. So with the projectors of the sixteenth and seventeenth centuries. They embarked on schemes to line their own pockets, but their projects also provided much-needed work for poor people. The motives of every projector mixed public and private interest in different proportions.

Three representative projectors offer themselves as examples to illustrate these diverse attitudes—selfish at one extreme, perhaps, but almost saintly at the other. Robert Payne was a projector who toyed with many schemes in the 1580s and 1590s. He wrote a booklet in 1583 on draining wet moorland, and another on making ponds on dry land. He wrote yet

---

[31] Ashton, op. cit. 199; John Houghton, *A Collection for the Improvement of Husbandry and Trade* (London, 1692), 76; Defoe, op. cit. 11, 17.

[32] See e.g. DNB *sub* John Hooper, whose liberality to the poor was unbounded, and Nicholas Ridley, who preached before Edward VI at Westminster on the need for better provision for the poor of London; G.R. Elton, 'An Early Tudor Poor Law', in *idem, Studies in Tudor and Stuart Politics and Government*, ii (Cambridge, 1974), 137 ff., esp. 151 ff.

[33] Including my predecessor, Professor J. Gallagher, giving the Ford lectures in 1974.

another treatise encouraging the settlement of English farmers in Ireland, and offered in the same work practical instructions on how to keep rabbits in small warrens. He was actively engaged in developing the spinning of jersey wool for stockings at Wollaton in Nottinghamshire, and in growing woad there as well. The woad-growing project started in 1585, but things did not go smoothly, and in the end quarrels broke out between Payne and his patron, Sir Francis Willoughby. The testimony of hostile witnesses made him out to be a rogue, ready to slide out of every difficult situation with a lie, and move on to the next irresponsible venture. But he talked the language of the commonweal. He wrote a well-informed, factually accurate, and business-like pamphlet on the way to grow woad and the profits it could earn. He described its merits as an employer of labour in eloquent terms;

If we were generally inclined to profit the commonweal as each man is to increase his own private gain, we might well keep continually winter and summer all our poor people on work to their great relief and comfort, whereby not only they might be sustained but also their poor young children trained up in some good and honest exercise, and not still to continue to idleness, the nurse of all vices, leading not only into many mishaps but also to the utter ruin and destruction of themselves and many others.[34]

In all that he said in print, he spoke the truth.

Payne planned to dovetail the spinning of jersey wool with the cultivation of woad in order to keep the poor of Wollaton in work in winter and summer. It was not an unrealistic scheme. Both occupations, as we shall see, were flourishing elsewhere, and would continue to flourish. When the Privy Council banned woad growing for a time, the Nottinghamshire J.P.s received many protests about the injury thereby inflicted on the poor, including those of Wollaton. Woad growing, men averred, had not in any way hindered the clothiers or farmers, as some complained; Wollaton was far from any clothing town or market, apart from Nottingham, and Nottingham itself was populous and had no industry with which to set people to work. Other villages around similarly lacked means of employing the poor. Payne's enterprise employed at least 400 people, so the

---

[34] Smith, op. cit. 27, 34, 40–6.

J.P.s claimed. Their report on his enterprise was entirely favourable and they supported its continuance.[35] Was Payne really just a rogue with a smooth tongue, as his former acquaintances in High Wycombe claimed? Could anyone on this evidence condemn him utterly?

Another projector was John Stratford, a man of many parts, again not easily labelled black or white. He was the younger son of a Gloucestershire gentry family and had to make his own way in the world. He had been brought up in a community in the Vale of Tewkesbury where status was not emphasized, where independent-minded freeholders mixed on almost equal terms with modest parish gentry, and where the whole community bore the burden of many poor and drove no one away. Stratford started to grow tobacco in his native parish in 1619, enlisting the support of all classes: the gentry rented him land for the purpose, tenant farmers grew the crop, and labourers performed the daily tasks of planting, weeding, and harvesting. When tobacco growing was banned, Stratford got into financial difficulties, and was pursued by his creditors. He pleaded for his liberty so that he could earn money to pay them off, and found a group of respected citizens of Winchcombe willing to testify to his diligence in discharging his debts, and his continuing concern to provide work for the poor. When tobacco growing ceased, Stratford turned to growing flax, employing sometimes 200 poor people in a day. One of two petitions to the Privy Council on his behalf bore the signatures of the clerk, bailiffs, and churchwardens of Winchcombe, the other bore the signatures of the parson and two local gentlemen. One of the latter was William Higford, who later wrote advice for his son revealing a strongly paternalist and humanitarian sympathy for his tenantry. The judgement of neighbours such as these surely rescues John Stratford from the charge of complete and utter self-interest.[36]

---

[35] Nottingham Univ. Library, Middleton MSS., M5/165/95.

[36] J. Thirsk, 'New Crops and their Diffusion: Tobacco-growing in Seventeenth-Century England', in *Rural Change and Urban Growth, 1500–1800*, ed. C.W. Chalklin and M.A. Havinden (London, 1974), 81–8, 92; *idem*, 'Projects for Gentlemen, Jobs for the Poor: Mutual Aid in the Vale of Tewkesbury, 1600–1630', in *Essays in Bristol and Gloucestershire History*, ed. P. McGrath and J. Cannon (Bristol and Glos. Archaeolog. Soc., 1976), 147–69; PRO SP 16/57, nos. 14, II and III.

The third example of a projector introduces the Cope family of Hanwell, a village in north Oxfordshire, not far from Banbury. The Copes were gentry in Henry VII's reign when William Cope was King's Cofferer and took up residence at Hanwell. The parish appears not to have had a resident gentleman before the Copes' arrival in 1498 and, given this fact, and the strength of the free tenantry in the Banbury neighbourhood as a whole, it is not unlikely that the parish was burdened with considerable numbers of poor. Lordless parishes with many freeholders tended to attract landless people, just as lordly villages repelled them.[37]

Sir Anthony Cope, the grandson of William Cope, inherited the Hanwell estate from his father, and in the course of his life gained a reputation, inside Parliament and out, as 'a hot Puritan'. He suffered imprisonment in 1587 for introducing a Puritan version of the Prayer Book into the Commons along with a bill for abrogating existing ecclesiastical law. At home he appointed John Dod, a young Cambridge fellow, to the living at Hanwell, entertained many distinguished Puritan divines in his house, and made Hanwell a celebrated Puritan centre to which people flocked from a wide area of the Midlands.[38]

The head of the family in Elizabeth's reign—the 'hot Puritan' Sir Anthony Cope—spoke the language of the commonweal with deep sincerity throughout his life. In 1597 he wrote to Burghley criticizing the weakness of a bill under discussion in the Commons, intended to curb enclosure. The amendments which he suggested were all designed to make the statute work more effectively. 'The execution of the law is the life thereof', he exclaimed, in a characteristic declaration of the zeal felt by all Commonwealthmen to improve the efficiency with which laws were administered. His earnest wish was to ensure that the poor and those who had been injured by enclosure and depopulation were relieved immediately. 'This law promiseth relief in some cases within six years and in other, God knows when', he wrote. The poor needed help now; so why not compel owners of newly

---

[37] VCH *Oxon*. ix, 113. [38] Ibid. 114, 119.

enclosed land to yield up some of their profits in weekly contributions to the poor?[39]

When the Cope family's sympathies with the poor are revealed in this way, the fact that they were also growers of woad on a considerable scale surely sheds a flood of new light on the motives of at least some projectors. In 1585 Sir Anthony Cope was growing 100 acres of woad at Hanwell. In 1616 his son, Sir William, was leasing 2,000 acres of marsh at Wickham Grange in Spalding parish, Lincolnshire, where he also grew woad. He grubbed up bushes, cast down molehills, banked the land against flooding, ploughed and cultivated for woad and corn. He also built woadhouses and woad mills.[40] Sir William is said to have done these things: in fact, of course, he must have employed many labourers to perform these tasks.

Is it straining credulity too far to suggest that the Cope family was growing woad *because* it gave employment to poor people? Sir Anthony Cope criticized the depopulation bill of 1597 because it promised pie in the sky. It promised help to the poor 'within six years' or 'God knows when'. Woad growing provided wages here and now, or, as Robert Payne, our first projector, explained, 'it does great good to the working man who otherwise kept his family on his own bare wages of 3s. 4d. a week.' '[By work in the woad fields] wife and children can bring this up in some periods of the year to 5s. or 6s. a week'.[41] Can we be absolutely convinced that Robert Payne was an arrant knave? Certainly John Stratford and Sir Anthony and William Cope were not.

In the following chapters, industrial and agricultural projects which were begun between 1540 and 1630 will be explored in greater detail. Some have been examined by earlier historians, and call for no more than passing reference. Others that have hitherto been deemed less important will receive more attention. The criteria by which some have been judged more important and others less have been laid down by our menfolk. Starch, needles, pins, cooking pots, kettles, frying pans, lace, soap, vinegar, stockings do not

    [39]   TED i. 86–8.
    [40]   BL Lansdowne MS. 49, no. 59; PRO C2, Jas. I, C22/82.
    [41]   BL Lansdowne MS. 121, no. 21.

appear on their shopping lists, but they regularly appear on mine. They may ignore them, but could they and their families manage without them? It is true enough that iron, glass, brass, lead, and coal were important industries in the nineteenth century, and that their condition in the six-teenth and seventeenth centuries needs investigation. But are we yet sure that they employed as much labour or contributed as much to gross national production in the seventeenth century as the common domestic goods that were liable to turn up in every household in the land?

The purpose of these essays, then, is to construct a more complete list of sixteenth-century projects than that con-sidered hitherto, and to explain the economic policies and circumstances that gave them birth. At the same time, some attempt will be made to give a glimpse of the scattered local communities that nurtured them, and explain how and why they so successfully reared them to maturity. Much of the argument on this score turns upon the quality of the goods produced and upon the classes who purchased them. Hence the title given to Chapter V. Attention will furthermore be given to the changing attitude of political economists towards the production of these consumer goods, which, by Adam Smith's day, were taken for granted in the English home. Many of them had been condemned in the 1540s as childish frivolities or unnecessary, even harmful, indulgences. By the 1670s their expansion was being positively encouraged as a means to employ more labour, and a new moral attitude towards consumer spending took hold. As Carew Reynel put it, when defending the idea of growing tobacco in England instead of banning its cultivation at home and importing it from abroad, 'Some say it is not so good as foreign [tobacco] ; however, if people will take it as they do, and it will go off [i.e. it will sell] , what matter is it?. . .It improves the rent of the land extremely as well as employing great numbers of people. . .and besides the tenant shall make £30 and £40 an acre all charges paid. . .all the objections that are against it cannot vie with the advantages that it produces.'[42] The new consumer society had become respectable.

[42] Carew Reynel, *The True English Interest* (London, 1674), 32–3.

II. THE CONSTRUCTIVE PHASE OF PROJECTS, 1540–1580

A Discourse of the Commonweal (1549) was, in part at least, a programme for the setting-up of new industries and introducing new crops. Another tract of the same year, *Policies to reduce this Realm of England unto a prosperous Wealth and Estate*, contained the same kind of arguments, and evidently reflected the same body of opinion. One chapter was devoted to 'the means to cause many kind of wares to be wrought within this realm which heretofore were wont to be brought from other countries'. The artificers who were promised work were some of the same craftsmen that we have already encountered in the *Discourse*: makers of caps, hats, points, pins, glass, worsted, painted cloths, knives, edge tools, pewter, silk, linen thread and linen cloth, gloves and purses.[1]

When was the policy first seriously initiated? Evidence that projects had already been started, and that new industries were already being set up to make articles formerly imported from abroad, dates not from 1549, the year of the *Discourse*, but a little earlier still, namely the last six years or so of Henry VIII's reign. Iron founding in Sussex is the first and best known; indeed, it was the one innovation of the sixteenth century to be singled out for praise by Stow in the first edition of his *Annals*. In 1540 a rumour was reported to the Privy Council by the English ambassador at the court of the Emperor Charles V that the Dutch were about to petition for a ban on the export of madder, woad, iron, and linen cloth to England. In 1543, at Henry VIII's instigation (so John Stow tells us), Peter Bawd, a French gunfounder, and Peter van Collen, a Dutch gunsmith, were invited to England, and perfected the making of iron guns, mortar pieces, and shot.[2] By 1544 at least 40 French ironworkers were working in the Weald and 3 furnaces were in use at Buxted, Hartfield,

---

[1] TED iii. 311–45, esp. 331–2.
[2] *L. & P. Hen. VIII*, xvi, 1540–41, 75; Stow, *Annales of England* 983. D.W. Crossley's recent edition of the *Sidney Ironworks Accounts, 1541–1573*

and Newbridge.[3] The industry was successfully established in time to serve the needs of Henry VIII in fighting the French. More ironworks were rapidly set up in the next four years until there were said to be over 50 scattered over the Wealden countryside by 1548.[4] In the words of its historian, Ernest Straker, the district had an almost complete monopoly of iron gun casting for the next two hundred years.[5] Grand words, and an impressive achievement. But it is not quite the whole story. If the Wealden ironworkers had depended on selling guns every day of the week they would often have starved. Sensibly, they established a second reputation for the manufacture of more homely wares. A century later, in 1657, if you wanted to set up a humble shop in Barbados and stock it with English goods, you were urged to go to Sussex to buy the small iron pots 'for the negroes to boil their meat'. Thence they could be had 'very cheap and [be] sent to London in carts at time of year when the ways are dry and hard'.[6]

This first example of a project, which was government inspired, prompts two general observations that will help us to interpret others. We know from other evidence that French ironfounders were working at Hartfield in Sussex in 1493, but the expansion of the industry is not evident until 1543–4. It is tempting to think that steady progress was made in Sussex between 1493 and 1543. This is almost certainly wrong. Nearly all new projects settled themselves in a district having some existing connection with the new enterprise. We shall see this well illustrated in the history of

(Camden Soc. 4th Ser. 15, 1975) follows the fortunes of the Robertsbridge and Panningridge ironworks from 1541 onwards. They were set up by Sir William Sidney on a dissolved monastic estate, acquired by him in 1539, and muster rolls show that 49 Frenchmen already lived in the neighbourhood in that year (ibid. 24). Although Mr. Crossley emphasizes the increasing domestic demand for iron at this time, its uses in war seem to have given the industry its prime stimulus (see ibid. 26, 31).

[3] E. Straker, *Wealden Iron* (London, 1931), 47.

[4] Ibid. 119.

[5] Ibid. 49. For the seventeenth-century history of gunfounding in the Weald, and forges making peacetime goods, disparagingly described as 'tinkers' shops', see H.C. Tomlinson, 'Wealden Gunfounding: an Analysis of its Demise in the Eighteenth Century', Ec HR xxix. 3(1976), 383–400, esp. 384–5.

[6] Richard Ligon, *A True and Exact History of the Island of Barbados* (London, 1657), 110.

woad growing and in the history of pin manufacture; here it is revealed in the history of ironfounding. Projects were never bright ideas appearing out of the blue that were put into operation no matter where. They clustered in places where facilities already existed to give the enterprise a promising start. But those facilities were frequently modest and did not have a past history that promised great things for the future. The new expansive phase thus marked an abrupt change of fortune, and yet it had a certain continuity with what had gone before.

This explains why disputes so often broke out later concerning the novelty of projects. The Norfolk weavers claimed that worsteds were not introduced by foreigners but had been made in Norfolk long before their arrival. Pin making was not new in Gloucester in the 1620s; there had been pin makers in the town long before. Woad was grown in England long before the sixteenth century. Both sides in this argument spoke truly. An old occupation *had* existed, but the projecting efforts of the sixteenth and early seventeenth centuries had, in fact, transformed it, either by introducing a new technique, or because changing economic circumstances had given a new stimulus, or both. The new technique might be a relatively small matter of detail, but it saved labour or materials and so reduced costs, or it produced a more attractive article; we cannot always be sure. Changing economic circumstances generally turn out to be a rise in the price of foreign imports, that drove men to produce the same article at home.

The second lesson about projects which is suggested by the ironfounding evidence, and is proved in other examples, is the speed with which a promising economic venture once launched, and apparently successful, was widely adopted. Although French ironfounders *were* already in Sussex in 1493, it is unlikely that they were gradually building up their enterprises until they received the publicity accorded them in the 1540s. It is much more likely that a *new* phase began about 1543 when the foreign gunfounder and the foreign gunsmith came to England at Henry VIII's invitation. The new methods which they introduced transformed the industry almost overnight, because they spread so quickly. Three furnaces were set up in Sussex by 1544; by 1548 there were over 50.

Successful projects spread like wildfire. We shall be able to demonstrate this more effectively in the history of woad growing, starch making, stocking knitting, and tobacco growing. Sometimes it took no more than three or four years, if that, to diffuse enthusiasm and practical skill, and find the adventurers with cash to take the chance. The speed with which news spread, propaganda worked, and projects started, is almost exhilarating to watch. Nor should we underrate the effectiveness of pamphlets and propaganda, the exhortations of the Commonwealthmen, and the official prodding of politicians and Privy Councillors in establishing projects. Official policy statements and public discussions among the Commonwealthmen so often coincided remarkably with what was actually achieved.

Ironfounding is not the only project that can be traced back to Henry VIII's reign. In the *Discourse of the Common-weal*, in a passage in which Sir Thomas Smith deplored the drain of bullion from the kingdom in payment for foreign goods, he mentioned not only iron, but oil and woad *because they cost one-third more in 1549 than in 1542*.[7] We have seen already how iron production started in 1543, because the fear loomed that foreign supplies might be cut off by a sudden edict. Here is a second contributory explanation. Foreign iron was costing too much. This price increase and the threat of an embargo on supplies from abroad almost certainly explain the beginnings of woad growing. Woad for the dyers customarily came in large quantities from the Azores, a Portuguese possession, as well as from France. Most of it was unloaded at Southampton. In the early years of the sixteenth century there was no great incentive to grow it in England, for it was relatively cheap. As two Italians, the Cavalcanti brothers, explained to Henry VIII's ministers, the customs duties on woad were remarkably low—no more than 2 per cent of its value.[8] However, the uncertainty of foreign imports coupled with Henry's debasements of the coinage in the 1540s changed matters radically. It became expensive, and prompted Sir Thomas Smith's complaint in 1549. In

---

[7] *A Discourse of the Common Weal* 16–17.
[8] HMC Salisbury MSS. xiii, 16.

fact, action had already been taken to promote woad growing at home: before 1548 land had already been leased for the crop at Lymington in Hampshire, on the edge of the New Forest close to Southampton. The evidence comes to light in an indenture involving Henry Bretayne, nominally of Monkton, Wiltshire, but surely in origin a Frenchman from Brittany, who had already erected woad mills at Lymington. The deed recording his lease of Hampshire land shows him in company with Thomas Derby, a gentleman of Cranborne, Dorset, who was also secretary of the Council in the West. It is found among manuscripts of the Cecil family at Hatfield House. If Cecil did not have a hand in inspiring this project, a lesser government official was certainly involved, and Cecil was informed about it.[9]

Woad was not an entirely new crop in England at this time. It had been grown in desultory fashion in different parts of the country in the Middle Ages; it was growing in Somerset, for example, in the fifteenth century. But inflation in the later 1540s forced men to reconsider the possibilities of growing more at home. The venture at Lymington in 1548 revealed a partnership between Henry Bretayne from Wiltshire, Thomas Heale of New Sarum in Hampshire, and Thomas Derby of Cranborne, Dorset. Subsequently, these three counties, Hampshire, Wiltshire, and Dorset, ranked among the six principal counties growing woad on a considerable scale in 1585. The other three were Berkshire, Somerset, and Sussex. While it is impossible to measure the spread of the crop in the intervening years, all the evidence points to a period of sluggish growth from the 1550s, followed by a sudden upsurge of popularity in the 1580s which astounded and also puzzled onlookers. The first experiments *circa* 1548 had not run into the sand. They had inspired confidence that the crop could succeed, for woad growing received outspoken public encouragement in 1559. The committee which drew up a programme of legislation for Parliament in that year numbered woad among its promotion schemes. If woad growing were extended 'as by some men's diligence it is already practised', it said, Englishmen would no longer have to rely on French woad, and, after all, 'no country robbeth England so much as France'.[10] Among the compilers of this legislative programme, it should be noted, were Sir Thomas Smith, author of the *Discourse of the Commonweal*, and Nicholas Bacon, William Cecil's brother-in-law.

In the late 1570s woad growers in England received even stronger encouragement for their efforts. Another substantial rise in the price of foreign woad took place, bemoaned by Hakluyt in 1579.[11] It represented such a threat to English supplies of dyestuffs that, in the same year, the Privy Council initiated an inquiry into indigo as a substitute for woad, which it hoped to procure from Muscovy and Persia.[12] The quarrel between Spain and the Netherlands further aggravated matters, by disrupting the supplies of Portuguese woad reaching the English clothiers. Spanish correspondence in the early 1580s shows that woad passing from the Azores to Antwerp was suspected of being used to pay for arms and ammunition for the Dutch rebels. On one occasion in 1581 Spanish agents were alerted in English ports to seize a woad ship that was expected to seek shelter there from the bad weather.[13] These several developments explain why woad cultivation suddenly surged forward in the years 1583 and 1584, arousing such alarm among the farming fraternity that a government inquiry was set up in 1585. Other contributory factors were a drastic fall in the price of grain in 1583 and 1584, which dropped on average by 25 per cent. Farmers complained that rents remained at their former level, yet they were prohibited from exporting bread-corn;[14] it is not surprising that they turned to a much more profitable crop. Woad growing had become almost too successful. It was growing in 1585 in at least twelve counties, occupying

[10] TED i. 329–30.

[11] TED ii. 52.

[12] J.B. Hurry, *The Woad Plant and its Dye* (London, 1930), 63. Instructions written by Richard Hakluyt to an agent, sent to Persia to study dyeing in 1579, are instructive. See TED ii. 51–3.

[13] *Calendar of Letters and State Papers. . .in the Archives of Simancas, iii, Elizabeth, 1580–86*, 71, 73.

[14] BL Lansdowne MS. 49, nos. 51 ff., esp. no. 58, fo. 139[v].

nearly 5,000 acres of land, and employing 20,000 men, women, and children for four months of the year.[15]

The *Discourse of the Commonweal* had remarked that foreign iron, oil, and woad, among other things, cost one-third more in 1549 than in 1542. The stimulus thereby given to domestic iron and woad production has been described. But it does not seem that any substitutes for olive oil presented themselves at that time, though there is plentiful evidence that they had become a serious quest by the 1570s, when the second round of price increases for foreign imports took place. The production of coleseed or rape then began to be energetically pursued, although it did not achieve marked success until about twenty years later, when the schemes for draining the fens started, and coleseed proved itself ideally suited to such soils. Domestic oil production thus made notable progress in the period 1570–80, and will be more fully considered in Chapter III. In the intermediate period the trail of the policy-makers who formulated the programme of projects must be followed, in order to show how they kept it on the agenda throughout the reigns of Edward, Mary, and Elizabeth.

Ironfounding and woad growing furnish the first and most substantial evidence of the projectors' interest, initiative, and *success* in promoting new occupations. An undated document, which, because of what followed, must be dated to Edward VI's reign, put forward a list of foreign industries that were deemed most suitable *for employing the poor*. Because of that last phrase, it may be associated with the Common-wealthmen and perhaps with the period of Somerset's rule. It was evidently written by someone who was familiar with the industrial scene in several European countries, and it put forward four proposals.[16] The first suggestion was to manufacture fustians, made of linen thread and cotton, in England. Fine quality fustians, it explained, were made in Milan, using cotton from Asia Minor; coarse fustians were made in Germany and Holland, with cotton from Africa and other Portuguese territories. To set up such an industry in

---

[15] Ibid., no. 54.   [16] BL Lansdowne MS. 110, no. 50.

England, the writer emphasized, it was essential to secure a regular supply of imported cotton.[17] The second suggestion was for the manufacture in England of worsteds, like those made at Valenciennes; these foreign cloths, it was said, already made use of wools from northern England as well as wools from the Baltic countries. The raw material in this case would not have to be imported. The third suggestion was for a linen cloth and canvas industry, which could be furnished with flax and hemp grown in England and Ireland. The fourth suggestion was for the working of iron and steel into manufactured goods. Here again, the writer pointed out, it was not necessary to count entirely on English metals for this purpose. They could be imported, following the example of other countries, which based their metalworking industries on imports.

This proposal introduced new principles on which industries might be set up in England. They might use raw materials drawn from other countries. It was a new lesson for the English to learn, and it was taught by observations made abroad. Men noticed that Italian and Antwerp silk makers, for example, relied on importing raw silk. Nearer home they noticed that English wool was being used to make foreign cloth, caps, and kersies; our skins—sometimes just leather offcuts—made Spanish gloves and girdles; our tin made foreign salt cellars, spoons, and dishes; our old rags made the Frenchman's white and brown paper. Even old shoes found a ready sale in France, presumably to be refurbished with new leather.[18] All these manufactures were then imported into England again at large expense. The possibilities for English industrial development were greatly enlarged when these truths about European industrial successes were borne in on English travellers abroad. Why did it happen in the 1540s?

Such ideas cannot sensibly be separated from the intellectual ferment which brought English humanists, including many holding posts in government, into contact with continental

[17] There is a tantalizing reference in a document of 1586 (concerning a paper making venture) to John Hales's scheme for making fustians in England, which, the author alleged, failed because of the actively hostile reactions of foreign competitors. (PRO SP 12/195, no. 132.)

[18] *A Discourse of the Common Weal* 63.

reformers and politicians. Humanists were men with a desire to use their intellectual gifts and knowledge for beneficent, practical ends. As Thomas Starkey—a humanist who studied in Padua and canvassed for a government post on his return to England in 1534—put it, 'In diverse kinds of studies I have occupied myself, ever having in mind this end and purpose at the last here in this commonalty where I am brought forth and born, to employ them to some use.' He pleaded for 'some part help [in] the restitution of the true common-weal'.[19]

The flow of cultural ideas which the humanists promoted was thus matched by an equally strong flow of ideas from abroad concerning economic and social policies. The practical consequences of those ideas have not yet been fully explored. Professor Elton has brought some of the evidence to light, in connection with foreign schemes of poor relief that were publicized in England by William Marshall, who then drew up his own scheme for the country.[20] Dr. Paul Slack has given a glimpse of social measures borrowed from abroad in the instruction from the Privy Council to English admini-strators of towns in 1543 that they should combat the spread of epidemics by first discovering, and then adopting, measures used in European towns.[21] Intelligent Englishmen were being exhorted to travel in Europe keeping their eyes and ears open.[22] The history of sixteenth-century projects in industry and agriculture demonstrates at every turn how Englishmen took these exhortations to heart, turning regularly to European countries for their models of economic advancement.

But who were the leading personalities in government who

---

[19] W.G. Zeeveld, *Foundations of Tudor Policy* (Cambridge, Mass., 1948), 46; F. Caspari, *Humanism and the Social Order in Tudor England* (Chicago, 1954), 111.

[20] Elton, *Studies in Tudor and Stuart Politics and Government*, ii, 137 ff.

[21] The Privy Council urged 'such of you as have travelled in outward parts to set forth such devises to be put in operation among you for avoiding the danger of contagion as ye have seen there kept'. (Corporation of London RO, Journal xv, fo. 49ᵛ.) I owe this reference to Dr. Paul Slack who cites it in his thesis, 'Some Aspects of Epidemics in England, 1485–1640', Univ. of Oxford D. Phil. (1972), 266.

[22] Indeed, throughout the world. For an excellent illustration, see TED II. 51–3.

watched over the early policy of projects? The most prominent men seem to have been Sir Thomas Smith and William Cecil. Sir Thomas Smith had originally embarked on an academic career at Cambridge but was drawn into court and government circles between 1540 and 1546. On the death of Henry VIII he finally moved from Cambridge and became a politician by entering the service of the future Duke of Somerset, Lord Protector under Edward VI. Smith thus declared himself a dedicated Commonwealthman. William Cecil was slightly younger but he was also at Westminster, training for government in the 1540s, and was ready to accept the post of secretary to Protector Somerset when it was offered to him in 1547. His later interest and support for projects was so clearly manifest when he became Elizabeth's servant that it was surely germinating in these years.[23] His method of informing himself on foreign developments in industry and agriculture, his retention of advisers and fact-finders who combed England and Europe and drew up reports on the feasibility of domestic projects, all bear strong traces of a method derived from the years of Thomas Cromwell's administration. Cecil pushed the method further, but the fundamental approach was the same.

Throughout his later career, William Cecil upheld the ideals of the Commonwealthmen and was deeply engaged in promoting projects. In his work and in that of Sir Thomas Smith (though we should not rule out the possibility that other officials as yet unidentified should take some credit as well) we see a continuous chain of influence running from Henry VIII's reign to the end of the century, and beyond into James I's reign, promoting all the projects that were enumerated in 1549, and continually searching for new. Essential commodities like iron, oil, salt, and woad came first in the list of their priorities, but less essential consumer goods followed quickly after. And it did not take long to discover, again from foreign experience, that to encourage new manufactures, especially those requiring foreign artificers, it was necessary for the state to give encouragement by issuing patents of monopoly. The first such patent, so far

[23] See below, pp. 52–3.

identified, was given in 1552 to Henry Smyth for the privilege of making glass; the second in 1554 (in Mary's reign, but possibly carried over from Edward's administration) gave to Burchart Cranyce a patent to search for and work metals.[24] With the issue of patents a fresh turn was given to the policy of promoting projects: it put them on a more solid footing, although one of the unforeseen consequences of patents was to inaugurate the scandalous phase of their history. But that is a later story to which we shall return.

Projects featured prominently in the writing of the later 1540s. What were the practical achievements? The Commonwealthmen were strong in government in the first years of Edward's reign, and their enthusiasm for projects to employ the poor was sincere. But the government was also deeply preoccupied with other concerns—the war in France, the siege of Boulogne, the defence of Calais, the defence of the Scottish border, and the risings in England, and many state papers discussed ways of discharging the ever-mounting burden of debt.[25] How could its ministers find time or energy to devote to the promotion of projects?[26] In fact, the needs of the army and its expense directed urgent attention to projects. The army on the move made large demands for domestic goods such as portable ovens, copper kettles and pans, brewing vessels, metalwares for horse tack like bits and stirrups, ropes, webbing, and canvas, not to mention soldiers' uniforms.[27] Since some of this equipment was being bought abroad,[28] it is surely no accident that the domestic manufacture of some of these articles was promoted by Edwardian projects.

Thus the Commonwealthmen's enthusiasm for projects that would employ the poor was reinforced by the pressing necessity to equip the army at lower cost, placing less reliance

[24] D.S. Davies, 'Acontius, Champion of Toleration and the Patent System', EcHR vii (1936), 64.
[25] Since these lectures were delivered, M.L. Bush's book has appeared on *The Government Policy of Protector Somerset* (London, 1975), which underlines more heavily still the government's preoccupation with war and its cost.
[26] For these anxieties, see e.g. PRO SP10/15, no. 73.
[27] See e.g. ibid., no. 11.
[28] A schedule of debts abroad and at home in Edward VI's reign and memoranda on devices for discharging them were either written by Cecil or annotated by him. (F.C. Dietz, *English Public Finance, 1558–1641*, Illinois, 1932, 33.)

on imported wares. The document which had commended the making of worsteds, fustians, linen, canvas, and metal goods became four serious projects. The first evidence of constructive steps to implement them centres upon the activities of the Duke of Somerset in 1549, that fruitful year. On a dissolved monastic site earlier granted to him at Glastonbury, he arranged to settle some Flemish clothworkers. In 1551, when Somerset fell, the care of the immigrants was entrusted to the Bishop of Bath and the local gentry, and for the next two years a considerable correspondence passed between them and the Privy Council. Thus we discover what the project was all about.[29] The Flemings had come to Glastonbury to set up the making and dyeing of worsted and says. Worsteds, such as those made at Valenciennes, had been named in the four earlier proposals for future projects. Something was plainly wrong with the worsteds that had been traditionally made in England, and which took their name from Worstead in Norfolk. They had once been a success abroad, but during the early Tudor period, when the export of woollen cloth was booming, the sale of worsteds had steadily declined. In the years 1510–20 exports had amounted to 5–8,000 pieces a year. By the 1540s they were down to 1,000.[30] The worsteds from Valenciennes, in contrast, were eminently successful, yet they used northern English wools as well as wool from Baltic countries. It was the *method of making and dyeing* them in which England was proving deficient.

But for what purpose did Somerset principally want foreign worsteds to be made in England? The evidence suggests two, and possibly three, purposes. The decline of the worsted trade was responsible for the decay of Norwich. Plainly, a revived worsted industry would help to solve the economic *malaise* of Norwich and the industrial region round it. The decay of all towns had been a prime stimulus behind the schemes of the Commonwealthmen, dating from the early 1540s,[31] but attention was more sharply focused on Norwich at the time of

[29] PRO SP 15/14, nos. 2, 3; SP 15/13, no. 74; SP 10/15, no. 55.
[30] P. Bowden, *The Wool Trade in Tudor and Stuart England* (London, 1971), 44.
[31] The decay of towns features prominently in *A Discourse of the Common Weal* 16, 78, 125.

Ket's rebellion. Secondly, a reinvigorated worsted industry would expand exports to their former level, and this was another desirable objective since this would help to pay for large imports. Thirdly, and here we can only speculate, it is possible that Valenciennes worsted was cheaper, or more hard-wearing, or both, than English worsted, and was needed by the army for uniforms. The worsted project certainly served two purposes, if not this third one.

In 1551 the Flemish households at Glastonbury numbered 34, later increased to 46. They received monastic land and monastic buildings for weaving worsteds and says *and* for dyeing them. As the first families moved in in 1551, £500 was spent on equipment, and the monastic brewhouse and bakehouse were allocated as dyehouses. The dyers immediately called for supplies of woad, madder, alum, and copperas. Weaving and dyeing here and elsewhere went hand in hand. Did it mean that even larger quantities of woad, madder, alum, and copperas were going to have to be imported? It did not.

The Flemings left Glastonbury with the accession of Mary and moved to Frankfurt, but the momentum set up by this project was maintained by others. In the end, six projects, not simply one, emerged from these modest beginnings. First, worsted making took on a new lease of life, in Norwich, and then spread to many other cloth centres of England. Woad growing had already started with the help of the French, as we have seen; madder growing was to be developed by Dutch gardeners a little later in the century. An alum project got under way, precipitated by a measure taken by the Spaniards *circa* 1553 to restrict the sale of alum except by licence.[32] This raised its price to the English dyer, and the use of English alum, previously deemed inferior, was reconsidered. The first patent to dig for alum in Devon and Cornwall was granted in 1562. Another patent to encourage the finding of alum *and* copperas in the Isle of Wight was issued in 1564.[33] By 1571 Bristol

---

[32]   TED iii. 136, 145.

[33]   E. Wyndham Hulme, 'The History of the Patent System', LQR xlvi (1896), 146–7. There is a possibility that alum was being dug in the Isle of Wight by a Portuguese in 1549 but the reference is ambiguous. The alum was at Southampton and could have been imported from Europe. On the other hand, Isle of Wight alum was known in the fourteenth century, though it was then said to be inferior to foreign alum. (VCH *Hants. & Isle of Wight*, v, 453.)

merchants were complaining that their trade in alum from Spain had decayed, now that better and cheaper alum was being procured in England.[34] Imports from abroad did not cease,[35] but a home industry had been set up. In the early seventeenth century it had found its feet in North Yorkshire, especially at Mulgrave,[36] and by 1662 English alum was being exported to Ireland, Scotland, and five continental countries (much the largest quantity, £14,900 worth, going to Holland) as well as to the East Indies and the Plantations.[37]

As for the search for copperas, we catch sight of it in the issue of the patent in 1564 to seek for alum and copperas in the Isle of Wight. It is almost certain that copperas was being collected before this date on the Essex coast, at Harwich, Walton, Frinton, and Brightlingsea. However, it was much more assiduously exploited after the Flemish came to Colchester in the 1560s, and we can only explain its new success by the superior skill which the Dutch showed in processing it.[38] The copperas industry expanded thereafter, and English copperas was counted as a regular export to France in 1604.[39] As an occupation it did not die out until the East Anglian cloth industry finally lost ground to the Yorkshire industry in the later eighteenth century. Until then Walton-on-the-Naze was the chief centre in Essex (lead tanks and pipes are still dug up there), along with Harwich whose copperas houses were famous. What did the local population get from all this? A new source of income for the women and children, who regularly gathered copperas after severe storms and sold it to the copperas boilers. They were still gathering it in the 1860s and 1870s, when the boiling houses had left Essex and the copperas had to be sent to London.[40] But Essex villages were not the only beneficiaries of this new by-employment. It was taken up in other parts of the country as well. In Kent it was gathered between Sheppey and Whitstable. The first works

[34] Hulme, op. cit. 147.
[35] See e.g. CSPD *1595–7*, 102.
[36] For the later history of the alum works in the reigns of James I and Charles I, see Thirsk and Cooper, 239–43.
[37] BL Add. MS. 36785.
[38] VCH *Essex*, ii, 411.
[39] Thirsk and Cooper, 444.
[40] VCH *Essex*, ii, 412–13.

were set up about 1590. In 1599 twenty poor people of Whitstable regularly gathered copperas; in 1636 a boiling house at Tankerton was sold for £1,000.[41] On Brownsea island, off the Dorset coast, copperas was a mainstay. Celia Fiennes gives us a glimpse of its value to the local population in the later seventeenth century. When she visited Brownsea, there was only one substantial house on the island, occupied by the governor; and the rest?—all little fishermen's houses, 'they being all taken up about the copperas'.[42]

The promotion of worsted cloth making and dyeing at Glastonbury thus had far-reaching implications, for it set up several industries having many different local centres. But what of the dyeing industry itself? It too was deemed to be in bad need of improved skills.

In a pamphlet written in 1553 William Cholmely had argued eloquently for an improvement in the English dyeing industry by copying foreign techniques. He himself had brought a dyer from Antwerp in 1551 and, in partnership with another Englishman, they had run a successful dyehouse in Southwark for the last three years.[43] Twenty years later Lord Burghley actively assisted the settlement in his home town of Stamford of a Dutch congregation, the leader of whom was Caspar Vosbergh, a dyer, who brought woad, teasels, alum, and copperas in his luggage.[44] At Wollaton in Nottinghamshire woad dyeing started in 1587 in alliance with woad growing. Robert Payne, whom we have already encountered growing woad there from 1585 onwards under the patronage of Sir Francis Willoughby, persuaded his employer to go one step further and set up a dyehouse that would dye wool with woad, which could then be spun into yarn for his jersey knitters to knit in winter. Payne negotiated on the matter with Randall Tenche, a dyer and clothier of Leeds, one of whose letters to Payne, opening with a notably fervent Puritan salutation, promised that he would not only undertake dyeing with woad but also set

---

[41] C.W. Chalklin, *Seventeenth-Century Kent* (London, 1965), 154–5. The first patent, however, was granted in 1565. See R.H. Goodsall, 'The Whitstable Copperas Industry,' *Archaeologia Cantiana*, lxx (1956), 143–4.

[42] *The Journeys of Celia Fiennes*, ed. C. Morris (London, 1947), 10–11.

[43] TED iii. 132–3.

[44] PRO SP 12/77, no. 65.

up the spinning, dyeing, and weaving of tapestry.[45]

Randall Tenche may not have been a foreign immigrant himself (Payne had encountered him casually one day on the road from Newark), but he was evidently a dyer with useful contacts, helping to diffuse foreign skills in traditional clothing towns, as well as introducing them to new centres. In the end, Payne's scheme for a dyehouse in Nottingham did not get going, but instead he erected a dyehouse in Wollaton between 1587 and 1588. His plans show how freely technical skills were transmitted between distant places.

Dyehouses in London in 1550, in Stamford in 1571, and in Wollaton in 1587; a patent in 1569 to dye frisadoes *in the Haarlem manner* at Christchurch, Hampshire, for export to Spain and Portugal: all these prompt us to ask how many other places in England took a hand in promoting dyeing in these years, and what technical progress was actually achieved? The subject has not yet been investigated as it deserves. In 1593 it seemed to one observer that the art was 'now growing to perfection'. By James's reign contemporaries were confident that great strides had been made, and this must surely be so or there would have been no Cockayne project in 1615–17. But that project concerned wool cloth. The dyers we have encountered were perfecting their art with worsteds. Englishmen certainly learned from the failure of the Cockayne experiment that the dyers of West Country wool cloth could not satisfy foreign requirements and standards. But the dyers of worsteds were based in eastern England, and out of Cockayne's sad experience a dyeing industry, with different goals, was salvaged. We know its weaknesses; what were its strengths? It is not for the historian to make guesses but it is very fruitful to ask the right questions. Did the strength of the English dyeing industry after 1617 lie in its success in dyeing worsteds (unaffected by Cockayne's scheme) and much humbler wares, dyeing cheap linen or canvas, dyeing coarser wool for blankets, or wools for the stocking knitters, in short, dyeing articles that mostly served

---

[45] Nottingham Univ. Library MSS., M 15/165/98. Randall Tenche lived under the tenters at Call Bank, Leeds. He was a searcher and sealer of cloth, and churchwarden, and died in 1629. I wish to thank Mr. Michelmore and Dr. Chartres for this information.

the home market, though their very cheapness, as we shall see, eventually won them a place in foreign markets too?[46] We may not answer that question confidently as yet, but the evidence seems to point in that direction.

Worsted cloth making was not the only project of Edward VI's reign. Another was the setting-up of a canvas industry, making poldavis and olerons for sailcloth. Imports of canvas from France were substantial. In 1565 a catalogue of foreign wares unloaded in the port of London showed canvas to be the fourth largest import in value, costing £32,724, plus another £600 for striped canvas.[47] The plan to reduce this expenditure also began in Edward VI's reign with the settling of Bretons in England to teach their skill to Englishmen. The documentary evidence is scanty, but Edward VI's officials made payment for his services to one John Orwell for undertaking this task, and although we are given no clue to John Orwell's choice of a centre for his project, his very name, Orwell, surely associates him with the Orwell estuary, that is to say, Ipswich and neighbourhood. Here hemp and flax were already traditional crops used for making Ipswich sackcloth, and here the sailcloth industry subsequently established itself.[48] It is not clear whether the Bretons who pioneered the undertaking in 1547–9 conferred any immediate benefits on the Ipswich industry. The superficial signs are that they failed. But the second attempt was much more successful: in 1574 another projector, John Collyns, applied for a patent to make mildernix and poldavis in the same district of Ipswich and Woodbridge. And when Richard Collins, his kinsman (and perhaps his son?), a poldavis maker of Ipswich, died in 1606, he was not a poor man. He drank out of a silver cup, had silver spoons on his table, and had complete confidence that his business would be carried on by his son-in-law, Edmond Goltie.[49] Persistence had finally brought success. Just how much painstaking care had gone into the perfecting

[46]   Richard Hakluyt had urged an agent going to Persia in 1579 to learn what he could about the art of dyeing linen cloth, for, he said, 'it hath been an old trade in England, whereof some excellent cloths yet remain; but the art is now lost, and not to be found in the realm'. (TED ii. 52.)

[47]   BL Lansdowne MS. 8/17, reprinted in Appendix I.

[48]   APC *1547–50*, 109, 404.

[49]   Hulme, 'The History of the Patent System...', LQR lxi (1900), 46.

of the manufacture can be gauged from an unusual description (undated, but Elizabethan) of fault-finding and fault-correction.

Ipswich sailcloths are like every day to be perfecter and better made than they have been by reason there is one Mr. Barber dwelling upon Tower Hill in East Smithfield who is the only buyer of all Ipswich cloths, and the Ipswich workmen and he, by agreement, hath two sealers, principal workmen indifferently chosen by themselves, the one by the workmen, the other by the said buyer, to survey, seal, and mark all true made sailcloths, being all brought to the said buyer's house in Ipswich by agreement, and there straight the workmen receive their money for all cloths that be sealed, marked, and the untrue made cloths rejected and unsealed, the workmen are fain to sell to loss, as they can agree, to the said buyer or otherwise.

The sealers being very good workmen tell straight the faults of the cloth refused to be sealed, if the yarn lack bucking, pinching, beating, or well-spinning, or otherwise be faulty in workmanship, upon the sealing day every week in the presence of all the workmen, whereby every man is made to see his own fault and is told how to mend it by conference together and a willingness the buyer keeps among them to teach one another and to win their cloths credit by true workmanship.

The Ipswich sailcloth industry was recognized by statute in 1603, the preamble of the act declaring that it had been unknown before 1590 when the skill was introduced from France.[50] Probably that is the date of its first real success. By the seventeenth century Suffolk sailcloth had a national and international reputation, *not* as the best sailcloth in Europe, but as the best sailcloth for 'our small ketches and vessels under 100 tons'. Flemish and Eastland sailors, too, commonly bought Ipswich cloths 'as they are serviceable enough for their price'.[51] This was the secret of their success. They served a particular purpose, and for that use they were good value for money. Suffolk canvas subsequently served the navy nobly, especially at the Restoration, when it made excellent sailors' hammocks.[52] In the years of war with France and Holland in the second half of the seventeenth century, when Dutch and French competition was removed, the English industry flourished

[50] VCH *Suffolk*, ii, 271; *Statutes of the Realm*, iv, pt. 2, 1049 (1 Jas. I, c. 24).

[51] VCH *Suffolk*, ii, 271.

[52] Ibid. ii, 272.

*un*naturally;[53] it had no competitors, and the canvas makers worked at full stretch. But in time of peace the canvas makers worked at a gentler tempo. They never achieved the supreme heights. They never stood alone as the best canvas makers of Europe. Nevertheless, many little coastal villages in Suffolk and Somerset owed their living to the trade.

Fustians and the making of metalwares were the third and fourth projects whose beginnings should be sought more systematically in Edward VI's reign. Both necessitated the import of foreign raw materials: cotton for fustians; steel and some iron for metalwares. Both industries deserve fuller examination, and only the briefest outline can be given here. Fustians were already being exported from Chester to Ireland in the 1560s; they may well have been made in Lancashire. By the 1590s, and probably much earlier, they were being made in quantity at Norwich, and attempts were being made to introduce them into York. By 1600 they were a booming Lancashire industry. By 1604 English fustians were being exported to France. By 1654 20,000 poor people in Lancashire alone were said to be employed in their manufacture.[54]

The making of small metalwares concerns many different branches of manufacture, some of which will be more fully discussed later. It is enough here to point to the makers of nails, lock, bits, spurs, stirrups, buckles, and arrowheads, whose campaign in 1603 to restrain chapmen from engrossing iron to their detriment, sends a momentary flash of light across the faces of crowds of men engaged in those occupations at that date in Staffordshire, Warwickshire, Worcestershire, and Shropshire.[55] Of others working in and around Sheffield

[53] R. Coke, *A Discourse of Trade* (London, 1670), Preface, printed in J. Thirsk, *The Restoration* (London, 1976), 120–1.

[54] N. Lowe, *The Lancashire Textile Industry in the Sixteenth Century*, Chetham Soc. 3rd Ser. xx (1972), 99; A.P. Wadsworth and J. de L. Mann, *The Cotton Trade and Industrial Lancashire, 1600–1780* (Manchester, 1965), 19–20; VCH *Yorks*, iii, 469; Thirsk and Cooper, 444–5, 258. The manufacture of fustians in England was alleged in 1669 to have begun with religious refugees who were skilled in making Milan and Genoa fustians (Thirsk and Cooper, 70). It is possible that the army's needs for uniforms in the 1540s first stimulated demand for domestic manufacture of this cloth. Milan fustian, lined with taffeta, was certainly used for doublets for the summer uniform of officers in Elizabeth's reign. (C.G. Cruickshank, *Elizabeth's Army*, Oxford, 1966, 93.)

[55] See the petition from West Midland metalworkers against the engrossing of iron, printed in Thirsk and Cooper, 188–90.

at the same period, Dr. David Hey has written with sympathy and insight.[56]

Thus, while the immediate success of Edwardian plans to set up fustian and metal-goods industries defies measurement, and was certainly modest, the firm intention to establish them was what counted most. As we have seen in other instances, men might make little or no headway at the first attempt, but they would continue to try; and before the end of Elizabeth's reign they could count remarkable achievements.

No trace can be found of a projecting policy actively pursued in Mary's reign. Publicity was given in 1555 to the efforts of some Norwich merchants in setting up the manufacture of russells and satins, two other types of New Drapery, in Norwich. These Norwich traders had watched the sales of their worsteds declining, while Italian russells, satins, and satin reverses were being made of Norfolk wool and reimported into England. They negotiated to bring Italian craftsmen to England, and yet another new group of cloths began to be made.[57] But this was a piece of private enterprise, and it may even have been started in Edward's reign. Of official projects in Mary's reign there is no sign.

Under Elizabeth, however, projects were launched on a new and much more expansive phase. In the 1560s religious persecution drove large numbers of Protestant artisans from France and Holland to seek refuge in England. Their plight played into the hands of Cecil and other like-minded Commonwealthmen. The first group of Dutch settlers was invited by the town council of Sandwich in Kent in 1561.[58] Other settlements followed in 1566 at Norwich,[59] in 1567 at Stamford, Maidstone, and Southampton, in 1568 at Colchester, and in 1574 at Canterbury. Smaller immigrant communities established themselves in market towns in the eastern and southern counties and also in the south-west. Ostensibly, the English government encouraged local authorities to take the first initiative, but, as we have seen, their initiatives were

---

[56] D. Hey, *The Rural Metalworkers of the Sheffield Region*, Occasional Paper, 2nd Ser., no. 5 (Dept. of English Local History, Leicester Univ., 1972).

[57] *Statutes of the Realm*, iv, 1 & 2 Philip and Mary, c. 14, 1555.

[58] TED i. 297.

[59] Ibid. 298.

remarkably in tune with Cecilian wishes, and official approval was readily accorded. The government could not have looked for a happier evolution of its long-laid plans to foster projects. The foreigners, coming to England to introduce new industrial skills, came under the best possible circumstances; they brought a relatively large group of skilled workers with them, and, being accompanied by their families, they were not likely to change their minds and depart without notice. A solid body of experience was attracted to English towns with some strong prospect that it would stay.

By these means many more of the New Draperies were introduced, first into Norwich and then into innumerable villages in Norfolk, Suffolk, and Essex. The success of the New Draperies was extolled by Norwich citizens in an eloquent address to the Privy Council in 1575.[60] By the early seventeenth century the New Draperies were being manufactured not only in East Anglia but in many other textile centres all over England.

The success of this project is a familiar story, but no one can say that its history is too well known to require further elaboration. The New Draperies represented innumerable different kinds of cloths whose number was constantly being enlarged; their spectacular success as a *group* has totally smothered curiosity in the history of each individual type of cloth, as well as obscuring the fortunes of associated handicraft industries which developed alongside the New Draperies and were also large, but separate, employers of labour. In Norwich, for example, one of the first centres in which the New Draperies started, lace making, ribbon making, and stocking knitting all became thriving, expanding occupations, simultaneously stimulated, if not started, by foreign craftsmen.[61] None of these allied industries has earned proper notice. Stocking knitting, indeed, ranked second only to the New Draperies as a user of long wool and an employer of handicraft labour. In 1615 it was calculated that two-thirds

---

[60] Ibid. 315.

[61] PRO E134, 44/45 Eliz. Mich.1 suggests that stockings were sometimes subsumed under the title of New Draperies, although in this lawsuit it was pointed out that some knit hose were made of wool, not of worsted.

of the long wool employed in the New Draperies went into the making of the cloth, while one-third went into the knitting of stockings.[62]

The beginnings of the stocking knitting industry, like all other projects, are entangled in the obscure history of a country handicraft that existed before the 1560s making wares for domestic use and purely local sale. But like the New Draperies the knitting industry underwent a revolutionary transformation when stockings became high-fashion goods. The new vogue appears to have developed as a result of an improvement in knitting techniques, partly connected with the use of finer wools, but perhaps also with the better shaping of stockings over the ankle and foot. Jersey wool, one type of fine wool increasingly used after the 1560s, was spun on a Jersey or Guernsey wheel. The technique was evidently derived from the Channel Islands and passed from there to Norwich, soon making Norwich the foremost centre for knitted jersey stockings. The other popular wool stocking was a worsted stocking, the knitting of which was copied from Italian examples. More luxurious and expensive were stockings knitted of silk, which copied Spanish and Italian styles. Italians, Spaniards, and French led the field in the knitting industry in the first half of the sixteenth century, and it is no coincidence that the growth of the English stocking knitting industry is first traceable in the 1560s when foreign refugees were settling in England in considerable numbers.[63]

Rapidly the English stocking knitters extended the range of their styles and their geographical centres. At the beginning of the seventeenth century stockings were being made in Wales, Gloucestershire, Cornwall, Devon, Nottinghamshire, Northamptonshire, Yorkshire, Northumberland, Cumberland, Westmorland, and Durham.[64] But as early as the 1590s it was an immense industry, employing *men and women* knitters, and the domestic trade was not the full measure of the business. Jersey, worsted, and woollen stockings were being sent to France, Holland, and Germany in consignments

[62] Thirsk and Cooper, 204.
[63] J. Thirsk, 'The Fantastical Folly of Fashion', op. cit. 50–73.
[64] Ibid. 56.

of 600 and 750 pairs at a time. By 1640, before the frame-work knitting industry is believed to have got into its stride, the foreign trade was prodigious. In that one year there went from London to the two ports of St. Lucar and Malaga alone 23,000 pairs of men's woollen stockings, 58,000 pairs of children's woollen stockings, and 53,500 pairs of worsted stockings for adults and children.[65]

Norwich was one of the most successful English towns in building not one handicraft industry out of ideas and skills brought into the town by foreigners, but several. But even the handicraft industries were not the full gamut of innovations introduced into Norwich. Another, which even the Common-wealthmen did not anticipate, was the flower-growing business, which established yet another occupation calling for little capital outlay, little land, but manual skill and the personal attention of the enthusiastic gardener. Its beginnings were very simple. Dutchmen coming from a country which had large concentrations of city dwellers and little spare land had a love of flowers to adorn their towns. The flower growers from Holland were encouraged to turn an interest and a hobby into profitable work when they encountered the curious botanists and country gentry zealously seeking new flowering varieties to adorn their gardens. Here was an appreciative clientele with heavy purses. The Dutch in Norwich, wrote Thomas Fuller in the 1660s, were 'the first who advanced the use and reputation of flowers in the city'. To him, they were 'pleasurable curiosities', in contrast with 'profitable crafts'.[66] But to the successful gardener, they were a livelihood. Today we see a thriving horticultural industry that meets a demand from all classes, and astonishes foreigners. It is an indulgence, perhaps, of an affluent society. In the sixteenth century it was an indulgence of gentlemen and the better-off middle class; it was only just beginning, and its economic significance should not be compared with the handicraft industries. It was nevertheless one more new occupation for hard-working men without capital.

---

[65] These calculations are based on the London portbooks in the PRO for 1640–41. I wish to thank Mr. K.G. Ponting and the Pasold Foundation for allowing me to use their transcripts of these documents.

[66] T. Fuller, *The Worthies of England* (London, 1952 edn.), 419.

Stockings and flowers were two very dissimilar occupations introduced into England in the 1560s by foreign refugees. In issuing their invitations to aliens the English city authorities set their sights on many more employments of great diversity. When Stamford invited Dutchmen in 1567 it issued a welcome first to weavers of bays, says, stammet, fustians, carpets, fringes, linsey wolseys, tapestry, silks, velvet, and linen, to hatters, rope makers, cofferers, craftsmen in metal who could make knives and locks, and workers with steel and copper.[67] The invitation to the Netherlanders from Maidstone citizens in 1567 asked for makers of bays, says, mockadoes, grograyn chamletts, russells, stammet, frisadoes, Flanders woollen cloth, patterned linen diapers, damask, plain linen, sackcloth, ticks for feather beds, arras and tapestry, Spanish leather, Flanders pots, paving tiles and bricks, and brasiers. It also called for makers of white and brown paper, corselets, headpieces, and all kinds of armour and gunpowder.[68] These lists bear a remarkable resemblance to Sir Thomas Smith's list of foreign imports in the *Discourse of the Commonweal*. He was still influential in Elizabeth's reign, sitting on a committee in 1559 framing plans for legislation that would prohibit the import of foreign trifles, and, if need be, encourage their manufacture at home.[69] It seems almost as if an official government document was in circulation offering to local authorities a standard list of manufactures to be encouraged. City officials adopted the list, modifying it as they saw fit, and with this in hand they conducted negotiations with potential immigrants.

In Maidstone the enduring success of the refugees turned out to be not the making of New Draperies or linen and sackcloth but the manufacture of linen thread. It was another of the foreign articles whose rise in price had been deplored in 1553.[70]

[67] J. Thirsk, 'Stamford in the Sixteenth and Seventeenth Centuries', in A. Rogers (ed.), *The Making of Stamford* (Leicester, 1965), 65.

[68] V. Morant, 'The Settlement of Protestant Refugees in Maidstone during the Sixteenth Century', EcHR 2nd Ser. iv (1951), 211.

[69] TED i, 327, 329-30. The composition of the committee which drafted these *Considerations delivered to the Parliament, 1559*, and the role of Sir Thomas Smith are discussed in S.T. Bindoff, 'The Making of the Statute of Artificers', in S.T. Bindoff, J. Hurstfield, and C.H. Williams, *Elizabethan Government and Society* (London, 1961), 81-9.

[70] TED iii, 145.

Maidstone had offered a welcome to makers of linen and sackcloth, that is to say, weavers of hemp and flax, probably in part because flax and hemp were already thriving crops in the district; if not, they soon became so. By 1622 the making of linen thread had outstripped linen cloth weaving and other new trades, and Maidstone became its renowned centre, pre-eminent in the kingdom. Thread, of course, is a lowly article that is generally dismissed with disdain.[71] Daniel Defoe's account of Robinson Crusoe's makeshift life on his desert island is completely vague about the way his hero set to work 'a-tailoring, or rather indeed a-botching' two or three new waistcoats and breeches. Whence did he procure his needles and thread? We are given no clues; Defoe did not give them a thought. They are humble articles, it is true, but it is very difficult to manage without them. Thread was needed in great quantity for sewing linen goods of all kinds, aprons, petticoats, shirts, sheets, napkins, rubbers (not yet called teacloths), and all the other innumerable domestic goods that were found in increasing quantity in the home by the late sixteenth century. Since, by the seventeenth century, these articles were commonplace even in the husbandman's dwelling, not a single family in the kingdom could dispense entirely with thread.

Fourteen projects which were launched in the period between 1540 and 1580 have now been identified. Some were forced into existence by the desperate need to find alternative supplies for foreign imports that had grown too expensive; some were concerned with supplying fancy wares to a more demanding consumer society that no longer wished to meet a high bill for imports. We see remarkable analogies with our present-day search for substitutes for expensive imports. One man uses methane gas from chicken manure instead of petrol; we discuss again the possibility of an engine that mixes hydrogen and oxygen and dispenses with petrol; distilled water has leapt in price by 25 per cent and so we are recommended to use the ice from defrosting our fridges; experiments begin again with straw to make paper instead of wood. We have seen for ourselves how quickly inventive men

[71] Fuller, op. cit. 253.

leapt into action in the summer of 1974 when the price of oil was sharply raised, and a balance of payments crisis ensued. They were equally quick off the mark in 1549.

A list can be compiled of 106 different articles mentioned by contemporaries in the sixteenth century as foreign imports which Englishmen seemed to regard as indispensable, and which ought to be made or grown at home. Hardly one was not capable of being produced in England. Those projects successfully launched well before 1580 were concerned with iron, woad, oil, fustians, worsteds and other New Draperies, canvas, metal goods, alum, copperas, dyeing, stocking knitting, the making of thread, and flower growing. Some of the others concerned frivolities and frippery like playing-cards, masks, busks, fans, and muffs which historians will doubtless be slow to treat seriously, even though by 1688 Gregory King estimated the 'annual consumption' of muffs at 50,000 (worth £10,000) and masks, busks, and fans at 200,000 (also worth £10,000).[72] But this still leaves a great number of other everyday necessities that called for new industries to be set up. In order to underline their importance in the life of ordinary English men and women, as well as their role in overseas trade, it is instructive to recite the shopping list of Lewis Hughes advising Englishmen in 1614 on what they needed to bring with them if they intended to settle in Bermuda. Such an adventurer had to choose his list with economy and care. 'Let them bring oil, vinegar, *aqua vitae*, barrel butter, pots, kettles, frying pans, trivets, bowls, trays, tankards, or pots to drink in, pails to fetch water in, and little barrels or jars to keep it in for their drink. . .Let them bring tongs, fire shovels, bellows, tinder boxes, brimstones, flintstones and steels, spits, dripping-pans, candlesticks, lamps, locks, spades, shovels, pickaxes, hatchets, whetstones, saws, hammers, piercers, pincers, and nails of all sorts. . . Also let them bring bedding; flock beds are better than feather beds. And for apparel for the summer, let them bring canvas or stuffs, blue linen and good buckram. . .Let them not forget to bring castile soap, pins, points, laces,

---

[72] Greater London Council Office, 'Burns Journal', fo. 203. I wish to thank Negley Harte for this reference.

[73] L.B. Wright, *The Elizabethans' America* (London, 1965), 204.

needles, thread, thimbles, shears and scissors,. . .fishing lines. . .and strong hooks.'[73] We have already noticed some of these wares because Englishmen aspired to set up their manufacture in the generation after 1540. The remaining items, so essential to seventeenth-century life, prepare us for the projectors' efforts that were to bear fruit after 1580.

III. THE SCANDALOUS PHASE, PART I, 1580–1601

In the late 1540s the idea of setting up new domestic industries that would reduce imports seemed a relatively straightforward affair. It was simply a matter of securing the services of foreign craftsmen who would introduce the skills to Englishmen. By the middle 1570s the ripples from this stone, dropped innocently into the water thirty years before, had begun to fan out in ever-widening circles, changing economic prospects and business attitudes in many unforeseen ways. By 1580 projects were becoming caught up in a complicated tangle of conflicting interests: they were being used by the Crown to further its financial interests, by local authorities to assist in the relief of the poor, and by private speculators who began to recognize what a gold-mine a successful project could be, and wanted their share in its profits. Projects became enmeshed in the web of royal schemes to relieve Crown debts and in the web of trading agreements between English and foreign governments. Lord Burghley started a file of documents on proposals *for* projects and complaints *against* projects: its continuation in James's reign was a thick file, now among the Cotton Manuscripts, entitled *Projects, Propositions, and Remonstrances*.[1] The remonstrances grew until they were as voluminous as the propositions; projects became scandals, and featured in the angry debates about monopolies in 1597–8, 1601, and 1624.

Thus we must follow the course of those many currents that between 1580 and 1624 muddied a once-clear stream. It is unnecessary to spend too much time on the use and abuse of monopolies; it is a tale that has been told many times. Yet some projects were deliberately encouraged by the government through the granting of patents of monopoly. We cannot follow projects and ignore monopolies. We must therefore consider both together, explain why scandals developed around monopolies, but demonstrate at the same

---

[1] BL Lansdowne MSS. 22 and 110; Cotton MS. Titus B V. See also Lansdowne MSS. 152, 81, and Cotton MS. Titus B IV.

time that a strong tide of healthy economic energy still surged through projects, relieving yet more families who would otherwise have floundered in penury. The period from 1540–1600 and beyond was a long hard struggle for working men and women, for their wages were eroded by inflation, and never caught up with the rise of prices. Projects saved their lives.

The idea of encouraging projectors by giving them a patent for the sole making of a new product, or for the sole use of a new technique, was first put into effect in England in 1552 with a patent for making glass, and in 1554 with a patent to search for and work metals in England.[2] After 1560 patents of monopoly flowed thick and fast. How and why did they start?

The origins of the patent system in England have provoked some discussion and disagreement. W.H. Price in 1906 decided that England was the 'birthplace of the system'.[3] Dr. Seaborne Davies, investigating the claim of Jacobus Acontius, the Italian philosopher, and one of the great figures in the history of toleration, to be the inventor of the patent system, has since decided in favour of the claim of William Cecil.[4] It seems more correct to describe the patent system as a widespread Continental practice, which was first copied in England in 1552, and then whole-heartedly adopted by William Cecil after 1560. Patents had been issued in Berne in 1467 for the manufacture and sale of paper, in Venice in 1469 for printing, and in Venice in 1507 for the making of mirrors.[5] It is evident from Cecil's papers that when he pondered an English problem and sought a politic solution, he turned to Europe for the benefit of other men's experience. It was a lesson that had probably been instilled in his youth, for Henry VIII's ministers had done the same. In later years Cecil's procedures were still more deliberate. He had some special investigators in his employ, with foreign connections (and also with foreign-sounding names, so that they may have been of foreign

---

[2] D.S. Davies, 'Acontius, Champion of Toleration, and the Patent System', 64.
[3] W.H. Price, *The English Patents of Monopoly* (London, 1906), 7.
[4] Davies, op. cit. 63 ff.
[5] Price, op. cit. 3.

birth themselves), who regularly plied him with ideas and information on economic projects in progress at home and overseas. For example, when Cecil became aware of the spread of woad growing in England and sought to check it by taxation, he called for information on the way it was taxed in Spain, Portugal, France, and Germany.[6]

The Continental method of encouraging inventors was brought more forcefully to Cecil's attention in the 1560s when increasing numbers of foreigners began to offer their services as inventors in private letters to Cecil. Their first argument was that privileges were essential to make the risks worth while. Acontius put the case most persuasively. 'Those who by searching have found out things useful to the public should have some fruit of their rights and labours, as meanwhile they abandon all other modes of gain, are at much expense in experiments, and often sustain much loss'.[7] The logic was compelling and could not fail to persuade reasonable men. Cecil accepted the system of patents as the best method by which he could achieve his objective of setting up new industries.[8] The preamble of an early patent in 1558 declared the government's desire to reward 'diligent travail' and 'give encouragement to others'.[9]

Patents were therefore granted to projectors; these gave them the sole rights of manufacture of an article, *according to the particular methods of which they were the true pioneers and inventors*. This rider is important.[10] The first patent after 1560 was awarded in 1561 to Stephen Groyett and Anthony le Lewyer to make hard white soap, equivalent

[6] BL Lansdowne MS. 49, nos. 44, 46, 47. Fuller in his *Worthies* (387) also described how Lord Burghley always consulted artificers in their art, and was instructed by a cobbler in the true tanning of leather.

[7] Price, op. cit. 7.

[8] As C.T. Carr puts it in his careful introduction to *Select Charters of Trading Companies, A.D. 1530–1707*, Selden Soc. 28 (1913), lix: 'monopolies [in the 1560s] were as yet part of an honest and unobjectionable economic policy'.

[9] Price, op. cit. 7.

[10] Sir John Neale, for example, believed that monopolies had originally protected new inventions and new processes, but had then been extended to old processes like the making of salt, starch, and paper. In fact, the salt, starch, and paper patents were no different from the rest. They all concerned new techniques. (J.E. Neale, *Elizabeth and her Parliaments, 1585–1601*, London, 1957, 352.)

in quality to the Spanish Castile soap that was made in Triana and Seville. The best soap made in England at this time was soft, mottled Bristol soap, 'very sweet and good', the patriots hastened to add, but unsuitable for fine laundry. Castile soap was the Lux of its age and was one of the expensive imports which English women refused to do without.[11] The patent conferred on the two foreign patentees the right of sole manufacture for ten years of Spanish Castile soap, *not* of soap in general. They had to submit their wares for inspection to the municipal authorities, and employ two servants who were native Englishmen.[12]

The next patent was granted in 1561 to a Dutchman for making saltpetre; the patent for making alum followed in 1562, replaced by another for alum and copperas in 1563. These were the much-needed raw materials for dyeing. Also in 1563 a patent was granted for the making of ovens and furnaces to George Gylpin and Peter Stoughberken, the latter evidently a Dutchman or a German.[13] What these ovens were is not exactly clear, but a number of clues suggest that a small oven, probably for domestic *and* industrial use, that economized in the use of fuel and was also portable, was being sought after. Its uses were many. The list of goods that had to be supplied to the army in the reigns of Henry VIII and Edward VI for the expeditions to France and Scotland remind us that transportable ovens, or field kitchens, were essential pieces of military equipment.[14] The patent granted to Gylpin and Stoughberken for their oven referred to the scarcity of wood fuel for the brewing and baking trades.[15] Yet another oven, produced by a German, Sebastian Brydigonne, was warmly praised in 1565 by some London

---

[11] Imports of soap *into London* in 1565 were valued at £4,422. This puts soap imports on a par with many other consumer goods, such as pins (worth £4,374), ticks for feather beds (£4,955) and Spanish leather (£3,691), i.e. in the intermediate range of imports, measured by value. The leading imports were wine and oil (£40–50,000 apiece) and certain other consumer goods such as linen cloth (£86,250), canvas (£32,724), and fustians (£27,254). (BL Lansdowne MS. 8, no. 17, printed below, Appendix I.)

[12] Hulme, LQR xlvi. 145.   [13] Ibid. 145–7.
[14] PRO SP 10/15, no. 11.   [15] Hulme, LQR xlvi. 146.

brewers, because of its economy in fuel.[16] Finally, a patent
was granted to Richard Dyer in 1571 for making furnaces
and transportable ovens and earthen firepots 'to hold fire for
seething meat'. Richard Dyer had learned the art while a
prisoner of the Spaniards, and armed with his patent, set up
his business in London without Moorgate.[17]

What the consequences of this innovation were for the
baking and brewing, even for the pottery, and other industries,
remains to be investigated. But its success must be inferred
from the fact that it featured among the innovations listed
by Howes in Stow's *Annals*, and it may well lie behind the
expansion of backstreet and small-scale industrial undertakings, requiring ovens and furnaces, which are a strong
theme in the history of several projects. The digging for
copperas, for example, required furnaces to keep the pans of
copperas boiling. Starch making and vinegar brewing (see
Ch. IV) likewise reflect the need for yet more small furnaces
and ovens.

Other patents issued in the 1560s include some well-known
ones, whose subsequent history has been thoroughly investigated, like the one granted in 1564 and 1565 to Daniel
Hochstetter and Thomas Thurland to search for metals,
especially copper, silver, and gold. 1565 was a bumper year
for patents: one was issued for the making of sulphur for
gunpowder, one for extracting oil from seeds, especially
from rapeseed, one to make Spanish leather (yellow leather
that was now in vogue in preference to black), one to mine
calamine, which, with copper, would make brassware,
especially woolcards (this launched the Mineral and Battery
Works), and one to allow the making of white salt by Francis
Berty, a native of Antwerp, according to the Dutch method
used for curing fish.[18] The *Discourse of the Commonweal*
had referred to the insufficiency of salt produced at home,
and its high price. This was the beginning of strenuous
English efforts—matched, incidentally, by equally strenuous
efforts in Holland, Scotland, and Denmark—to produce salt

---

[16] Ibid. 146.
[17] Stow, *Annales of England . . . continued by Edm. Howes* (London, 1615),
948; Hulme, LQR lxi. 45.
[18] Hulme, LQR xlvi. 147–8.

at home and escape dependence on foreign supplies. French salt could no longer be relied upon, once the Huguenots made it their practice to seize the salt stocks of La Rochelle whenever they were locked in struggle with the French King. Spanish and Portuguese salt supplies also were liable to be disrupted whenever relations with England deteriorated. Thus all foreign salt became alarmingly expensive, and salt evaporation at home became another project. Its subsequent history deserves more of our attention, but suffice it here to say that salt making made some headway at first at Yarmouth where salt was used for salting herrings, and was markedly successful at Newcastle on Tyne, because of the abundant coal locally available for boiling up the saltpans. In the long term this area became a major producer. By the early seventeenth century South Shields had 200 saltpans and an annual output of 10,000 tons. In 1700 prodigious quantities of salt were being shipped from Newcastle, especially to Lowestoft and Yarmouth.[19]

After 1565 the encouragement of foreign inventors by patent was a well-established procedure. Between 1566 and 1596 patents were issued for making window glass (1567), for the dyeing and dressing of cloth in the Flemish manner (1568), for making frisadoes (1569), for collecting madder that grew wild in Ireland, and dyeing skins with it (1568), and for making Turkish knife-handles of horn (1571). In 1574 the patent was granted for making mildernix and poldavis (sailcloths), already mentioned, and making drinking glasses (1574). In 1577 a patent was granted for making sulphur, brimstone, and oil. After that, some patents reverted to old projects with new promises—to make white salt, and salt upon salt, and to make oil (train oil, this time, from fish). In some cases, the former patents had expired, in others new processes were to be used. Yet some entirely new projects were also encouraged for making armour and horse harness (1587), making starch (1588), cutting iron for nails (this was Bevis Bulmer's patent of 1588), making white writing-paper

[19] A Discourse of the Common Weal 42; E. Hughes, 'The'English Monopoly of Salt in the Years 1563–71', Eng. Hist. Rev. xl (1925), 334–50; BL Lansdowne MS. 86, no. 73; R. Howell, Newcastle upon Tyne and the Puritan Revolution (Oxford, 1967), 21; PRO E190/207/13.

from rags (1589), making flasks for touchboxes, powder boxes, and bullet boxes for small arms (1591), making aqua composita, aqua vitae, and vinegar (1594), making playing-cards (1598), and mathematical instruments (1598).[20]

If memory serves the reader well, he will recognize many of the articles mentioned in these patents as having already appeared in lists of foreign imports that were deplored, or in lists of skills that were positively desired. The granting of patents was not without rhyme or reason. But in the 1580s possibly, and by the 1590s certainly, some of the patentees were no longer inventors and skilled craftsmen, but courtiers, merchants, and speculators who planned to hire the services of such craftsmen, while they themselves shouldered the main financial risk. On the face of it, this development was sensible, and perhaps inevitable, but it brought the patent system into disrepute. How did this happen?

It is hardly surprising that skilled technicians turned out sometimes to be unskilled business managers. When their financial resources proved insufficient for the task they set themselves, they welcomed the offer of help from a rich patron. Thus merchants of London and courtiers began to feature in patents, which passed on to them privileges earlier granted to much less wealthy men. But the situation had now become more complicated, because of the more grasping attitude adopted by the Crown towards projects. As soon as projects became successful native industries, the customs receipts from foreign imports of these same articles fell, and the Crown's revenues suffered. Flourishing projects therefore spread gloom in the Exchequer.

The Crown's concern at this development is clearly reflected in a letter written by Customer Thomas Smith in June 1576 to the Lord Treasurer. Smith was evidently answering a question that asked him how damaging to the Crown's customs was the manufacture of New Draperies at home. He acknowledged that the growth in native manufactures

---

[20] Hulme, LQR xlvi, 149; LQR lxi. 45–51. This is not the complete list. Patents for engines that would dredge, drain, grind, raise water, pipe a water-supply, and refine pit coal have been omitted since they did not directly result in the production of consumer goods.

of late years, especially of bays, says, frisadoes, owlterfines,[21] and such like, was now substantial, and, in truth, 'much hindered Her Majesty's customs inwards', but he preferred to look at the gains to the nation in another direction. 'In my opinion it is not only beneficial to Her Majesty in her customs *outwards*, but also profitable to our Commonwealth, for it cannot be that such number of these commodities can be wrought in this realm by strangers only, but that they must set many of the poor people of this realm on work.' The original letter from the Lord Treasurer had evidently voiced the further suspicion that the manufacture of the New Draperies was causing decay in the making of broadcloth and kersies. 'I am not of that opinion', retorted Thomas Smith, 'but that there is as many made now as hath been in times past, and as much worn within the realm now as before times hath been; and sure I am that there is as many carried out of the realm now as in times past, as may appear by the custom books.'[22] In other words, Smith took the view that the market for traditional cloths as well as the New Draperies was expanding both at home and overseas, and what the Queen lost in customs inwards was compensated by her gains from customs outwards. But the Queen's ministers were not so easily persuaded. Their anxieties persisted: they lie at the centre of that other lively controversy in 1585 about the spread of woad growing in England. Her Majesty was aggrieved that her customs from the import of foreign woad had diminished.

Hence new projects began to be presented in a fresh form to forestall criticism: would-be patentees promised the Crown a percentage of their profits to offset any loss that might be incurred in customs revenues. It meant that projectors now played for higher stakes than before, and more strenuous efforts had to be made to see that they did not turn into losses.

The financial difficulties of Elizabeth, and later of James,

---

[21] A project had been set up at Coventry in 1568 to manufacture owlterfines and cromplistes, cloths that were a speciality of Armentières in France (PRO SP 12/46, nos. 4–8). This remark suggests that the project was not unsuccessful. But compare VCH *Warws*. viii, 167.

[22] BL Lansdowne MS. 22, no. 32.

also affected the policy towards projects in yet another way. Some of Henry VIII's debts to his faithful servants of more than thirty years before had still not been paid. Some of these patient creditors saw an opportunity of recovering their money by offering a project. This accounts for the appearance of some gentlemen and nobility among patentees. Monsieur Bucholt, a Frenchman, received an oil and sulphur patent from Elizabeth to compensate him for debts owed him by Henry VIII, and Sir Richard Coningsby got his notorious patent to make playing-cards because James I owed him £1,800.[23] The new complexion of these financial transactions doubtless owed something to the fact that William Cecil took control of the Queen's finances as Lord Treasurer in 1572, and for the next decade steadily pursued his aim of reducing debt and increasing and stabilizing the Crown's regular income.[24]

When comparatively well-to-do and influential men began to receive patents of monopoly, the privileges that they received were much more rigorously exploited. Inventive craftsmen who had earlier received patents were men of limited resources, who had difficulty in guarding their secrets, and could not afford to employ agents and informers to suppress competing enterprises. Their new techniques tended soon to become public knowledge. That many of their wares made heavy demands on labour and small demands on cash for the raw materials was in a sense their undoing. When labourers had to be employed in great numbers, they quickly learned as much as their employers, and could then set up business on their own. This is why so many projects in the 1560s and 1570s developed rapidly into established occupations that were dispersed in a multitude of geographical centres. But when richer patentees appeared on the scene in the 1580s the repressive threat to enterprise, already inherent in industrial patents, but so far latent, was more fully exploited. These patentees had the resources to hire agents to poke and pry in all corners of the realm, and to suppress competitive enterprises, often with a completely unscrupulous

[23] BL Lansdowne MSS. 22, nos. 20, 21, and 23; 160, no. 90.
[24] Dietz, *English Public Finance, 1558–1641*, 32–48.

disregard for the strict letter of their privilege.[25] When their
diligent searches to destroy their competitors raised an outcry, they defended themselves by charging their imitators
with making inferior goods, an accusation whose economic
significance will be explored later. Here it is important to
notice only the valuable clues embedded in these charges
that the new manufactures were spreading into many scattered
places throughout the kingdom. Provincial M.P.s in the
Parliamentary debates of 1601 spoke bitterly of the activities
of agents of patentees, crushing the efforts of small producers
in modest workshops in their local market towns and villages.[26]
'Bloodsuckers of the Commonwealth' was the name given
to these agents and searchers by Mr. Martin, M.P. 'I speak
for a town that grieves and pines, and for a country that
groaneth under the burden of monstrous and unconscionable
substitutes [i.e. agents] to the monopolitans of starch, tin,
fish, cloth, oil, vinegar, salt, and I know not what.' 'If these
bloodsuckers be still let alone to suck up the best and princi-
pallest commodities which the earth there hath given us,
what shall become of us from whom the fruits of our own
soil and the commodities of our own labour, which, with the
sweat of our brows (even up to the knees in mire and dirt)
we have laboured for, shall be taken from us by warrant of
supreme authority, which the poor subject dares not gainsay.[27]

Wealthy patentees never succeeded in destroying flourishing new industries, but they were a constant irritant, and
their attentions fell upon particular regions of the country in
a wholly arbitrary way. We have a glimpse of the nuisance in
the activities of the Duke of Lennox's agents when he was
granted the aulnage of the New Draperies, and turned his
attention to the dues he could collect on knitted stockings.

Stockings and most of the New Draperies had entirely
escaped the patent system because these industries had
started, and dispersed themselves widely among ordinary
people, before the policy of granting patents of monopoly
got into its stride. The industries had spread like wildfire
in the 1560s especially after the initiatives taken by the

---

[25] Heyward Townshend, *Historical Collections* (London, 1680), 230–1.
[26] Ibid. 230.   [27] Ibid. 234.

government to settle foreigners in Sandwich, Norwich, Colchester, and Halstead. But because the new types of cloth sold so well, it was inevitable that sooner or later, when the Crown's finances received fresh scrutiny, they should be regarded as suitable objects of taxation. Broadcloths had been subject to aulnage for centuries.[28]

The collection of aulnage on New Draperies began in 1578 when the right to collect it was granted to two patentees, Sir George Delves and William Fitzwilliam. In 1580 Norwich was granted the farm of the New Draperies within the city, and the record of its collection shows dues being levied on stockings; stockings were often subsumed under the heading of New Draperies.[29] However, the small numbers charged in the first year establish that the administration was far from efficient.[30] In 1585 Delves and Fitzwilliam resumed collection in Norwich until 1592, and had their patent renewed in 1594 for another 21 years. The rate then charged on stockings was set at $\frac{1}{2}d$. per dozen.[31] Delves and Fitzwilliam forthwith sent their agent to various centres of the New Draperies in Yorkshire, collecting information on the quantities produced. He identified the stocking knitting centres as Doncaster, Richmond, Barnard Castle, Askrigg, and other small townships in the Richmond neighbourhood. The patentees intended to delegate the collection of the aulnage to one or two local dealers in stockings who regularly sold their wares in London.[32] A lawsuit later initiated by Delves and Fitzwilliam in 1602 reveals deep uncertainty concerning the articles embraced by the term New Draperies—not surprisingly, since the cloths so named were increasing in number and variety, and using many different combinations of wool, silk, and

[28] An undated paper in a volume of the Lansdowne MSS. which contains many documents on the decline of the Queen's Customs, advocates the charging of a duty on, and the sealing of, New Draperies. (BL Lansdowne MS. 110, no. 63.)

[29] I have drawn freely in this paragraph on Dr. K.J. Allison's detailed account of the aulnage on New Draperies in his unpublished thesis, 'The Wool Supply and the Worsted Cloth Industry in the 16th and 17th centuries', Univ. of Leeds Ph.D. (1955), ii. 609 ff. I wish to thank Dr. Allison for permission to do this, and Mr. J.P. Cooper for drawing my attention to this carefully investigated account.

[30] Norwich Record Office, Aulnage Accounts, 1580–1610, Press D. Case 17, Shelf D.

[31] PRO E134, 35 & 36 Chas. II, Hil. 19.

[32] PRO SP 12/252, no. 2.

linen yarn.[33] Probably Delves and Fitzwilliam were only too glad to surrender their patent three years later, in 1605, when it passed to the court favourite, the Duke of Lennox.[34] In his hands we see for the first time what resources could be deployed by a well-to-do member of the nobility, to exploit a grant of this kind, and harass provincial craftsmen and traders.

The fresh patent of 1605 did not specify the rate to be charged on stockings, and uncertainty still prevailed as to whether stockings were embraced under the title of the New Draperies or not. According to one witness in a consequent lawsuit, aulnage was levied at first at a rate of 1d. per dozen pairs, while, according to another, the rate was $\frac{1}{4}d$. per dozen.[35] An order of the Barons of the Exchequer in 1606 declared that aulnage was not payable on stockings, but that they should pay a subsidy, thereafter levied at the rate of 4d. per 64 lb. Nevertheless, in all later litigation an aulnage on stockings was taken for granted and always so named.[36]

Disputes started almost at once with the Norwich dealers who claimed that the aulnagers' charges were excessive. The Duke of Lennox had appointed searchers to collect his dues, and had launched his claims upon Norwich first of all. Ten agents were needed to uphold his rights in Norwich, reinforced by a gentleman, Anthony Gibson, in London who gave legal advice when needed, while he in turn referred tricky questions to Richard Hadsor of the Middle Temple, Lennox's learned counsellor at law. It was Richard Hadsor who prepared an answer to the protests that reached Cecil as early as 1606 (perhaps through the Commons, perhaps through private petitions) against Lennox's patent.[37]

Lennox's methods were brisk and thorough. His agents claimed to search the carts of Norwich carriers before they set off to London. When one Norwich carrier refused to allow his carts to be so inspected they pursued him to his

---

[33] PRO E134, 44/45 Eliz., Mich. 1.   [34] CSPD *Addenda, 1580–1625*, 457.
[35] PRO Stac. 8, Bdle 90, no. 19.   [36] Ibid.
[37] CSPD *1603–10*, 306.

first stopping place on the road to London, Attleborough, where a second attempt to search the carrier's cart was resisted. Not to be thwarted so easily, Lennox's agents then dispatched one of their number hot foot to London to consult the Duke of Lennox himself. Mr. Hadsor of the Middle Temple was called upon for advice, and as a result five men in the service of the Duke betook themselves to an inn at Ware in Hertfordshire, called for the aid of the local constable and headborough, and waylaid the Norwich carrier as he entered the village. His carts were driven to the inn, packs of stockings, gartering, and other items were removed and carried to London where Anthony Gibson, Lennox's deputy, unpacked them and triumphantly proved that the goods were unsealed.[38]

Not until about 1614 did Lennox's agents appear in Richmond, Yorkshire, to lay claim to the aulnage on stockings there. They called the dealers together, waved the Letters Patent in front of them, and asked for £10 for arrears, and another £10 by way of payment for the future.[39] By 1629, and probably much earlier, stocking dealers in Northampton and Doncaster had been mulcted of aulnage, and in all cases the collection was farmed for a lump sum to local traders. Nevertheless, the rights of Lennox's patent were still disputed, and some dealers paid while others did not. Occasionally a dealer was suddenly arrested, and 'for peace and quietness' he would pay his arrears and promise to pay for the future. But in the same town there were other stockingers who were never asked to pay, and never had their stockings examined. Thus Ursula Hicks, a stocking knitter in Richmond, had never been asked for aulnage in forty years, while Ambrose Appleby of Barnard Castle had been arrested for non-payment.[40] What happened in the numerous other knitting centres all over the kingdom, at Wells and Taunton in Somerset, at Tiverton in Devon, not to mention the knitting centres of Wales, it is impossible to say. What is certain is that the aulnage collectors appeared and disappeared in a totally unpredictable way.

[38] PRO Stac. 8, Bdle 90, no. 19.   [39] PRO E134, 2 Chas. I, Mich. 38.
[40] Ibid.

Since the patentees of the aulnage arranged the collection of their dues by means of the principal local traders who dealt with London, the small producers of New Draperies sensibly took evasive action. A dispute in Norwich reveals how the makers of lace and gartering entrusted their wares for London to small traders, bypassing the recognized dealers, or sold them to chapmen who toured the country selling at fairs.[41] We can be sure that the stockingers resorted to the same ruse. In short, the patent to farm the aulnage which was originally intended to yield cash to the Crown, and the aulnage system itself which was intended to maintain standards of workmanship and keep up a good reputation for English goods in overseas markets, positively promoted the dispersal of cheap wares of any and every quality, unexamined, unsealed, and ungraded throughout the kingdom. It was then but a short step for the same clothiers and stockingers to arrange the sale of their wares overseas, again bypassing the recognized merchants. This was not difficult wherever foreign markets greedily absorbed English manufactures. This was certainly the case in Spain when its trade with England reopened in 1605, and cheap English stockings and cheap English cloth were in high demand. It became a principal grievance of the recognized merchants trading to Spain and Portugal in 1617 that they had to compete unfairly with cloth makers and stockingers 'who make their wares and send them themselves to Spain, not dealing through merchants'.[42] In this way yet more country wares made their way unobtrusively to their customers overseas, again unsealed, unsorted, and ungraded.

The vexations caused by the Duke of Lennox's aulnage patent afford a glimpse of the consequences of all patents. They did not root out industrial enterprises everywhere, and many individuals, like Ursula Hicks of Richmond, a knitter of forty years' standing, were entirely overlooked. But they were a sore irritation to the entrepreneur who conducted business on a scale that made him conspicuous. And when he employed others he could not fail to become

---

[41] PRO E134, 6 Jas. I, Easter 38.
[42] BL Lansdowne MS. 152, 244 ff.

conspicuous. This meant that it was in villages and hamlets that men were best able to work and trade unnoticed, whereas they could not escape attention in towns. Industry was thus driven more systematically into country places, while the resentments of the towns were most loudly and eloquently proclaimed—by the M.P.s of Warwick, Reading, and York, for example, in the monopolies debates in Parliament. The widows in outhouses and cottages to whom Cecil referred sarcastically—or was it only light-heartedly and playfully?—in his Parliamentary reply did not raise their voices.[43] But it would be foolish to underrate their increasing numbers in villages, hamlets, and farmsteads.

The free and healthy growth of new industries had been an objective of the Commonwealthmen, but the path they had blazed was losing its way in a dense, thorny thicket. Yet the original aspiration was still upheld by the multitudes of people who thronged the doors of Westminster Hall as the monopolies debates proceeded, crying out that they were Commonwealthmen, and asking for compassion for their grief, 'they being spoiled, imprisoned, and robbed by mono-polists'.[44] The high ideals of the Commonwealthmen, how-ever, were not entirely submerged by the scandals. Many new occupations that had by now shown their value as employers of the poor began to occupy a high place in the list of industries to be developed in parish workhouses. Legislation in 1576 had made provision for a work stock to employ paupers in their homes or in workshops, and to discipline the idle in Houses of Correction. It has long been known that paupers were thereafter put to work on various cloth making tasks, using wool, flax, and hemp. But the exact nature of that work calls for more precise definition. It included a number of the newly flourishing occupations that had been fostered since the 1560s. The House of Correction at Win-chester, for example, planned to provide hat making, glove making, and nail making for men, as well as cloth making and dyeing; for women it offered the spinning, carding, and sorting of wool, the carding of hatters' spools, the dressing of flax,

---

[43] Heyward Townshend, op. cit. 249–50.
[44] Neale, op. cit. 383.

and the knitting of stockings.[45] Among the finished articles to be made at Winchester were kerseys and felt hats, which were to be dyed with woad on the premises. Since laymen locally were said to have provided much of the stock, we may safely guess that they supplied home-grown woad, for the county of Hampshire was a principal centre of cultivation. Work was planned for 80 men and women in Winchester, and three or four storehouses within 10–12 miles of the city were to be set up, giving out spinning work that would keep the House of Correction fully supplied with yarn.[46] These plans for dispersing successful projects among the poor were now developing forcefully and winning increasing support from public-spirited men and town authorities all over England. The keeper of Worcester gaol in the early 1580s had the bright idea of employing poor prisoners in his custody on woad growing. He provided them with work on 30 acres of woad near the city, 'whereby they are greatly relieved'.[47] In 1597 the corporation of York granted the freedom of the city, a ten-year monopoly, a house rent free, and a loan of money to a man from Hartlepool who promised to set up the making of fustians in York and employ 50 poor people.[48] The same policy almost certainly explains why knitting schools were founded in large towns in the early 1590s, in York by 1590, and in Lincoln and Leicester by 1591,[49] while at Eaton Socon in Bedfordshire a woman was hired to teach bone lace making to poor children in 1596.[50] In the seventeenth century the list of these suitable occupations for the poor was to lengthen further to include pin making, lace making, and button making, as at Salisbury in the 1620s.[51]

Thus while monopolists interfered with the spread of new occupations, under other influences their advance was

---

[45] VCH *Hants*. v, 424.   [46] BL Cotton MS. Titus B V, no. 145.
[47] BL Lansdowne MS. 49, no. 43.   [48] VCH *Yorks*. iii, 469.
[49] Thirsk, 'Fantastical Folly' 60. It is significant that in 1570 Norwich's suggestions of work for the poor were restricted to grinding malt and spinning and carding wool. The range of choice of occupation was much wider by the late 1570s.
[50] J. Godber, *History of Bedfordshire* (Luton, 1969), 222.
[51] P. Slack, 'Poverty and Politics in Salisbury, 1597–1666', in P. Clark and P. Slack, *Crisis and Order in English Towns, 1500–1700*, (London, 1972), 181.

sustained. The legislation on workhouses and parish stocks dispersed them in new places. An even stronger stimulus was administered by the second round of price increases in foreign imports which began somewhere between 1568 and 1571 and which were described by John Grey, a draper residing in Hamburg, as stemming from Spanish policy in the Low Countries. Duke Alva would only allow English goods into the Netherlands under licence, and at heavy charge. This drove up the price of English goods sold there; the same licence system for Dutch exports drove up their price in England by 30 to 40 per cent. John Grey gave examples of the sharp rise in prices in 1571 (since 1568) of hops, madder, linen, cloth, and pins. Hops formerly cost 14s. and 16s. per cwt but now cost 45s. and 50s., madder formerly 20s. per cwt now cost 38s. and 40s., a Flemish ell of Ghentish cloth had been $7\frac{1}{2}d$. but now was $11d$. or $11\frac{1}{2}d$.[52] No wonder that hops and madder growing, linen, and pin making were enthusiastically taken up as projects in the following years. By the early 1580s, moreover, trade with other European countries was in trouble. From 1581 to 1585 Venice levied imposts on English goods traded by the Levant company in retaliation for imposts levied in England by a patentee on imported Venetian goods.[53] More price rises followed. In 1582 government ministers read with gloom a document reciting the imposts levied in late years on English goods in France.[54] Projectors seeking home-made substitutes redoubled their efforts. Among these were men seeking substitutes for foreign oil.

The *Discourse of the Commonweal* had issued the first call to oil projectors in 1549. Oil cost one-third more in 1549 than in 1542, it declared.[55] One of the main sources of supply was Spain, and in 1553, when Spain stopped the sale of alum abroad, except on licence, William Cholmely put the obvious next question. 'What if Spain did the same with oil? How should we then have oils to work our wools withal?'[56]

[52] CSPD *Addenda, 1566–79,* 356–7.
[53] PRO SP12/185, no. 51.
[54] Ibid. 81.
[55] *A Discourse of the Common Weal* 16–17.
[56] TED iii. 136.

A new note of urgency had entered the discussion, but no solution was as yet in sight. Although from 1532 onward, throughout the remainder of Henry VIII's reign, the growing of hemp and flax was encouraged by statutes that insisted on half an acre being grown for every 60 acres of tillage, the purpose was clearly to promote the linen and canvas industry, not to procure oil from the seeds. When Elizabeth revived her father's policy on hemp and flax growing in 1563, she still had in mind the needs of fishermen for nets and sails, and the work given to spinners and weavers in making linen and canvas. The extraction of oil was nowhere mentioned.[57] Yet in one region of England at least—around Lynn in Norfolk—coleseed was already being grown in 1551 and used for oil.[58] Was it the result of the alarms first raised in 1549? It is not impossible. However, the Norfolk experiment was not widely known; national economic necessity was not yet compelling enough to spread the news further afield. Stronger action to promote coleseed growing came from foreigners arriving in England in the second half of the 1560s. In 1565 a patent was issued to Armigil Wade and William Herle for making sulphur and oil from seeds.[59] The progress of this project in the next ten years is unclear, but the government kept the project alive by looking sympathetically at all fresh schemes. In 1571 Giles Lambarde proposed a device for making oils for English clothiers; in 1572 a bill was introduced into Parliament to encourage the making of oils in England.[60]

By 1576 other external circumstances made the success of this project a pressing necessity. Oil imports from Spain could no longer be counted on because of continuing political difficulties between the two countries. The price had become 'extreme dear' and was 'like to be dearer by reason of the abundance that every year more than the other is carried out

---

[57] Statutes of the Realm, 24 Hen. VIII, c. 4, renewed in 28, 31, 33, and 37 Hen. VIII; also 5 Eliz. c. 5, though this was repealed by 35 Eliz. c. 7.

[58] E. Kerridge, The Agricultural Revolution (London, 1967), 236.

[59] Hulme, LQR xlvi. 147. Wade and Herle were, in this case, agents negotiating on behalf of foreign artisans. Documents in BL Lansdowne MSS. show that they were advisers to Cecil on projects to be set up in England, and also on many other government matters. See e.g. Lansdowne MS. 21, no. 23 et passim; BL Lansdowne MS. 110, no. 51.

[60] H.W. Brace, History of Seed Crushing in Great Britain (London, 1960), 15.

of Spain into the West Indies'. William Herle, who had now become an intimate adviser of William Cecil on projects of various kinds, presented a memorandum that explored many aspects of the problem and put forward certain definite proposals.[61] The making of oil within the realm 'of seeds, herbs, roots, minerals, etc.' was especially necessary for the sake of the soap and cloth making industries, though it was also needed for lighting, cooking, in medicines, and for paints. At present there were only about four or five people in the kingdom who 'in very imperfect or unprofitable manner make oil of seeds'. Were these the men of Norfolk? William Herle took pains to get his facts right. We must take his statement seriously, though it meant that getting oil from coleseed was still at the experimental stage and not making much headway. In Flanders and France, Herle announced, great numbers of idle people were employed in extracting oil, and in manufacturing processes that depended on it. Both countries, indeed, imported hemp and flax from England for this purpose. Such exports, he urged, should be restrained so that oil as well as cables, ropes, nets, fishing lines, linen and sackcloth, twine, pack thread, and sewing thread, girth webbing, bone lace, dornix, and fustians, could be made at home. Hemp seed, flax seed, and coleseed, he reiterated, made good oil for soap and cloth making.

The practical measures urged by Herle were that the statutes encouraging the growing of hemp and flax be reinforced, and that a larger acreage of land should be sown with coleseed. Indeed, he added, these crops 'will be more gainful to the owners and farmers of land than any corn'.[62] The reader of this report—almost certainly William Cecil—reached for his pen and underlined these words, not to sound a note of alarm, as one might expect—the woad-growing craze that seemed to imperil corn supplies had not yet begun—but to add stronger arguments in approval. If these crops were more profitable than corn, the gain would drain more land, he noted in the margin. Coleseed and hemp, as everyone knew, were excellent crops on newly drained fen. Thus the

[61] BL Lansdowne MS. 22, nos. 30 and 31.
[62] Ibid., no. 31.

plan to produce oil at home was linked with drainage projects, and gave fresh encouragement to yet another group of inventors and projectors—those who were commending their designs for windmills and drainage engines.

The decade 1570–80, then, marks the serious beginnings of the oil project. William Herle favoured the granting of a fresh patent for making oil, which was duly conferred in 1577 on William Wade and Henry Mekyns, alias Pope, a London jeweller, to make sulphur, brimstone, *and* vegetable oils that would replace whale or train oil in soap making and the dressing of cloth.[63] Other claims for patents were evidently turned aside, though William Herle had also commended the claims of the Frenchman, Monsieur Bucholt, who was owed various sums of money by the Crown going back to Henry VIII's reign, and who hoped to recover them by making sulphur and oil, the oil being got from olive trees that he proposed to plant. An Italian, Michel Andrione, also asked for royal favour for a scheme to make good oil at Colchester and Colebrook, though he did not divulge its source.[64] By 1579 seed crushing was certainly producing some oil for in that year Laurence Mellowes was locked in argument with the soap makers of the City of London because they would not pay him a fair price for oil that he had crushed from seed within the realm.[65]

As the oil project gathered momentum so did the projects for fen drainage. With increasing regularity in the 1570s flooding in the fens had engaged the Privy Council. In the early 1580s it examined practical proposals by drainage engineers, and a general drainage bill was drawn up in 1585; in 1589 Humphrey Bradley of Brabant submitted his treatise on the cause of flooding in the fens and the methods of draining them.[66] Agriculturists began to experiment with the growing of coleseed (by 1603 it was being exported from Boston),[67] and at the same time clothiers were experimenting

[63]   Hulme, LQR lxi. 47.
[64]   BL Lansdowne MS. 22, nos. 20, 21, 23, 29.
[65]   Brace, op. cit. 15–16.
[66]   H.C. Darby, *The Draining of the Fens* (2nd edn., Cambridge, 1968), 13–19.
[67]   R.W.K. Hinton (ed.), *The Port Books of Boston, 1601–1640*, Lincs. Rec. Soc. 50 (1956), 23.

with the use of rape oil in cloth making. As it turned out, long years of trial and error still lay ahead before the use of rape oil was perfected, but we can follow the story mirrored in the details of the life of Benedict Webb.[68]

Benedict Webb was a clothier of Kingswood, in Wiltshire. In 1579 he was apprenticed to a French merchant in London who immediately sent him abroad. He observed foreign cloth making techniques in Paris, Rouen, and in Italy, and returned to set up in business in Taunton, Somerset. Webb became the pioneer in the manufacture in England of Spanish cloth, otherwise known as medley cloth, but he also became the most notable and successful pioneer in the use of rape oil in cloth making. He first set up an oil mill at Kingswood in 1605; by 1618 he was expanding production and enjoying the confident support of other local clothiers who used his oil—increasingly so, after 1621. Twenty-two of the principal clothiers of Gloucestershire, Wiltshire, and Somerset gave evidence in 1626 of the excellent quality of Webb's rape oil. By this time he was growing coleseed not only in Kingswood but also in the Forest of Dean, renting 550 acres alone from one landowner for the purpose. The Forest of Dean did not long remain the home of rapeseed, however; the fenlands of eastern England proved a much more congenial habitat. Coleseed extended its domain as fenland drainage progressed, especially in the second half of the seventeenth century. William Dugdale wrote ecstatically in 1657 of the coleseed he saw growing in the Bedford Level, while on the Isle of Axholme, beyond Santoft on the road to Thorne, he passed four windmills used for bruising rapeseed and making oil.[69]

Some prejudices lingered among clothiers at the use of rape oil in cloth, probably because the cloths were not always properly scoured after fulling; worms were said to breed in the cloth if it lay packed for too long.[70] But there is no doubt of the successful use of rape oil in the textile industry and for other industrial uses including lighting. Home-produced oil

[68] E. Moir, 'Benedict Webb, Clothier', EcHR 2nd Ser. x (1957), 257–64, from which all details in the following paragraph are drawn.

[69] Brace, op. cit. 20.

[70] Thirsk and Cooper, 499–500.

attracted an excise in 1643, a sure sign of its commercial importance, and oil mills multiplied.[71] In the course of the seventeenth century the cultivation of rapeseed, and the crushing of rape oil, became two commonplace occupations in the eastern half of England. Among the many counties that benefited, from Yorkshire through Lincolnshire to Huntingdonshire, perhaps Cambridgeshire should be singled out as the first of them all, and Wisbech as the principal port. A Wisbech gentleman testified that between 1632-1633 and 1640 he made about £300 a year from coleseed.[72] In 1719 a thousand tons of rape oil were said to be shipped annually from Wisbech, and in 1735 seven mills were at work in the town crushing seed. No wonder that Wisbech could afford street lighting with oil lamps before York, Coventry, or Birmingham.[73]

That oil mills were pressing rape oil is a reasonable assumption. This was their principal purpose but it was not their only one. Rapeseed is the most productive in oil; nowadays the seeds yield $25\frac{1}{2}$ per cent of oil, whereas linseed yields $20\frac{1}{2}$ per cent, and hempseed 16 per cent.[74] But linseed and hempseed oils were not to be despised, and they contributed something to domestic oil production. The campaign to promote hemp- and flax-growing that was under way from Henry VIII's reign was far from being a complete failure, but, as the acreage of flax and hemp was enlarged, the greatest benefit from these crops went to the cloth industries.

That seventeenth-century writers always seemed to write in disappointment about English hemp and flax was because they did not see them growing in every parish in the kingdom. But as Walter Blith expressed it in his book of husbandry in 1653, writing of hemp—it 'would be far the better but that it

---

[71] Brace, op. cit. 19.

[72] Kerridge, op. cit. 237.

[73] Brace, op. cit. 27; M. Falkus, 'Lighting in the Dark Ages', in *Trade, Government and Economy in pre-industrial England*, ed. D.C. Coleman and A.H. John (London, 1976), 259-60. For the Russell family's dealings with Wisbech oil mills in 1743-4 in connection with their Thorney estates, see Beds. RO, Russell Collection, R4/4045/12-13.

[74] Brace, op. cit. 16-17.

is not made so national'.[75] All politicians and writers agreed monotonously on the necessity to grow these crops at home. The import figures explain why. Linen cloth was the largest single import into London in 1565, worth £86,250. Wine, the second largest item, cost little more than half that amount—£48,634. In addition to this, imported flax cost £13,217, thread (which must mean flaxen thread, since sackcloth thread, made of hemp, was listed separately) cost the large sum of £15,745, i.e. more than flax. Canvas cloth, made from hemp, cost £32,124, plus another £600 for striped canvas; hemp cost £4,038, ropes cost £2,759, and sackcloth thread £1,600. Ticks for feather beds were almost certainly made of hempen cloth and cost another £4,955.[76] It is therefore not surprising that so many economic writers in the sixteenth century urged Englishmen to grow their own flax and hemp and improve their techniques of making linen and canvas.

The achievements of the linen cloth industry must be reserved for brief comment below: it was built largely on imports of foreign yarn, which, for quality with cheapness, could never be equalled by English growers.[77] But English flax and hemp made perfectly acceptable coarse cloth,[78] and perfectly satisfactory thread, rope, fishing nets, and lines. In scattered villages all over England hemp and flax growing were pursued on a scale sufficient to support a substantial local industry. In the Isle of Axholme, for example, men and women wove canvas for sacks, around the Wash the fen-landers grew both crops and wove linen and hempen cloth.[79] Flax grown around Maidstone was the mainstay of its thread industry, the thread itself having the reputation in the

[75] W. Blith, *English Improver Improved* (London, 1653), 255. The same words were used by Joseph Blagrave in *The Epitome of the Whole Art of Husbandry* (London, 1685), 180. See also Heyward Townshend, op. cit. 188, and Anchitel Grey's *Commons Debates* iv, 161.

[76] BL Lansdowne MS. 8/17.

[77] See this verdict in 1681 by John Houghton in *A Collection of Letters for the Improvement of Husbandry and Trade* (London, 1681), 112–15; also in 1698 by W. Davenant in 'An Essay on the East India Trade', in *Discourse on the Publick Revenues*, ii (London, 1698), 44.

[78] W. Blith, op. cit. 256.

[79] J. Thirsk, 'The Isle of Axholme before Vermuyden', *Agric. Hist. Rev.* i (1953), 21–2; Lincs. Archives Office, Probate Invs., *passim*.

mid-seventeenth century of being the 'best thread in England',[80] Hemp and flax growing in Somerset made Yeovil famous in the seventeenth century for hemp and linen thread, and some of the finer-quality linen thread may have been used by Yeovil's bone lace makers, though they also used Antwerp thread (doubtless finer still).[81] The coarser hemp thread made sacks and sails. It evidently served John Ash, one of the sack weavers of Stoke under Hamden, near Yeovil, who wove for a Reading merchant sackcloth that was almost certainly destined to make corn and malt sacks for the grain trade of the Thames Valley.[82] It is true that flax and hemp had long been traditional crops in both Somerset and Dorset, but we must give credit to Christopher Cockerell of Elham in Kent, who was commissioned by a group of West Country gentlemen in the mid-1620s to move to the south-west and teach the art of cultivation and the processing of flax. He stayed in Somerset and Dorset for thirteen years,[83] directing his attention to places where fenland was being drained at the same time. The local industry expanded and modernized itself to keep abreast of its rivals abroad. Bridport in Dorset used locally grown hemp for making the best hawsers, cables, and ropes for ships, also traces and halters for horses, and even ropes for the hangman (called Bridport daggers).[84] In Scarsdale Hundred in Derbyshire, flax was widely grown in the seventeenth century to make cottons.[85] Staffordshire hemp, growing everywhere in the county, according to Robert Plot, was the basis of the substantial linen industry which in 1700 was centred on Bilston, and extended to Wednesfield, Willenhall, and Sedgley.[86] In the Wolverhampton

[80] Blith, op. cit. 260.

[81] VCH *Somerset*, ii, 426.

[82] This was John Ash who died in 1619. (PRO Prob 11/134, no. 97.)

[83] VCH *Somerset*, ii, 423–4; HMC 7th Report (Taunton Records), 694.

[84] VCH *Dorset*, ii, 344–8. For an illuminating example of the way in which distant regions were linked by their industrial specialities, see the census of Ipswich's poor in 1597 which named Hewge Russell, a newcomer from Bridport, Dorset, as 'the chief workman of ropemakers'. (*Poor Relief in Elizabethan Ipswich*, ed. J. Webb, Suffolk Rec. Soc. 1x (1966), 139.)

[85] VCH *Derbyshire*, ii, 372.

[86] Robert Plot, *The Natural History of Staffordshire* (Oxford, 1686), 109. I am indebted for information on the situation in Staffordshire in 1700 to Roger Vaughan, whose thesis will have more to say on the industry of these places.

district, it was considered second only to metalworking. At Rowley Regis the specialities were rope and thread. These are only a few of the examples that could be enumerated, which give a glimpse of the thousands of men and women the length and breadth of the kingdom who got part at least of their living from the growing and working of flax and hemp, and who supplied the home market with its routine requirements in rope, nets, sacks, ticking, and thread.

But what of the scandals encircling projects? There were mumblings against monopolies in Parliament in 1571. In 1601, the indignation of the Commons reached such a pitch that Elizabeth was obliged to cancel many patents. The truth is that the scandals were much better publicized in London than the constructive achievements of projects in the country-side. Yet in 1601 they had a commendable record. Oil crushing from rapeseed, flax and hemp growing, and the manufacture of goods from their fibres were all making solid progress. On the success of oven and furnace making we must withhold judgement until the evidence is more fully investigated. But fresh possibilities of work were being offered to labouring men and women, and workhouses too had begun to employ paupers on the better-established schemes. What is more, some of these projects were being carried over into Ireland.

The setting-up of English plantations in Ireland had been propounded to Thomas Cromwell in the 1530s and again discussed in Edward VI's reign. The idea began to be put into effect in 1563–4 in Leix and Offaly, but was much more energetically pursued in Munster after the Desmond rebellion was crushed in 1583.[87] Almost instantly English projectors saw the potential demand for consumer goods from the newly arriving English planters. They were right: all the essential and luxury wares that were said to waste England's treasure in the 1540s began to appear among Irish imports in the 1580s and 1590s. The opportunity of establishing these new industries in a country that had more fuel, and much cheaper labour, was quickly seized. In 1584 just as the woad growing craze was working up to a climax in England, licences

[87] K.S. Bottigheimer, *English Money and Irish Land* (Oxford, 1971), 7–12.

were issued for woad and madder growing, and for rape oil production, in the Flemish manner, in Ireland. Sir Francis Walsingham not only took a personal interest in this project, he also helped to finance it. (William Cecil appears to have had his woad project on the island of Helbry.) This venture had its amusing episodes, but basically, it was a serious project, seriously pursued. Wild madder already grew in Ireland,[88] and it served well enough for dyeing Irish cloth, but by English standards the processing of the dye was inexpertly done, and in consequence it was unsaleable outside the country.[89] Nearly twenty years before, in 1568, a patent had been granted to Peter Backe, a native of Brabant, to collect madder in Ireland.[90] The new licence, issued in 1584, was showing results by 1588 when 13 tons 1 hogshead of green madder were landed from Ireland in the port of Chester.[91] As for the woad project, detailed accounts show with what care the equipment and the work-force were assembled.[92] . The under-takers were a Fleming from Tournai, Peter Desmaistres, and John Williams, a London merchant, newly returned from the Low Countries.[93] They did not intend to live rough in Ireland, and along with the shovels, spades, axes, baskets, and other gear which they assembled for their tasks, they laid in plentiful supplies of beds, tables, benches, linen (nothing so coarse as hempen) sheets, pillowslips, and table-cloths. They gave priority to woad over madder in the first stage, since it gave a quicker return; cultivation began in 1585. At the end of the first year these two managers were dismissed, and another was engaged by Walsingham. Who was he? None other than Alexander King, Cecil's roving reporter,

---

[88] The roots of wild madder do not give such a brilliant red colour as culti-vated madder, but they yield a rosy pink dye that is favoured nowadays by arts and craftsmen. (Geoffrey Grigson, *The Englishman's Flora*, London, 1958, 348.) I wish to thank Mrs. Marion Stowell for this reference.

[89] A. Longfield, *Anglo-Irish Trade in the Sixteenth Century* (London, 1929), 182–3.

[90] Hulme, LQR lxi, 45.

[91] Longfield, op. cit. 184.

[92] PRO E101, Bdle 540, no. 19. Other references are contained in State Papers Ireland, but they are not fully listed here since I hope to publish elsewhere a fuller account of woad growing in England and Ireland in the sixteenth and seventeenth centuries.

[93] PRO SP 63/113/51.

who had travelled round England in 1585, meeting all the woad growers and discussing with them the benefits and drawbacks of the new crop. His survey had been undertaken when the government, panic-stricken by the acreage now occupied by woad, had banned its cultivation and drawn loud protests. In his new role as *promoter* of woad in Ireland, Alexander King engaged a number of different experts to take responsibility for the woad plantations in different parts of the country. Who were they? None other than some of the men whom he had interviewed on his tours of England.

At the end of the second year of woad growing in Ireland, it became clear how impossible it was to supervise centrally a crop that was being cultivated in many scattered places. One of the advisers at the centre of things in Dublin urged Walsingham in 1586 to license individual woad growers at a yearly rent and leave them to their own devices. What happened to woad growing thereafter we do not know. Decentralization brought the official records to an end. But the projecting fervour was not quenched. Peter Desmaistres retained the madder and oil licences, and laid new plans to put these into operation. John Williams set to work with the aid of a Dutchman to begin the making of thread and starch in Ireland.

Since the Irish plantation in Munster met with disaster in 1598 it is likely that all these projects came to an abrupt close.[94] But we should not pass premature judgement on this score. One or two may have caught on with the Irish and continued thereafter. We shall see in the history of tobacco growing in England (Ch. IV), how a projector's new crop could speedily be taken over by poor peasants if its agricultural routine suited their circumstances and the right market was found. But even if the Irish episode had no lasting results, it broadened the horizons of English projectors. In the next phase of projects, from 1601–1624, as more schemes unfolded in England, trials almost automatically started overseas, not only in Ireland, but across the Atlantic, especially in Virginia.

---

[94] Bottigheimer, op. cit. 12.

IV. THE SCANDALOUS PHASE, PART II, 1601–1624

A substantial number of projects supplied consumer goods that could never be deemed essential to life. As imports they had been much more severely frowned on officially than hemp, flax, oil, and portable ovens. Even when they began to be produced at home, they were still considered to be frivolous and unnecessary, unfit to occupy the labours of honest Englishmen. However, their manufacture at home halted the drain of bullion, they provided much work, and, because of public demand, they persisted.

This chapter directs attention at three such consumer industries. To trace their beginnings is an uphill task. Take, for example, the pin industry. Historians have decided that pins are commodities beneath notice, and more than one editor of historical documents has printed valuable references to them, but omitted the word entirely from his volume's index. In fact, enormous numbers of pins were used in the sixteenth century, and for a long time the bulk of them was imported. Accordingly, they were named by Sir Thomas Smith in the *Discourse of the Commonweal* in 1549 as one of the commodities that ought to be manufactured in England.[1]

In an age of conspicuous consumption, when changing fashions in dress were followed by people of all classes, pins were surely one of life's necessities. They were as essential to the tailors, dress makers, hat makers, and lace makers as were nails to the carpenter and joiner. In the home too they were used in large quantities. The children in Sir Henry Sidney's household at Penshurst in Kent each received an allowance of 3s. worth of pins to last them six months.[2] This was the equivalent of nine days' wages for a male labourer at 4d. a day. 'Is there no small pins for my cuffs? Look in the pin

[1] *A Discourse of the Common Weal* 63.
[2] Kent Archives Office, Sidney MS. U1475, A 56 (2), Accounts for Michaelmas 1573–Easter 1574.

cushion. Pin that with a black pin.[3] These were standard sentences for translation in a textbook for teaching French to English boys, published in 1605. Not a soul in the kingdom could entirely dispense with pins.

Everyone agreed that the demand for pins was enormous. In 1597 £40,000 worth of pins and needles were said to be imported.[4] In 1609 it was claimed that £60,000 worth of pins were used in England every year.[5] At the same time, it was persuasively argued that the English pin makers could not produce all the different types of pins in sufficient quantity and at the same cheap price as the Dutch.[6] Some types of pins were probably more cheaply made in England than Holland, but others plainly were not.

Just how many qualities and types were on sale is difficult to determine. Some pins were coarse, some were fine; some were made of iron (and presumably rusted easily), some were made of brass. It was not easy, declared one contemporary, to distinguish iron pins from brass pins when they were new.[7] Hence one of the complaints about deceits in manufacture. One list of pins runs to nineteen different kinds, another to thirteen, varying according to weight and type of metal.[8] The principal difference was between red pins and white pins (possibly the difference between brass and iron?) but they were also done up in differently sized packets. Moreover, styles and shapes varied: there were long white pins and short white pins, double cawkins, angel pins, and red number pins. A draper's shop in Kirkby Lonsdale in 1578 stocked 16,000 pins at $9\frac{1}{4}d$, a thousand, and 1,000 pins of another kind costing 18d. , plus rowd (=rolled?) headed pins worth 13d.[9] Thus it had a goodly quantity but not a very wide selection.

---

[3] M. St. Clare Byrne (ed.), *The Elizabethan Home* (London, 1949), 40. The standard wage for men rose from 4d. to 1s. a day between 1500 and 1650. Contemporaries cited 4d. a day as an average in the 1580s, but 8d. in the 1620s. See below, p. 173.

[4] BL Lansdowne MS. 84, no. 21.

[5] BL Lansdowne MS. 152, fo. 328.

[6] Ibid. fo. 316.

[7] Guildford Muniment Room, LM 1331/36. I wish to thank Mr. J.R. More-Molyneux of Loseley Park for allowing me to consult these MSS.

[8] PRO SP 39/9, no. 6; BL Cotton MS., Titus B IV, fo. 160.

[9] J. Raine (ed.), *Wills and Inventories from. . .the Archdeaconry of Richmond*, Surtees Soc. xxvi (1853), 279.

Quantities of this kind nevertheless give a glimpse of the labour employed in this industry. Every pin had to be pointed with a file; every knob of every pin had to be put on by hand. With complete unanimity, contemporaries averred that pin making employed labourers in their thousands. We must surely believe them. Between 2,000 and 3,000 were said to be employed in pin making in London and the suburbs in 1608.[10] Children started work at the age of eight, and for the lame and the legless, for disabled soldiers and crippled paupers, pin making was one of the few occupations that enabled them to earn an independent living.[11] Yet this industry had developed in the sixteenth century almost from nothing. Almost, but not quite. Pins made of iron had been manufactured in the country for at least one hundred and fifty years,[12] but they failed entirely in the first half of the sixteenth century to compete with the Dutch. The bulk of the pins used in England by that time came from Holland. However, the policy of reducing imports and encouraging domestic manufacture affected pins as well as other goods, and at some date in the 1560s or 1570s pin making with brass wire imported from Sweden and Germany started. It reflected the newly learned lesson that industries might well flourish in England even though the raw materials came from abroad.

It is likely that Dutch immigrants had a hand in inaugurating this new phase in the history of pin making, but the chronology of innovation is confused. The Dutch had a technique whereby two men could point more pins than a hundred, working with a file, had done previously.[13] This is doubtless the reason why Holland had earlier driven the English pin makers out of business. Now Dutchmen introduced the technique into England. Then the Mineral and Battery Works was set up and the manufacture of brass wire began in England. Competition between English and Dutch pin makers grew fiercer but the English still laboured at a great disadvantage. They failed to copy from the Dutch—at least at the beginning—

[10]   BL Lansdowne MS. 152, fo. 333.
[11]   BL Lansdowne MSS. 84, no. 21; 160, no. 68, fo. 240; 152, fos. 322, 324.
[12]   BL Lansdowne MS. 160, no. 68, fo. 240.
[13]   BL Cotton MS. Titus B V, fo. 304 (n.d.).

their method of employing paupers in workhouses to make pins. This was the main source of labour in the Dutch pin making industry, and it was said to be the reason why Dutch pins could be so cheaply produced. The paupers were housed, fed, and clothed at public expense, and the wire was supplied from the common stock of the workhouse.[14] The standard English account of this practice was somewhat jaundiced: the Dutch pin makers, they said, were maintained 'in perpetual slavery', whereas in England pin makers were free men. English pinners, they proudly maintained, could not have endured 'so hard diet' as the Dutch.[15] But the sad fact remained that, in consequence, English pins cost more.

In the wrangling about whether to restrict the import of foreign pins or to allow freedom of trade, and in the frequent changes of policy that accompanied these debates, we have some measure of the economic importance attached to the industry. Foreign pins were banned in 1563, allowed by proclamation in 1564, and allowed by statute in 1565. They were banned again in 1571 and the prohibition was regularly renewed for the rest of Elizabeth's reign. But a summary of the law in 1608 stated that, despite all the statutes, foreign pins were continuously imported by Englishmen and foreigners.[16] Legislation could not intimidate merchants in the face of insistent market demand.

The competitive struggle in the years between 1600 and 1620 grew more intense. Some Dutch pins cost half as much as their English equivalent; on average all Dutch pins cost one-third less.[17] The Dutchman's specialities were the very low priced pins which were most in demand in England, and represented 80 per cent of the market.[18] The Dutch were also far better than the English at making pins for use with very fine cambric and lawn. The English, on the other hand, were competitive in the manufacture of medium-quality pins, although these were still described by some as 'gross and stiff' pins.[19]

[14] BL Lansdowne MS. 152, fos. 322, 323.
[15] Ibid., fo. 328.
[16] Ibid., fo. 319.
[17] Ibid., fos. 324, 332.
[18] Ibid., fo. 324.
[19] Ibid., fo. 317.

In the competition between Dutch and English no holds were barred. The Dutch gave their pins private marks and wrapped them inside a blue paper. The English wrapped theirs in white paper. But each charged the other with counterfeiting these private marks and packing the pins in the wrong coloured papers.[20]

The English pin makers in the early years of James I's reign had shrill voices, so that the wrangling between them and would-be monopolist importers of Dutch pins filled many yards of parchment, and they made sure that Parliament heard and read every word. But while the Londoners wrangled, the possibilities of this expanding domestic industry were being exploited in a much freer atmosphere in the provinces. An old pin industry survived in Gloucestershire from the fifteenth century, in the vicinity of the Forest of Dean and in Gloucester. Schemes were laid for bringing Osmund iron from overseas to Bristol, turning it into wire at Tintern and delivering it for pin making at Bewdley, Gloucester, and Bristol, as well as London.[21] These plans reflect a different mood and a new phase in the industry's development in the south-west. The government's notes on pin making in 1609 recommended greater production of English wire from English wireworks in order to make the raw material more cheaply available to poor pin makers.[22] The English industry in the provinces was gathering strength.

By the early 1620s the old Gloucester pin making industry had advanced sufficiently to be commended as a scheme to provide work for the poor. In 1623 John Tilsley, son of a chapman of Abenhall, who had been apprenticed to a wire-drawer of Gloucester, proposed a scheme to Bristol corporation for teaching poor children pin making.[23] It was accepted; in 1626 he undertook the same task for Gloucester Corporation, teaching thirty boys at a time and paying them a weekly wage which increased as they became more proficient. The idea spread and in 1627 one of the public-spirited

[20]   Ibid., fos. 322, 317.
[21]   BL Cotton MS. Titus B V, no. 134, fo. 355 (n.d.).
[22]   BL Lansdowne MS. 152, fo. 328.
[23]   This and the following paragraph are based on Mr. R.A. Lewis's unpublished pamphlet on pinmaking, lent to me by the Gloucester City Museum and Art Gallery. I wish to thank the author for allowing me to draw on his research.

inhabitants of Berkeley, Glos., meeting Tilsley at Gloucester Assizes (the Assizes were one of the best places for publicizing projects), persuaded him to come to Berkeley and start an industry there, again teaching thirty pin makers at a time.

Pin making in Gloucestershire had a continuous history for two centuries thereafter. John Tilsley's son, Philip, ran a flourishing pin business in Gloucester, which in 1632 was said to keep eighty boys and girls in work, and which made him a personal fortune of £20,000. Five of his apprentices also became independent pin makers in the same City. Tilsley's brother was just as successful in Bristol. In 1735 pin making was the chief manufacture of Gloucester, and still involved nine different tradesmen and nineteen distinct operations. As for the quality of the pins made, this had evidently improved so much that silence fell upon the subject of Dutch competition. In 1683 one writer claimed that English pins excelled 'all that are made in any other part of the world'.[24]

To summarize, the pin industry had started as a project of the 1540s; it benefited by technical innovations in the period 1560–80, and by the 1620s had become a strongly entrenched industry in parts of Gloucestershire as well as London and a workhouse industry in some other places, such as Salisbury. By the 1650s it was also a mainstay of the market town of Aberford, Yorkshire.[25]

Two consumer industries now call for attention that were not envisaged when the constructive policy towards projects first developed in the 1540s, but which appeared on the scene some twenty or more years later, unannounced and unanticipated. They were the accidental consequence of foreign immigration. Immigrants, as all experience teaches, wish to have the food, drink, clothes, and household and industrial goods to which they have been accustomed at home. The Dutch and French brought strong likes and dislikes with them; Englishmen adopted them too, and new industries resulted, providing occupations, this time mainly in towns. One of these unexpected guests was starch making. The first recorded reference to 'starch' in *The Oxford*

[24] S.J., *The Present State of England* (London, 1683), 266.
[25] *Barnabae Itinerarium, or Barnabee's Journal* (7th edn., London, 1818), 29. I wish to thank Mr. Brian Haigh for this reference.

English Dictionary is dated 1440. In what sense, then, can starch making be described as a new occupation in the late sixteenth century? Various stiffening agents were used before this, but probably nothing was produced on a commercial scale: milk stiffened lace, gum arabic was used for nets and silks, size was employed for dark-coloured cloths and woollens.[26] The root of *arum maculatum* (cuckoo-pint), so Gerard's *Herbal* tells us, made pure white starch, but it blistered the hands. Starch that was made from wheat had been introduced into northern Europe in the fourteenth century,[27] but it was not until the fashion for starched ruffs came in in the sixteenth century that it was needed in large quantity and became an article of commerce. When this happened, the Dutch not only supplied the fine lawn of which the ruffs were made; they became masters of the method of making starch from wheat.

We have no detailed sixteenth-century account of the process, but the more general descriptions of it from that period do not conflict in any way with that given by Robert Plot, who observed it in Oxford in 1677.[28] It was laborious work, requiring time and care but no expensive capital equipment, nothing more than a roomy shed or workhouse, many tubs and barrels, and plenty of water. Bran was steeped in water with rock alum (another use for alum, which was also the projectors' concern) for 10 to 14 days, then rinsed through three different tubs, finishing with a rinsing in clear pump water. The resulting fine washed flour then stood in its own water for about a week, more pump water was added, and the smallest bran that settled at the bottom was strained off. The tubs were left for another day, the water was then drawn off entirely, the starch left to dry for two more days, rinsed lightly with more pump water, then cut out of the tubs in great pieces with sharp trowels. It was packed into troughs with holes in the bottom, through which the remaining

[26] D. Hartley, *Water in England* (London, 1964), 322. I wish to thank Miss Christine Bloxham for this and several other references to starch making cited below.

[27] Wadym Jarowenko, 'Starch', in *Encyclopaedia of Polymer Science and Technology* (New York, 1970), xii, 787.

[28] R. Plot, *Natural History of Oxfordshire* (Oxford, 1677), 280–7.

water drained; it was laid on cold bricks to dry for two days and then on a baker's oven (that newly invented portable oven that was so economical in fuel, perhaps?) where it dried for another four days. Some was then ground to a white powder for powdering the hair, the rest was dried on a hot stove. The whole process took over a month to complete.

Some starch was imported from abroad in the 1530s and 1540s; but its manufacture in England was probably first introduced into London in the early 1560s, along with the first sales of lawn and cambric. Edmund Howes in his edition of Stow's *Annals* recalled the first appearance of these novelties on the London scene in 1562. The new fine linen fabrics, lawn and cambric, were sold by Dutch merchants in yards and half-yards only, the English linen drapers not daring to buy larger quantities. Then the Queen, whose ruffs had always hitherto been made of fine holland fabric, had new ones made of cambric, but no one knew how to starch them. She had to find a Dutchwoman who was familiar with the art, and thus it was that the wife of Gwillam Boone, the Queen's Dutch coachman, became starcher by appointment to Her Majesty. In 1564 Mistress Dinghen van der Plasse, from Teenen in Flanders, came as a refugee to London and set up a starching business among the Dutch community. Her work was superb and her compatriots paid her handsomely. English women were attracted by the neatness and delicate appearance of the Dutchwomen's linen (Dutch paintings explain the attraction); they too made ruffs of cambric for themselves and took them along to Mistress Dinghen to be starched. Then they ventured to make them of lawn 'which was at that time a stuff most strange and wonderful'. Finally, Mistress Dinghen took some of their daughters as trainees, charging £4 and £5 to teach them how to starch, and 20s. for showing them how to prepare it. Ruffs fast became essential wear with men as well as with women who wanted to keep up with the fashion—they were sometimes 9 inches deep and 12 lengths to a ruff, if your neck was long enough.[29] Three new urban occupations had thus been

[29] John Stow, *Annales of England,* continued by Edmund Howes (London, 1615), 867–9.

created: ruff making, starch making, and weekly starching.
What employment did starch making afford? An undated
Jacobean document, describing those licensed to make
starch, claimed that there were 19 starch makers in and
around London, and that King's Lynn and Norwich had the
same number as London, making such large quantities that
every fortnight 40 horseloads were taken from Norfolk to the
counties of Nottinghamshire, Staffordshire, Lincolnshire,
and Yorkshire. Others licensed to make starch dwelt in
Oxford, Northampton, Wisbech, Ely, and Peterborough, all
making large quantities.[30] In 1609–10 starch manufacture
was said to consume considerable quantities of wheat in
Bristol and Gloucester, as well as in London, and in 1612 a
list of starch makers named one at Berwick, two at Newcastle, two at King's Lynn, and seven in Norwich, as well as
the Londoners.[31] These numbers are not impressive, but on
closer investigation it becomes clear that those who were
counted, and sometimes named individually, in official
documents were the lions in the business. A proclamation in
1608 referred to the humble suit 'of *the better sort* of the
starch-makers',[32] these were the men who made their voices
heard in government circles, and who appear in the surviving
records. The legislation and proclamations against starch
making shed light in much darker places.

The account which follows is based to a large extent on
statements in proclamations, the explanatory preambles of
which are not generally treated seriously. They deserve a
different assessment. The manuscripts of William Cecil,
Lord Burghley, reveal that he possessed a quite remarkable
information service. Thomas Fuller in the later seventeenth
century reported Burghley's reputation for always consulting
artificers in their own art.[33] The reputation was well earned.
We see this in the inquiry into woad growing. Alexander King
travelled all over southern England questioning woad growers,

---

[30]   BL Cotton MS. Faust. C ii, fo. 119.

[31]   BL Lansdowne MS. 152, fo. 130; Cotton MS. Titus BV, fo. 315.

[32]   J.F. Larkin and P.L. Hughes, *Stuart Royal Proclamations*, i: 1603–25
(Oxford, 1973), 189.

[33]   See above, pp. 52–3; E.P. Cheyney in *A History of England*, ii (London,
1926), 289, also noted how carefully Burghley scrutinized requests for patents,
and called for reports on their consequences.

J.P.s, and labourers. He reported thoroughly and conscien-
tiously, and since he became acquainted with the leading
woad growers in places as far apart as Hampshire, Worcestershire, and Suffolk, we can understand how some of the same
people came subsequently to be recruited to oversee the
growing of woad in Ireland.[34] Another such investigator was
William Herle who wrote memoranda to Lord Burghley on
such matters as the salt industry.[35] It would not be unprofitable to study more systematically the missions undertaken by
some of these roving reporters. Suffice it to say that words
from some of their reports can be recognized in the phrases
of subsequent proclamations. The evidence points to the
existence of an efficient and fair-minded government information service in Elizabeth's reign, and although it did not
maintain the same high standard under James, it continued to
function more modestly as some of the Cotton Manuscripts,
that include the papers of influential Privy Councillors,
testify.

The proclamations therefore deserve careful reading as
responsible statements of fact, distilled from a much larger
file of information. When they harped on the fact that more
and more people were turning to starch making for a living,
we should give credence to that possibility. The inherent plausi-
bility of the statement is strengthened by examples already
given of new occupations that spread rapidly. Stocking
knitting and woad growing are two of those whose rapid
diffusion is well documented. Another from this period is
tobacco growing: tobacco was a new field crop in Winchcombe, Gloucestershire, in 1619, and quickly proved itself
to be ideally suited to the needs of men who had a small
amount of land, and no capital, but who were willing to work
hard with their hands. At the end of the first year the
growing of tobacco was banned by the government, and the
original projectors gave it up entirely. One of these men,
indeed, subsequently received a patent to stamp out tobacco
growing wherever he found it. Yet seven years later it was
being grown in 39 places in Gloucestershire, 17 places in

---

[34] See above, pp. 76–7.
[35] BL Lansdowne MS. 21, no. 23.

Worcestershire, and one in Wiltshire. Fifty years later, in 1670, it was growing in 22 counties in England and Wales and in the Channel Islands. From the late 1620s it was generally recognized as a poor man's crop that yielded him a good profit in return for much hard labour. If a new occupation suited the circumstances of poor men, nothing in the world could stop it from spreading like wildfire.[36]

Starch making in towns caught on as successfully as tobacco growing in the country. Its early history was rehearsed with historical accuracy in a proclamation of 1607 which described it as 'a thing newly taken up' in Elizabeth's reign, and 'grown in few years very frequent and to be much used'.

Some twenty years after the vogue for starched ruffs came into England, in 1585, Cecil carefully planned a speech to Parliament in support of a bill against the making of starch. We can read it in its first draft, and then in its polished form. Although Cecil wore starched ruffs himself—his portrait in the Bodleian Library shows him wearing some, while sitting somewhat ponderously on a mule—he could put on a very convincing display of Christian remorse at the criminal waste of a staple food in the vain pursuit of sartorial display. 'Is it not a very lamentable thing that we should bestow that upon starch to the setting forth of vanity and pride which would staunch the hunger of many that starve in the streets for want of bread?' England had enjoyed peace and plenty of corn for twenty-seven years, but if men reached back in their memories seven years earlier still, they would recall a scarcity of such severity that people made their bread of acorns. 'Such times have been many times and such times may come again.' The abuse of starch had grown apace not merely because more people were wearing ruffs but because ruffs had increased in size and splendour. Double ruffs had been the fashion a few years before, now it was long ruffs, 'grown so outrageously and to such unconscionable length'. And presumably, the bigger the ruff, the more it rubbed your neck, the dirtier it became, the more often it had to be starched, and the more you had to spend on starch.

[36] Thirsk, 'New Crops and their Diffusion: Tobacco-growing in Seventeenth-century England', 76 ff.

Politicians might choose to wait patiently for the fashion to die out, Cecil conceded, but he preferred to take some practical steps to hasten the day; the choice lay between taxing ruffs or curbing starch making.[37] Cecil chose the latter course, and in 1588 handed over the monopoly of manufacture to patentees, who retained it from 1588 to 1601. But storms of protest at the starch monopoly caused Elizabeth to revoke it in 1601, and restore 'the liberty of all men'. In James's reign starch making 'continued in many places of this realm', and the consumption of wheat grew alarmingly. It became especially offensive in years of grain scarcity, yet a total ban on starch making was out of the question because it would take away the living of so many people. A solution was found in a system of licensing. The proclamation of 1607 insisted on starch houses being licensed by magistrates, and allowed nothing but pollard wheat and bran to be used in the manufacture.[38] A year later (in July 1608) a new proclamation admitted that more and more people, who had never before made starch, were setting up in the business, and in order to reduce the consumption of good edible wheat special permission was given to use musty, imported wheat that had been damaged by sea water.[39] By 1610, however, this had encouraged 'a far greater number of persons even in all parts and places of the same our realm and dominion. . .daily more and more' to set up starch making, and another proclamation became necessary.[40] Inferior persons were now said to be using starch, thus indicating that the lower orders had taken to wearing starched ruffs, or at least starched collars. The making of starch was again prohibited, but as the government did not wish to deprive 'the better sort of our said subjects' of their much-needed starch, nor to increase its price by creating a shortage, permission was given to import it from abroad. J.P.s, mayor, constables, and others were

[37] BL Lansdowne MS. 43, no. 73.

[38] Larkin and Hughes, op. cit. i, 537. A Starchmakers' Company of London was incorporated at this time (1607) but it was suspended in 1610 and domestic manufacture forbidden. Plans were laid to reincorporate it in 1612 but nothing resulted. In 1619 illicit makers were licensed again. In 1622 the Starchmakers' Company was reconstituted.

[39] Larkin and Hughes, op. cit. i, 188 ff.

[40] Ibid. 237 ff. The same facts are stated in BL Lansdowne MS. 152, fo. 120.

exhorted to enforce this order. But was it likely that officials would deliberately destroy the livings of many labouring men for the benefit of the *Dutch* starch industry? The argument began to develop into a controversy about natural justice: why should Englishmen be prevented from following an honest trade, while foreigners were allowed to sell the same prohibited wares brought in from abroad? It was 'directly against the law and the good of the Commonwealth'.[41]

Seven months later, in August 1610, a fresh proclamation showed that local officials had not responded obediently to James's call. Starch making continued, and some of the worst offenders against His Majesty were now said to be the formerly respectable grocers, chandlers, and retailers, who bought starch cheaply from small, illicit starch makers, 'needy and mean persons [who] are stirred with small profit'.[42] The uncooperative mood of local officials in suppressing this new local industry was illustrated by an episode at Yarmouth. A summons from the Privy Council in 1620 to one of the bailiffs asked him to explain why he did not aid 'those who came down about the starch-making'. He was evidently reluctant to assist the royal representatives. Yet his fellow bailiffs and the justices of the county enthusiastically testified to his diligence in serving their town.[43]

In defence of recalcitrant local officials, it should be said, however, that they often had the tacit, and some-times the explicit, approval of the King's ministers in interpreting royal commands in their own way. The J.P.s of Surrey made the revealing disclosure that the Lord Chancellor himself had given his approval when they re-frained from executing the proclamation of 1610 against starch. 'In these and like cases,' they said, 'where letters have been written to JPs, the Lord Chancellor has often told them that the Lords do rely so much upon their discretion to whom they write, that if there be anything in their letters seeming harsh either in law or otherwise, they should in their wisdom moderate the same in the execution, presuming the tenor of such letters to be rather *in terrorem* [to strike

41 BL Lansdowne MS. 152, fo. 123.
42 Larkin and Hughes, op. cit., i, 252.
43 CSPD *1619–23*, 162.

fear] than otherwise.'[44]

In 1619 the starch makers were again allowed to carry on their trade under licence. The proclamation of 1620 explained that 'many of our poor subjects did live and maintain themselves by making of starch'.[45] A fresh development in the industry was noticed at the same time. 'Diverse persons of wealth and ability' were secretly employing 'great stocks and sums of money, and therewith set on work in making of starch persons of little or no ability, who, being questioned for their offences, are ready to fly, or being found out have no substance or estate to yield any fine'.[46] Evidently some kind of putting-out or subcontracting system was evolving; the substantial starch makers were learning to live with the small men. Some of these 'poor starch-makers' were men with starch houses beside the Thames, who were mentioned by name in 1621, as protests built up against the winkling-out of unlicensed starch makers[47] The house of one Duffield, 'a very poor man', was broken into and his starch carried away when he was not at home. Jacob Meade, starch maker, was restrained from making starch for ten weeks, and *so had no means of feeding his 200 pigs*. Michael Francis, starch maker, was restrained for twenty-three weeks, and his pigs starved in consequence.[48] What were the pigs doing amid the starch tubs? They were evidently fed with the bran and pollard meal that was strained from the starch in the course of the refining process. These men had resourcefully devised two complementary occupations for themselves, starch making combined with pig fattening along London's riverside.

It is, of course, impossible to estimate the numbers of men employed in starch making in the early seventeenth century, but it is difficult to argue on this evidence that it was a paltry industry employing only a handful of

---

[44] BL Lansdowne MS. 152, fo. 118.
[45] Larkin and Hughes, op. cit. i, 473.   [46] Ibid. 474.
[47] W. Notestein, F.H. Relf, and H. Simpson, *Commons Debates, 1621* (New Haven, 1935), vii, 513–5.
[48] Ibid. 514–5.

people.[49] Having seen how quickly other projects caught on, we must take seriously the uproar against starch making. It was plainly a town industry and it started in London. Starch houses quickly sprang up in sheds and outbuildings amid domestic houses, where the unpleasant smell of starch and the fires which were stoked for drying the starch were a nuisance and a hazard. One starch house was so near the chancel of St. Mary Overbury's Church in Southwark that the noise disturbed the congregation at divine service, and once the church and whole borough were nearly burnt down.[50] Starch making then spread to the larger provincial towns whence starch was dispatched to counties far away; Norwich, for example, supplied Staffordshire and Yorkshire. In the early seventeenth century the starch makers even had hopes of a market abroad, in Spain where starch making was prohibited.[51] Whether their hopes were realized is not revealed, but English starch found its way to Ireland in the late sixteenth and seventeenth centuries and in the 1660s some went regularly to the Plantations and occasionally to Italy.[52] The main users of English starch, however, were English women, all over the kingdom; and when English housewives ceased to bother with the starching of ruffs, they turned their energies to starching pillowcases, napkins, and tablecloths. Starch remained firmly on the shopping list of the English housewife. In the account of one busy landlady, Joyce Jefferies of Hereford, we see starch being bought in 1638 in packs of 12 lb. at a time.[53] If we buy it at all these

[49] Indirect evidence may be found in various statements on the quantity of materials used in starch: (i) a seemingly well-informed expert (probably c. 1612) claimed that one starch house in London used 1,500 quarters of wheat in less than a year, while ten other starch makers steeped 40–50 quarters apiece a week (BL Cotton MS. Titus B V, fo. 315): (ii) 100,000 tons of starch were said to be made in England yearly, but this is a suspiciously round figure (BL Lansdowne MS. 152, fo. 126 (July 1612)); (iii) in the time of John Packington's patent (1594–1601) it was alleged that 600 cwt of starch was sold in London every week (BL Cotton MS. Faust. C ii, fo. 119); (iv) bran was short in London in 1609–10 and the starch makers were blamed by the brown-bread makers who used it for horsebread, and by the colliers and brewers who fed it to their horses and cattle, and now had to buy oats, which had consequently doubled in price (BL Lansdowne MS. 152, fo. 130).

[50] BL Cotton MS. Titus B V, fo. 315[V].
[51] Ibid., fos. 315 ff.; Titus B IV, no. 85.
[52] Longfield, Anglo-Irish Trade 191; BL Add. MS. 36785.
[53] BL Egerton MS. 3054, fo. 26.

days, we buy it in 4-ounce packets.

Another unanticipated and unplanned consumer project of the later sixteenth century was vinegar making and the distilling of spirits. Vinegar is *vin aigre* (bitter wine) and traditionally it was made from wine lees or from wine that had gone sour. Before the mid-sixteenth century malt vinegar was not a commercial article, although it was brewed in private houses on a small scale. When the Dutch introduced beer made with hops, they made it possible for *commercial* beer brewing to begin, because hopped beer will keep for a long time without deteriorating, unlike ale. By the early sixteenth century, when commercial beer brewers were entrenched in London and Canterbury, many were of Dutch and German origin.[54] Their numbers were much augmented by the Dutch refugees who arrived in the 1560s. As more beer was brewed in the later sixteenth century, so the brewers found themselves with more dregs that could be made into vinegar. The commercial brewing of vinegar began, stimulated, we may suppose, by the fact that the Dutch had a taste for malt vinegar, whereas it was less familiar to Englishmen. In the early days at least, they were prone to call it 'corrupt vinegar, made of corrupt beer and ale'. Complaints were submitted to Lord Burghley in 1576 against the makers of this 'corrupt vinegar' who congregated in London and in St. Katherine's, Whitechapel, Shoreditch, and St. Thomas's, Clerkenwell. In addition to making straightforward malt vinegars, called 'alegar' and 'beeregar', they were accused of flavouring these liquors with unwholesome dredges and colourings, using elderberries, *tournesole*,[55] and privet berries. To the gourmet some of these may sound interesting and tasty variations on standard malt vinegar, but some of the

---

[54] P. Mathias, *The Brewing Industry in England, 1700–1830* (Cambridge 1959), 3–4.

[55] I am much indebted to Mrs. Carolina Lane for investigating the identity of *tournesole*, and establishing that it was *Chrozophora tinctoria* (a member of the modern Euphorbiaceae), a herb that has its origins in the Mediterranean region and has been used as a source of red and blue dye since prehistoric times. It was described by Gerard in his *Herbal* as the 'small tornsole' used in France to colour jellies, wines, meats and 'sundry confectures'. Privet berries were used in dyeing and tanning. (A. Pratt, *The Flowering Plants of Great Britain*, 2nd edn., London, 1899, 231.) I wish to thank Mrs. Marion Stowell for this reference.

mixtures were undoubtedly unwholesome and they greatly bothered the Tallowchandlers of London, makers of traditional brews.[56]

By 1593 good malt vinegars seem to have become acceptable to the Englishman's palate, but their unreliable quality gave cause for alarm. Lord Burghley deputed Alderman Anthony Radclyff to carry out an investigation, and he sought out 'the substantialest men' in the business. Those using good beer and ale as ingredients wanted to debar the rest, but 'they who are poor and find more sweet by making it of weaker beer or ale or of worse stuff no doubt will repine at any new grant to restrain them', he reported. Evidently there were reputable makers and there were the back-street brewers. But strong or weak, beer and ale were not the only ingredients. Radclyff probed deeper, and was puzzled why so many people bought the hogwash and dregs of the coolback [sic]. He was not content to be fobbed off with the statement that these liquors were bought only by desperately thirsty felt makers and weavers. He persisted, and found that distillers of aqua vitae and vinegar also bought dregs, and worked them up secretly in their houses, mixing them with weak beer. Prowling around the back streets of London, he chanced to enter the yard of a vinegar maker just as the brewer's drayman was delivering some barrels of dregs collected from private houses. The drayman, when challenged, admitted selling the barrels to the vinegar maker for 1s. 8d. to 2s. a barrel.[57]

Radclyff reported to Lord Burghley what were the correct ingredients for these liquors: malt vinegar should be made from the best beer if it was to keep well. Seamen on long voyages had found that much of this new vinegar did not keep properly. He passed on an interesting snippet of gossip that, during the wars in the Low Countries, the Flemish had bought great quantities of beeregar in England to cool their guns, as had the Spaniards also. It had sold at a great price, but the demand had now fallen off. Presumably the quality of the beeregar had not mattered greatly, and the inflated

[56] BL Lansdowne MS. 22, no. 19.
[57] BL Lansdowne MS. 74, no. 10.

demand for it had further encouraged the back street brewers.[58]

Under Dutch influence, aqua vitae and aqua composita similarly began to taste good to Englishmen. These drinks had traditionally been made of wine and wine lees, or of ale specially made for the purpose. But when wine grew too dear (along with so many other imports from abroad), Flemings and other strangers began to use the dregs and washings of beer, hitherto used only to feed pigs. They too bought up the dregs of barrels from inns, alehouses, and private houses, almost entirely dispensing with wine. Cecil's reporters concluded that the abuses in vinegar making and distilling needed reform, but hesitated to suggest solutions. If a few reputable brewers were allowed to monopolize the trade, the supplies to the market would diminish and the price would rise. Prices would have to be fixed or the abuses would never be remedied. Another report reaching Cecil agreed about the abuses and thought reform necessary in the interests of men's health, but 'at the same time the trade doth concern so many poor men's livings that it is impossible to bring it to one man's hand by licence'. Moreover, the trade had been in use for a long time, and legal opinion had pronounced firmly against the Queen's right to vest an old trade, practised by many, in the hands of one nominee.[59]

Despite these doubts, Richard Drake received a patent in 1594 to make vinegar, aqua composita and aqua vitae from ale. After the grant was passed, Lord Burghley hastened to insert a further clause allowing others to continue to make vinegar from wine lees, and allowing vinegar of all kinds to be made freely for domestic and charitable purposes.[60] After two years' experience of the workings of the patent, however, bitter complaints reached Burghley in 1596 from 'poor makers and traders of vinegar, alegar, *aqua vitae* and *aqua composita*'. The patentees had acquired their privileges by condemning others for the abusive use of dregs, lags, and unwholesome stuff. But now the patentees themselves were bulk purchasers of the same dregs. The liquor was the same

[58]   Ibid.
[59]   BL Lansdowne MS. 74, nos. 10 and 11.
[60]   Hulme, LQR lxi, 50–1.

as before, but the profit was turned from poor men—'your poor artists'—to Master Richard Drake. Drake's servants were scouring the town to drive out competitors; they seized from Hans Sturm aqua vitae that was ready to be sent overseas (sales by Flemings in London to customers abroad had been described in 1593 as substantial[61]); they forced Roger Adeney to surrender two hogsheads and 25 gallons of aqua vitae. The patentee was suppressing 'poor men in the trade who are forced to give it up'.[62]

This monopoly was one which Elizabeth agreed to abolish in 1601, and thereafter the vinegar makers and distillers of aqua vitae were liberated from controls. Roger Adeney, who had suffered the attentions of the patentee, Richard Drake, continued his modest business in St. Olave's parish, Surrey, until he died in 1619. He was indeed a poor man, just as the petitioners to Lord Burghley had earlier described him. In his will he called himself proudly a vinegar maker, and died a fervent Protestant, proclaiming Jesus Christ 'my saviour and redeemer, steadfastly believing that by virtue of his bitter death and passion I shall have remission and forgments [sic] of all my sins and that in the last day I shall reign with him in that celestial kingdom which never shall have end. This my hope and belief is firmly enclosed and laid up in the bosom of my heart', he declared. We do not know his total fortune, but his goods were speedily divided: ten shillings to his son, and the rest to his brother, Roger.[63] Those who spoke up in Parliament against monopolists, fought to defend poor men such as this.

In 1565 vinegar to the value of £1,000 had been landed at the Port of London from abroad.[64] We do not know whether this was wine or malt vinegar, but the Dutchman's malt vinegar was destined to win favour over the Frenchman's wine vinegar, and to be most commonly used in English cooking, though the more correct names for malt vinegar— 'beeregar' and 'alegar'—went out of common use.

The Dutch scored a second victory over the English by

[61] BL Landowne MS. 74, no. 12.
[62] BL Lansdowne MS. 81, no. 21.
[63] PRO Prob. 11, 133.
[64] BL Lansdowne MS. 8, no. 17.

persuading them of the goodness of distilled liquors, aqua vitae, strong waters, and 'extraordinary drinks', and more distillers were called into existence. Some of the new consumers of these spirits were drowning their sorrows, but not all. Aqua vitae was regularly carried on board ship for seamen and their merchant passengers to keep out the cold. But another reason for its increasing consumption in the early seventeenth century was that more was being prescribed by physicians and apothecaries for the sick and the aged, 'in time of sudden qualms and pangs to help their old and decayed stomachs'.[65] In 1621 it was alleged that all strong waters (and they included more esoteric liquors such as wormwood water, cinnamon water, and aniseed water) were being produced in increasing quantity. The distillers in London, Westminster, and the suburbs now numbered 200 households, and, with their apprentices, servants, porters, carriers, and salesmen, they counted 5,000 people employed in the business. These statistics, presented by the distillers themselves, are the usual round numbers, but the fact that the distillers now found the apothecaries beginning to make these waters, and trying to monopolize the manufacture of those sold as medicines, substantiates their argument that demand was increasing and for new purposes.[66] It became one of the essential drinks of Englishmen in good health and in sickness, at home and overseas. The good ship *Talbot* sailing for Massachusetts in February 1629 carried for its 100 passengers and 35 crew 20 gallons of aqua vitae as well as 2 terces of beeregar and 40 tons of beer. In 1662–3 English aqua vitae was being exported to the Plantations (5,619 gallons worth £1,685. 14s.), to Africa (204 tuns £8,160), to Russia (1,546 gallons £463. 16s.), to the East Indies (953 gallons £285. 18s.), and in token quantity (2 hogsheads) to Portugal. Strong waters were popular in Africa (1,609 gallons £482. 14s.) and Spain (1,596 gallons £478. 16s.), and small quantities also went to Germany, Portugal, Scotland, France, and Italy.[67]

The period 1601–24 was a flourishing one for projects but

---

[65] Notestein, Relf, and Simpson, op. cit. vii, 77 ff.

[66] Ibid. 77–80; iv. 108; v, 259.

[67] *Records of the Mass. Bay Colony*, i (1853), 26–7. I owe this reference to Mrs. Carolina Lane; BL Add. MS. 36785, *passim*.

it was also their most scandalous phase. The scandals were only rarely publicized in debates in Parliament, for although Members of Parliament must have known the harsh reality of monopolies, as seen from the back streets of Southwark, Reading, and York, they did not often describe them in detail on the floor of the Commons, or, if they did, reporters rarely bothered to note them. One brief glimpse is given, however, in the speech of Mr. Spicer of Warwick in 1601 who described how 'the agents of *aqua vitae* and vinegar came not long since to the town where I serve, and presently stayed the sale of both these commodities'. Their manner was threatening: 'If the sellers would not compound with them they would take them to the Privy Council.' He, Spicer, viewed the patent: it gave liberty to people to sell aqua vitae for six months more; the agent, however, gave the people only two months.[68] For once, we feel ourselves amid the throng of shopkeepers and customers in a busy provincial town. In general, however, the Parliamentary speeches about monopolies present the subject in a theatrical way that drains away any sense of contact with reality.

In 1601 Elizabeth bowed gracefully to the storm against patents and admitted that her grants concerning salt, salt upon salt, vinegar, aqua vitae, aqua composita, the salting and packing of fish, train oil, blubbers of livers of fish, poldavis and mildernix, pots, brushes, bottles, and starch had not proved to be beneficial to her subjects as she had intended, but had injured 'many of the poorer sort of her people'. Without further ado, she declared these patents void.[69] She hesitated about some other patents, promising remedy to aggrieved subjects who took their complaints to law. She also agreed to end the restraint on woad growing and to allow people 'who think it for their good to employ their grounds to the use of sowing of woad', to do so freely. Only she begged them not to inflict the smell on her when she came in her progresses to see them in the country.[70]

[68]   Townshend, *Hist. Coll.* 230–1.
[69]   Price, *Patents of Monopoly*, 156–9. The Speaker, delivering the news to Parliament of the ending of the starch monopoly, reported the Queen's sardonic comment that 'those that desire to go sprucely in their ruffs may with less charge than accustomed obtain their wish'. (Townshend, op. cit. 250.)
[70]   Price, op. cit. 156–9; Townshend, op. cit. 250.

Although Elizabeth faced a storm of anger against patents in 1601 (and earlier still, in 1597–8), in fact the number of manufacturing, as opposed to trading, patents issued between 1591 and 1600 (6) was less than half the number (14) issued between 1580 and 1590.[71] Harrington ascribed the reluctance to grant patents in the 1590s to the hostility of the Keeper of the Great Seal, Lord Ellesmere, who was said to be 'a great enemy to all these paltry concealments and monopolies'. 'To corrupt him with gifts' was 'impossible'. This may well explain (as Wyndham Hulme suggested in 1900) why William Lee failed to get a patent for his stocking frame, why Hugh Platt received so little encouragement for his many foreign novelties, and why Harrington was denied a patent for his water-closet.[72] A different mood held sway as soon as James took up the crown, but his generous grants of new patents were not more palatable to his subjects than those of Elizabeth. He was brought up sharply at the beginning of his reign by the famous lawsuit of *Darcy* versus *Allan* in 1603 concerning the patent for playing-cards. James saw the need to tread more cautiously and adopted the device of appointing councillors and Crown lawyers as referees to certify all patents before they passed the royal seal.[73] But resentment simmered. Parliament discussed patents in 1606 and again in 1610, pleading that 'those of the poorer sort. . .living hardly upon these manufactures are. . . very greatly hindered and utterly undone'.[74]

In 1603 James had suspended all monopoly grants, pending their scrutiny by King and Council, but he exempted from this order all corporations and companies enjoying monopoly privileges.[75] This had encouraged the setting-up of companies of manufacturers of the new wares. Instead of one man assuming the monopoly and sharing the privilege

---

[71] Hulme, LQR lxi. 52. Different figures, given by E.P. Cheyney (op. cit. ii, 290), include trading patents. For the debates of 1597–8 and 1601, see Neale, *Elizabeth and her Parliaments, 1584–1601*, 353–5, 376 ff.

[72] Hulme, LQR lxi, 53; Price, op. cit. 30.

[73] Robert Zaller, *The Parliament of 1621. A Study in Constitutional Conflict* (Berkeley, 1971), 128.

[74] E.R. Foster, *Proceedings in Parliament, 1610* (New Haven, 1966), ii, 268–9.

[75] Carr, *Select Charters* lxvi.

with his nominees and agents, as hitherto, associations of the more substantial men in the trade were formed, who agreed to pay James an annual sum for the privilege. The Starch-makers' Company of London had come into existence in 1607, and other new industries (the pin makers included) formed similar organizations.[76] But this only provoked a fresh outcry as non-members suffered interference with their work and experienced the oppression of privileged corporations. Since the years between 1610 and 1620 were especially fruitful in projects, the conflict between competing interests in the new industries sharpened further. 'Proclamations and patents', wrote Chamberlain in 1620, 'are become so ordinary that there is no end, every day bringing forth some new project; the few monopolies complained of at the King's accession were multiplied by many scores.'[77]

Matters came to a head in 1621 when a bill against monopoly, largely the work of Coke, was presented to the Commons. Coke's views on monopolies were made clear in the *Institutes*: they were against the liberty and freedom of the subject, and therefore against the common law of the realm. The bill put forward in 1621 did not pass, but a similar instrument was put on to the statute book in 1624.[78] It restricted the grant of monopoly rights to genuine inventors for fourteen years only. It did not entirely remove abuses, however, for privileges granted to towns and to corporations were allowed to continue; would-be monopolists continued to form corporations.

The significance of the struggle in Parliament against monopolies has been much discussed in a constitutional context, and so has the influence of the common lawyers in upholding a view of the common law which, in the economic context, strengthened the tide flowing in favour of free trade and free industrial growth.[79] We have peered into the quieter

---

[76] James I insisted in a proclamation of 1607 that starch should be made only from bran. The setting-up of a Starchmakers' Company in 1607, therefore, meant restricted, supervised manufacture. (Notestein, Relf, and Simpson, op. cit. vii, 438–9.)

[77] Carr, op. cit. lxxi, quoting PRO SP Dom., Jas. I, cxvi, 13.

[78] Zaller, op. cit. 126–8.

[79] D.O. Wagner, 'Coke and the Rise of Economic Liberalism', EcHR vi (1935–6), 30–44.

waters underneath and tried to see the economic significance of that Parliamentary struggle for working men and women, who were entering the new industries. The heightened bitterness of the conflict between monopolists and free traders may reasonably be seen as a reflection of the industrial success of projects. They were yielding rewards to projectors, and giving work to large numbers of people in many different parts of the country. The tools and expertise of many of these trades were easily acquired by men with little capital, who were not slow to see their opportunities. The monopoly rights claimed by a few Londoners were an affront, not to say an irrelevance, when seen against the wide diffusion of new occupations in towns and villages all over the kingdom. In summing up the effects of the monopoly system in its more scandalous phases, then, we must bear in mind the evidence adduced here to show that the rights of monopoly for particular projects were continually changing hands, especially in James's reign, and that the policy itself was continually vacillating between alternative courses of action. It was never efficiently enforced throughout the realm. Monopolists handled their victims roughly. When one M.P. in the Commons debate in February 1621 publicized the case of 200 looms having been laid down by a monopolist's threats and bullyings, he probably was not inventing the whole incident. But monopolists' victims were more likely to be Londoners or citizens in large towns. A great number of small producers escaped notice and carried on with these occupations undisturbed.

The programme of projects launched by the government in the mid-sixteenth century had become by James's reign part of the luggage carried by every aspiring young merchant and apprentice who made his way to London. The procession of Dick Whittingtons of the early seventeenth century, trudging down Highgate Hill with a list of projects tucked in their knapsacks, and powerful optimism in their hearts, may well have inspired the telling of the Dick Whittington story, for it is not known to have been narrated before 1605.[80] Some of these hopeful young men had very varied careers that

[80]   DNB *sub nomine*.

involved them in more than one project, and took them to more than one country as the scene for their experiments: they journeyed with their projects and hopes to Wales, Scotland, Ireland, Virginia, and the West Indies. By way of illustration, the career of John Stratford is instructive.

Stratford was the younger son of a gentry family, living at Farmcote, a hamlet in an idyllic spot in Winchcombe parish, Gloucestershire.[81] He was apprenticed to a salter in London. More notable projectors in the same company were Sir Robert Mansell, who held one of the monopolies of glass manufacture, and Sir Nicholas Crisp, who also came from Gloucestershire, later set up a madder plantation at Deptford, and is said to have suggested many inventions for water mills, paper mills, and powder mills.[82] The Salters' Company seems to have been the nursery of a multitude of projectors.

When Stratford completed his apprenticeship, he traded under his master's eye in Cheshire cheese and woollen stockings. Then about 1601 he set up in business buying goods, chiefly rough flax, but also wheat, rye, and linen yarn, from the Eastland merchants. Some of the rough flax he put out to flax spinners in London and the countryside. At the same time Stratford was engaged in a trade in tallow, potashes, soap ashes, oil, and kitchen stuff, in partnership with his brother, and this partnership was extended in 1616 when Stratford set up a soap boiling establishment in Thames Street and employed a soap boiler, John Ollyffe.[83] When the Netherlanders began to export to England flax ready dressed in place of the former undressed flax, Stratford's flax business decayed, and he decided to return to his native parish of Winchcombe, and organize the planting of tobacco. In the first year this extremely labour-intensive crop, growing on 100 acres, cost £1,400–1,500 in wages. But the government banned tobacco growing at the end of 1619 for the sake of another colonial project—the settlement and prosperity of

<hr>

[81] For the sources of this biographical information on John Stratford, see Thirsk, 'Projects for Gentlemen, Jobs for the Poor' 147 ff.; see also Thirsk, 'New Crops and their Diffusion', *passim.*

[82] J. Steven Watson, *A History of the Salters' Company* (Oxford, 1963), 70; Blith, *English Improver Improved*, 239.

[83] PRO Req. 2, Bdle 308/45.

[84] PRO Stac. 8, Bdle 266, no. 24.

the Virginia plantation—and this was the beginning of John Stratford's serious financial troubles that led to many lawsuits. John Ollyffe, Stratford's soap boiler at Thames Street, was offered a job in Scotland by the patentee of soap boiling in Scotland, and presumably went off there. His partner in tobacco growing went home to Nottinghamshire and got a patent for suppressing tobacco growing wherever he found it, though, as we have seen, his efforts made little impact. John Stratford stayed in Winchcombe, working to pay off his debts. He had leased land at very high rents for four years ahead to grow the superbly profitable crop of tobacco, and the courts of law made him continue to pay those rents although he was no longer allowed to grow tobacco. He turned to flax growing instead, and employed in the first season 200 people on a crop of 40 acres. Others were engaged to dress the flax and even to weave a small amount of linen cloth—'only for trial', he explained.[85] In all his many projects, monopolies and monopolists only once affected his business when the Virginia Company managed to procure the prohibition on tobacco growing.

Stratford subsequently wrote a treatise about his experience, the purpose of which was to demonstrate the amount of work for the poor that flax and other projects afforded.[86] He calculated that 40 acres of flax grown and made into linen cloth gave work to 800 persons a year, reckoning 300 men at 8d. a day, 300 women at 6d., and 200 young people at 3d. Thus 40 acres of flax yielded more profit to the grower than 160 acres of corn and grass. Indeed, one acre of flax made into linen cloth yielded more work and wages to the poor than a crop of wool raised on 400 acres of pasture, when made into broadcloth. 'Accordingly do they beyond the seas where the sowing of flax is much used, raise a benefit to their own poor and commonwealth more than we do in this kingdom by our pasture', he argued. He went on to urge the crushing of the flaxseed for oil. Benedict Webb, he said, was making great quantities of rape oil for the clothiers as a substitute for olive oil. Flaxseed too made good oil for paint,

[85] PRO C2, Jas. I, S3/11; SP14/180/79.
[86] PRO SP 14/180/79. The date is *circa* 1624. See also a shorter treatise containing the same arguments, SP 16/57/28, dated *circa* March 1627.

and also for good sweet soap that was little inferior to that made from olive oil. At present, he alleged, flaxseed was being carried overseas to be made into oil which was then brought back to England and sold at an excessive price (Benedict Webb had also stated this as a fact). Linseed oil ought to be pressed in England. Flax had other uses, moreover. Flax sheaves and the chaff from threshing the flaxseed made good fuel for the fire. He himself had used nothing else for a whole year. (Was this one of his economy measures while paying off his debts?) Finally, he had great hopes for the future manufacture of linen with home-grown flax, since the flax imported from abroad was 'the refuse of other countries'; not unnaturally, foreigners kept their best flax for themselves. He saw no reason why England should not find in hotter countries a market for linen as buoyant as the market it already had in colder countries for woollen cloth.

Stratford's message was eloquent and its tone that of a Commonwealthman of a former age. A successful flax growing and linen industry would transform the idle poor from an intolerable burden into a profitable asset to the Commonwealth 'paying for food and clothing and [living] according to God's ordinance by the sweat of their face in a more religious order'. As suitable land for flax growing he pointed to 'mean land' such as the uplands of remote forests, chases, and other commons, now nourishing none but idle people and breeding weak and unserviceable horses and sickly sheep. And to forestall the critics who feared a decline of corn growing, he concluded thus: 'The more flax we sow, the greater quantity of tillage it will beget, as the sowing of woad does prepare the land the better for corn afterwards.' He was a fervent advocate of tillage rather than pasture: tillage maintained 100 people where the equivalent land in pasture maintained only 20. It was a public duty to employ the many thousands of poor people in producing at home all the corn, hemp, flax, tow, cordage, wickyarn, match, thread, tapes, linen yarn, linen cloth, fustians, hops, hempseed oil, and linseed oil, that were now imported. The poor of Winch-combe—not a mass of nameless people to Stratford, but individuals whom he knew—must have been before his eyes as he embraced in his words both those who begged and stole 'for want of the help of work' and those who were ashamed to beg, would not steal, and would 'rather endure much misery'. As we have seen, Stratford practised what he preached;[87] in 1627 the clerk, bailiffs, and churchwardens of Winchcombe, the parson and two local gentlemen addressed letters to the Privy Council vouching for Stratford's good work in employing the poor of the parish.[88]

Stratford's career sheds light on one man's personal involvement in several projects, and his informed advocacy of others. We catch a glimpse of stocking knitting, soap boiling, tobacco growing, flax growing and linen weaving, oil pressing from rapeseed and linseed, and woad growing. As the background to Stratford's career we see an ever-changing kaleidoscope of partnerships in business in London, that formed and broke up, and formed anew, while in the country-side of Gloucestershire, in the town of Winchcombe, hard hit by the dissolution of its abbey, we see woad growing, tobacco growing, flax growing, and stocking knitting coming in as occupations for working men and women in the seventeenth century to alleviate poverty. In neighbouring Tewkesbury, another poor town, similarly hard hit by the dissolution of its abbey, we find tobacco growing, stocking knitting, and woad growing. Until very recently the best place to see woad in golden flower in May and June was on the Mythe, a red marl cliff above the Severn just outside Tewkesbury.[89] If London sometimes appears to command most attention in the history of projects because the scandal of monopolies made most noise there, it is in distant regions of the country that we must look for the more impressive evidence of their con-structive economic consequences.

[87] Stratford's evidence about his flax growing and flax dressing in Winchcombe is supported by independent evidence in PRO E134, 10 Car. I, Mich. 9.

[88] PRO SP16/57/14, II and III.

[89] Grigson, *The Englishman's Flora*, 57. I wish to thank Mrs. Marion Stowell for this reference.

V. THE QUALITY OF GOODS AND THE QUALITY OF CLIENTS

The goods which came on to the market in greater quantity than ever before as a result of projects promoted the growth of a consumer society. Their success is readily demonstrated in any random comparison between the standard household goods of husbandmen living in the first half of the sixteenth century and those living in the later seventeenth.[1] Before 1550 their houses contained the basic furniture, benches, a table, stools, and beds, a small amount of domestic linen, and essential cooking and eating vessels. By the end of the seventeenth century people had a choice of so many different qualities of linen for domestic use and personal wear that it is impossible to count them;[2] many more iron, brass, and copper pots lined the shelves of kitchen, buttery, and dairy; there were innumerable different qualities in pewter ware. 'We change the fashion of our pewter as often as we change the fashion of our hats', wrote a correspondent in the *Philosophical Transactions of the Royal Society* in 1675.[3] For personal wear, people could choose between a host of different colours, designs, and weights of knitted stockings. The shops were stocked with 11 or 12 different kinds of thread, with lace, fine and coarse, in several different colours, tape, ribbon, inkle—the range of haberdashery was quite as varied as anything in a large drapery store today. Diet similarly offered a much wider range of choice in food. The best orchards of the gentry yielded a choice of 60 different varieties of apples, 20 of pears, 16 of cherries, and 35 of apricots and plums. Such was the selection found in the orchard of Rowland Okeover of Okeover in the Dove valley in Staffordshire in the second half of the seventeenth

[1] See e.g. Margaret Cash (ed.), *Devon Inventories of the Sixteenth and Seventeenth Centuries*, Devon and Cornwall Rec. Soc. N.S. ii (1966), *passim*. Note the contents of an Exeter draper's shop on pp. 164–7.

[2] See e.g. Thirsk and Cooper, 252–3 (for 1641) and (for 1657, listing foreign linens) BL Thomason E 1065 (21).

[3] *Philosophical Transactions*, x–xii, no. 116, 26 July 1675.

century.[4] If you ordered lettuce seed from London *circa* 1677 you could choose between the cabbage lettuce, the Humbar, the Roman, the Arabian, the Savoy, the rose, the red, and the curled. If you wanted onions, you selected between the Strasburg, the red Spanish, the white Spanish, the French, and the English onion. Cucumbers could be long, short, or prickly. Even cress, which always looks the same in our greengrocers' shops today, could be Indian, garden, broad-leaved, or curled.[5]

When we survey the magnificent range of choice available to the customer in seventeenth-century England, we are compelled to think deeply about the economic significance of quality and variety in consumer goods, and the influence which different classes of customers exerted upon producers. In our present-day inflationary economy, the range of choice is steadily diminishing—only three or four kinds of apples in the greengrocers, two or three kinds of pears, no more small tins of paint, only large ones, only pint bottles of milk, no half-pints. To some extent the inconveniences we might suffer through this diminishing range of choice—in manufactured goods, at least—is mitigated by the existence of a flourishing market in second-hand articles; the scale of prices for cars, washing machines, and dish washers is much longer than that in the manufacturers' catalogues, because the second-hand market is comparatively efficiently organized while remaining free from official interference. In the seventeenth century, no second-hand market on the same scale existed. Instead the virtual freedom accorded to rural industries permitted a wide range of manufacturing enterprises to exist alongside one another, some large, (employing 10 or 20 people on the premises), but much more frequently small (employing the family members and perhaps one servant). They were scattered all over the kingdom among country communities that varied greatly in their class structure, material wealth, and local resources. Consequently, they produced wares of varied patterns, qualities, and prices that gave their customers a wide range of choice. We have

[4] Plot, *The Natural History of Staffordshire* (Oxford, 1686), 227.
[5] John Harvey, *Early Gardening Catalogues* (Phillimore, Chichester, 1972), 66–7.

seen that the projects that were being promoted from the 1540s onwards were in large part responsible for fostering the consumer society. It now becomes necessary to identify those characteristics of their manufacture and marketing which especially promoted this wide range of quality, style, and price.

Throughout the sixteenth century Tudor governments held fervently to the view that industry should be practised in the town, agriculture in the countryside. 'Cities and great towns are only, or for the most part, to be maintained by manual arts, occupations, mysteries, and sciences', said a memorandum on the Statute of Artificers in 1573 (?). 'And therefore it appeareth convenient that apprentices should be *there* brought up and instructed in the said arts and sciences, and not in such other towns and places where men ought to live by husbandry and labouring of grounds.'[6]

This was the theory of the matter. In practice things were very different. As the same memorandum admitted, 'But yet, contrary to the meaning of the law, a number of apprentices are brought up and taught occupations [i.e. industrial occupations] in husbandmen's houses, which turneth to a superfluous increase of artificers, and to the decay and ruin of such cities as should set forth the honour and strength of the realm.'[7] A wealthier class of people also promoted this confusion of industrial and agricultural occupations. These were gentlemen clothiers. As John Coke described it in *The Debate of the Heralds* (1550), 'In England. . .you clothiers dwell in great farms abroad in the country having houses with commodities like unto gentlemen where as well they make cloths and keep husbandry; and also grass and feed sheep and cattle, taking thereby away the livings of the poor husbandmen and graziers.'[8] In the course of the severe depression in the Essex cloth industry in 1629, one of the grievances of the specialized weavers was that clothiers took apprentices whom they transferred from cloth making to husbandry 'when trading serves not', 'being men able to hold land as well as their trade'.[9]

[6]   TED i. 354 (my italics).   [7]   Ibid.
[8]   TED iii. 5.   [9]   Thirsk and Cooper, 229.

The separation of functions between agriculture and industry could not be satisfactorily maintained. But in so far as the government did succeed by regulation and exhortation in preserving industry in the towns, what it preserved there were industrial occupations that catered for the rich. The clock makers, goldsmiths, silversmiths, jewellers, perruque makers, and parchment makers were found in towns and not in villages. In addition, goods that were not made exclusively for the rich, like knives and stockings, became increasingly differentiated by quality and price, and again the highest-quality craftsmanship was found in the towns. The reverse proposition, that all poorer-quality goods were produced in the countryside, does not completely represent the full facts, but it is broadly correct. The country areas were the main producers of the cheaper quality wares.

To take but three examples, one of the principal knife manufacturing centres lay in south Yorkshire. The best knives were made in Sheffield itself, the inferior and cheaper common knives were made in the villages round about.[10] In the pottery industry, slipware and coarse pottery were made in rural areas, while the fine pottery, such as creamware, saltglaze, and delft ware, was centred in the larger towns.[11] Knitted stockings were so varied in their patterns and the kinds of yarn used to make them that it is not easy to establish all the many qualities. But ordinary woollen and worsted stockings were made in rural areas scattered in many parts of the kingdom, while the finest wool stockings were jersey stockings, the manufacture of which was centred at the beginning, at least, in Norwich (with a subsidiary centre at Yarmouth) and in London. Silk stockings, the most expensive of all, remained an almost complete monopoly of London until the second half of the seventeenth century. When the framework knitters petitioned for incorporation in 1655, their appeal emanated from London craftsmen only, who were wholly concerned with the knitting of silk. Only in the later seventeenth century did silk knitted wares become

[10]   D. Hey, 'Sheffield and its Region, 1660–1800', unpublished paper delivered to the Urban History Group, 1972.
[11]   L. Weatherill, *The Pottery Trade and North Staffordshire, 1660–1760* (Manchester, 1971), 7.

considerably cheaper, and only then did the Leicestershire and Nottinghamshire framework knitters seriously take up silk knitting.[12]

Evidence on the different qualities of many other mass-produced wares needs to be more systematically analysed before this working hypothesis can be fully tested, but it appears to be true of other goods, such as lace, metalwares, and linen, that the best quality was made in the towns (the very best of all in London), while cheaper qualities were made in the rural areas.

What were the economic and social circumstances of rural industrial workers? A number of different explorations in this field in recent years have shed light on their economy. In the early stages of their growth these industries did not depend on a full-time, specialized work-force. It was the rule, rather than the exception, for craftsmen to have a landholding that provided food for the family, and perhaps even some surplus to sell. Industrial employment was thus an additional source of income, supplying more ready cash, but occupying the family for only part of their time. Pasture farming regions, not arable areas, supported this kind of dual economy. Corn farming was too labour intensive, and left no time for other pursuits. As the inhabitants of Hertfordshire explained to James I when they rejected his suggestion that the New Draperies might be established in their county: 'The county of Hertford doth consist for the most part of tillage...it has better means to set the poor children on work without this new invention than some other counties, viz. by employing the female children in picking of their wheat a great part of the year, and the male children by straining before their ploughs in seed time, and other necessary occasions of husbandry.'[13]

For this and other reasons,[14] industries found their most congenial home in pastoral regions where people had time on their hands that could be devoted to industrial work, and

[12] Thirsk, 'Fantastical Folly' 68–72.
[13] J. Thirsk, 'Industries in the Countryside', in F.J. Fisher (ed.), *Essays in the Economic and Social History of Tudor and Stuart England* (Cambridge, 1961), 87.
[14] Ibid., *passim*.

where they also had the freedom, and the land, to attract additional workers if their industry flourished sufficiently to call for yet more labourers.

Most consumer industries, moreover, depended on simple tools that were not expensive, and if a workshop or forge was needed, a shed beside the house was sufficient. When John Tilsley agreed to train thirty young people to be pin makers first in Gloucester and then in Berkeley, all he asked for was a house. In eighteenth-century Gloucester, the pin makers' premises consisted usually of no more than a house with a workshop in the yard.[15] In Staffordshire, the usual domestic pottery was one room of a house or a one-room building outside; the nail maker's workshop was a shed near the house.[16] In 1711 a tobacco-pipe maker of Hastings, Sussex, lived in a two-roomed house, one up, one down, and made his pipes in a shop next door which contained the clay and all his working tools. This also afforded a chamber above for beds for his apprentices.[17]

The simplicity of the industrial structure supporting substantial rural industries requires emphasis, for some economic historians have a strong desire to turn it into something far more elaborate, and look for capital accumulation where nothing so grand was needed or was taking place. The capital resources that were required by merchants in the *trade* were not required by the producers of these consumer goods. Of course, they depended heavily on merchants from the towns to sell their wares further afield, but production could flow smoothly for a long time without transforming the simple industrial base; an increase in demand was met by the employment of yet more workers from among those under-employed in the countryside. A description of the way of business of makers of Welsh cottons in the early seventeenth century presents a fresh, and little known, description of a

[15] I wish to thank Mr. R.A. Lewis for allowing me to draw on his research into the pin industry, contained in his unpublished pamphlet, lodged at the City Museum and Art Gallery, Gloucester. The upper floor of a house in Westgate Street, Gloucester, which was used by pin makers, is now the Folk Museum.

[16] Weatherill, op. cit. 45; M.B. Rowlands, *Masters and Men in the West Midland Metalware Trades before the Industrial Revolution* (Manchester, 1975), 27.

[17] East Sussex Record Office, Probate Inv. no. 186. I wish to thank Mr. Stephen Porter for this reference.

system already made familiar to us in the famous statute of
1555 describing the simple business organization of the
Halifax cloth workers.[18] The makers of Welsh cottons were
'for the most part poor people dwelling amongst the moun-
tains of Wales. And many times two or three of them do lay
their stock together to make one piece, and when it is ready
most commonly the owners with the weavers and walkers
thereof do come with the same to the market of Oswester
[=Oswestry], being ten, twenty, thirty, forty or more miles
away distant from their dwellings. And there they sell the
same for ready money (for they never give any credit). And
at receipt of the money, the walker taketh his wages, the
weaver his wages, and then the poor owners divide the rest.
And either in the same market, or in some other market
near unto their dwellings, they bestow the money again in
wool and so keep themselves at work.'[19]

As rural production expanded, differences between the
quality of wares made in the town and those made in the
country emerged more conspicuously. But at the same time
the expansion of the rural industries multiplied the range of
choice faster still. The ground was already prepared for
this, since the centres of manufacture for new projects were
never chosen in a completely haphazard or arbitrary way.
Projects tended to build upon existing structures, however
rudimentary. They positioned themselves in places where an
earlier tradition of manufacture, or some associated occupation, existed already. This meant that as industries or the
growing of new crops expanded, they made long geographical
leaps, from one successful centre to another having an
embryonic industry or other facilities that offered the same
promise. Woad growing moved from Hampshire into cloth-
working districts in Berkshire, Gloucestershire, Wiltshire,
Sussex, and Suffolk, where deep pastures provided suitable
land, *and* cloth makers demanded quantities of woad dye. At
Midhurst and Godalming, in Sussex, many of the growers of
woad were actually dyers.

Inevitably, the variety of local conditions in these widely
dispersed centres of rural manufacture gave rise to many

---

[18]   TED i. 187–8.
[19]   BM Cotton MS. Titus B V, fo. 252.

more differentiated articles. The stocking knitters, for
example, used different yarns that were procured locally,
and in addition to this they incorporated their own distinctive
patterns and colours. We have already noticed how quickly
stocking knitting, which started in the 1570s, had spread by
1600 into at least ten different counties of England and
Wales.[20] Some of the salient characteristics of their local
industries can be positively identified, or we can make near
guesses. The cheapest stockings of all were made in the four
northernmost counties of Westmorland, Cumberland,
Durham, and Northumberland, where the local wool was
coarse and hairy. Such stockings were described by Defoe in
the early eighteenth century as 'very coarse and ordinary'.
Probably they resembled the thick fishermen's stockings
nowadays worn under wellington boots. In more southerly
counties like Gloucestershire, where short wool was available
from the Cotswolds, it is reasonable to guess that the woollen
stockings knitted in towns like Tewkesbury and Winchcombe were less coarse than the stockings of Westmorland.
But they were still not as fine as worsted stockings, which
were knitted wherever the New Draperies were made in
eastern England, and which were differentiated from northern
woollen stockings by their prices. Northern woollen stockings
in 1578 cost on average 12*d.* – 18*d.* a pair, whereas the best
worsted in 1590 cost as much as 8*s.* – 9*s.* Finer still were the
jersey stockings which Mary Queen of Scots wore next to her
skin on the scaffold (with a pair of more decorative worsted
stockings over them). These were made in large numbers in
Norwich and Yarmouth. Silk stockings at the same period
might cost 20*s.* a pair, and would be made in London.
More variety still was achieved by embroidery, using gold
and silver thread for 'quirks and clocks', but gold and silver
thread was very expensive, and again it was only the knitters
in London who regularly went in for these refinements.[21]

Lace varied similarly in quality. Sir Henry Sidney of
Penshurst, Kent, bought in 1578 bone lace of gold and silver
costing 6*s.* 8*d.* and 7*s.* a yard. Fine white lace cost even more,

[20] Thirsk, 'Fantastical Folly', 56. This number omits Cheshire, since the first
evidence of a stocking knitting industry there has not been substantiated.
[21] Ibid. 57–9.

8s. 8d. a yard (almost certainly an import). But he did not despise a cheaper range, so cheap, indeed, that it may well have been English lace made in Buckinghamshire. This was white and black lace (seemingly mixing the two colours) which cost 2s. 4d. and 2s. a yard, while yellow crown lace cost only 16d. a yard.[22] Purchases of thread for the same household, to stitch sheets, towels, napkins, and pillowcases, consisted of coarse brown thread at 2s. a pound, and fine brown thread at 3s. a pound. Both these were very cheap thread, and we may wonder if they came from Maidstone, so near to the Sidney's home at Penshurst, before the foreign refugees improved the quality. These are speculations, but they are not altogether idle if they prompt more purposeful searches into the early condition of an industry which later developed so successfully. In the seventeenth century it was generally agreed that Maidstone made the best thread in England. This same account gives us a firm clue to the comparative standing of the Coventry thread industry at that time: in 1549 it had been said to be in decay. But in 1578 the 'blue Coventry thread' used in the Sidney household cost 7s. a pound, compared with only 2s. and 3s. for the brown thread (possibly made in Maidstone). Finally, white silk thread for the Sidneys' personal use cost 12d. for half an ounce, or 32s. a pound, and almost certainly came from Spain.[23]

Purchasers and producers enjoyed positive economic advantages because of this variety. Buyers could find just the right article to suit their purses and their practical needs, producers of whatever quality knew that they could always find buyers, if not among the rich nobility who could be expected to pay a high price, then among the middle classes, and if not there, then among the lower ranks of husbandmen and craftsmen. If all these potential clients disdained their wares, then they might still find a market among less choosy, probably poorer, people still in Spain, the Azores, or the West Indies. The Southampton merchants who bought green

[22] Kent Archives Office, U 1475—A 53/3, A 50/12, A 58 (i). Yet another kind, called 'knet lace' cost 2s. 2d. a yard.

[23] Kent Archives Office, U 1475—A 53 (iv), A 50/12. See also below, p. 121, for comparisons with prices of thread in Kirkby Lonsdale.

woad in the Azores, for example, paid for it with the bad or coarse short cloths which English clothiers were unable to sell at home.[24] When the English pin makers asked for a complete prohibition on the import of Dutch pins, the importers of these pins objected that 10,000 poor Englishmen would be put out of work indirectly by such a measure. These were the makers and dealers in cheap goods that had no sale or use in England, and were sold in Holland in exchange for pins. Conyskins, shreds and lists of cloth, coarse bands, woollen stockings, and Monmouth caps, made of refuse wool, had some sale in England, they said, but the additional market in Holland was important also, setting thousands of English poor on work 'to dress, to spin, to card, to weave, and to dye'.[25]

The cheapest markets overseas were the last resort, however. The home market was capable of absorbing a wide range of qualities and this was one of its greatest merits, guaranteeing the livelihood of thousands of rural craftsmen. The virtues of variety were described by the makers of Welsh cottons in James I's reign, when legislation threatened to enforce upon them a standard weight and width for their cloth. Welsh cottons were cheap cloths, most of which were used for lining. Some linings needed to be thick and warm, but garments like waistcoats and children's coats required a light-weight lining. The quality of Welsh cottons varied accordingly, and so did their price. Fourpence a yard was the cheapest, but the best cost 2s., six times as much. So many were the differences in weight and width between these two extremes that the grades in between rose in farthing steps. The prime differences in quality and weight were regional: Denbigh cottons cost 8d. or 10d. a yard; Merioneth cottons 12d., 16d., 20d., and 2s. a yard; Montgomery cottons 8d., 12d., 16d., 20d., and 2s. a yard. But within the framework of these regional differences, other differences were haphazard and peculiar to every individual weaver.

As a result, goods at many different prices were available to every class of purchaser, and their sale did not depend upon the whim and fashion of one small section of the

²⁴   BL Lansdowne MS. 49, no. 58.
²⁵   BL Lansdowne MS. 152, fo. 324.

population. Everyone could find the price and quality that suited him. If there had been only one quality of cotton cloth, a great proportion of the population of North Wales would have been made idle. As their makers explained, 'the poorer sort of people (who use these linings most) have 6d. or 8d. to bestow upon a yard, when they have not 12d. or 16d. to bestow'. The makers of Welsh cottons had a market so large that they did not fear its sudden collapse. Not surprisingly, they bitterly opposed the government's attempt to standardize the width, length, and weight of their cloths. Their instinct was correct. This was a policy designed for the benefit of large merchants trading overseas. It was not in the interests of the cloth makers, for it restricted the range of their products, narrowed the home market for their wares, and made them dangerously vulnerable to trade depressions. A generation later, *circa* 1670, the stocking knitters of Leicester, harassed by the threat of new regulations that would have imposed higher standards of manufacture on them put forward a similar argument. 'It is not the curious making of a few stockings, but the general making of many that is most for the public good, for that sets more people on work, as well children as others, and when the stockings are made up and sorted, there are amongst them some for all sorts of people. . .if none but fine stockings be made the poor must go without'.[26]

The government's policy to standardize production and maintain quality was a constant quest throughout the reigns of Elizabeth, James, and Charles and was revived again during the Interregnum by the Council of Trade in 1651.[27] Viewed in the light of the strong competition which English manufactures faced abroad, the policy seemed sensible enough. Overseas merchants who had difficulty in finding customers for English goods always blamed their troubles on the falsity of the wares they were selling; 'frauds and adulterations', they were called, for they involved the mixing of different materials—the mixing of copper with gold and

---

[26]   BL Cotton MS. Titus V B, fos. 252 ff; H. Stocks (ed.), *Records of the Borough of Leicester, 1603–88* (Cambridge, 1923), 536–8. I owe this reference to Mr. Charles Phythian-Adams.

[27]   For this concern in the Interregnum, see Thirsk and Cooper, 255–8.

silver thread, for example, or the mixing of silk with linen thread in ribbons and points. But the standardization which the government strove for was, in fact, inimical to industrial growth and the expansion of the home market; and, as we shall see, when analysing the overseas market, it was in some respects inimical to the expansion of the foreign market too. In the deflationary circumstances of the seventeenth century, selling was a tough assignment sometimes, but the production of wares of many different qualities and prices positively assisted selling rather than the reverse, by enlarging the circle of purchasers who could afford them. The freedom to produce cloth of all standards, shapes, and sizes was essential to manufacturers, and to buyers of limited means.

Overseas merchants and the highly skilled craftsmen who lived mostly in towns wielded the greatest influence over policy, and spoke most loudly when trade was depressed and required a helping hand. Producers of cheaper-quality industrial goods mostly dwelt in the countryside, had different interests, and rarely made their voices heard in Parliament. Yet they were successful in resisting the policy of standardization, largely because the government was powerless to enforce its regulations in rural areas. The government long cherished a memory of the relatively successful and efficient regulation of urban industry through the gilds. The Statute of Artificers in 1563 was built on the confidence that the scope of such regulation could be enlarged and extended, even though the circumstances of urban and rural life in the mid-sixteenth century were rapidly changing. Still more ambitious proposals were put forward in the years of trade depression between 1622 and 1625 to control the manufacture of the New Draperies in the *rural* areas by incorporating the J.P.s of every county as Governors for the New Drapery, and making all the inhabitants members. All the cloth made in each county was to be examined, as it passed through each stage of manufacture, for length, weight, standard of dyeing, and finish.[28] The scheme was never put into operation, and, of course, it could never have been enforced. Regulations even in the towns became less and

[28]   Ibid. 222–3.

less effective. The Statute of Artificers was certainly enforced, but only in a haphazard way, and hundreds of artificers lived outside the law, practising crafts in which they had not been apprenticed.[29]

During the scandalous phase in the history of patents, when patentees' agents roamed the countryside demanding cash and hush-money in an almost random way, they could not destroy the broad foundations of rural industries. Provided that these offered saleable wares, they flourished quietly and without ostentation. They had a steadily loyal clientele because they offered a lot of serviceable goods—nothing expensive, just everyday necessities, plus some fancy wares that were cheap and cheerful, and came within the purses of working men and women. It is true that fortune smiled benignly on them throughout the seventeenth century. Three generations of men lived through an age when prices stabilized or fell, and the real value of wages rose. The upper classes, inevitably, complained about the high wages commanded by labourers, and deplored the money that they spent on luxuries. 'The lowest member, the feet of the body politic, are the day labourers,' wrote Edward Chamberlayne in 1669, 'who by their large wages given them, and the cheapness of all necessaries, enjoy better dwellings, diet, and apparel in England than the husbandmen do in many other countries.' In contrast, he claimed, the nobility, the gentry, and the clergy after the Restoration set a sober example, favouring plainness and comeliness, less prodigality and more modesty in clothes; 'only the citizens, the country people, and the servants appear clothed for the most part above and beyond their qualities, estates, or conditions, and far more gay than that sort of people was wont to be heretofore'.[30] It might well appear to some that all this indulgence in material things corrupted the spirit, but it also provided much work for the country men and women, who wove Welsh cottons, made lace, knitted stockings and caps, made hats, ribbon, buttons, and thread. The wheels of rural industry turned ever faster.

But how, it must be asked, did the wide selection of

[29]   PRO SP 12/93, nos. 27–31.
[30]   Edward Chamberlayne, *Angliae Notitia* (London, 1669), 445, 85.

consumer goods that were being produced in England after 1570 find their way so surely to all their potential customers? This question directs our attention at the organization of the home market. Local market towns were the immediately obvious selling places for new wares. Sometimes they had a long-standing reputation in the district for selling similar goods, though they were now being produced by a new technical process or to satisfy a new demand. Sometimes the new industries or agricultural occupations, like woad growing, were located in areas where other associated activities indicated that the potential demand was strong. Thus when traditional wares, of new design, were put up for sale, customers were ready to hand. Thereafter the reputation of a good market was carried as quickly as the wind far and wide. Among the upper ranks of society, among gentry, yeomen, and merchants with an eye for good business, an almost encyclopedic body of knowledge existed by the late sixteenth century about where the best markets were to be found for different types of goods, and gentlemen or their servants, not to mention merchants, travelled long distances in search of their special needs.[31]

After 1600 when English colonists settled on the other side of the Atlantic and learned new ways of farming and new foods to eat, they nevertheless looked to particular places in England to supply them with humdrum household tools and wares that had been familiar equipment at home. When cargoes were loaded at Bristol for voyages to Virginia between 1619 and 1633, the weeding and holing hoes and felling axes were procured from the Forest of Dean; Benedict Webb, based in Gloucestershire, supplied the broadcloths; some of the stockings were woven linen stockings from Ireland, while the others, knitted of wool, and shipped from Bristol, surely came from the Midland counties, perhaps even from Tewkesbury and Winchcombe, whence the passengers

---

[31] When the Hatcher family of Careby in Lincolnshire wanted a bull, they went to Derbyshire, but, for a horse, they went to Northamptonshire. When Sir Henry Sidney was at Ludlow, Shropshire, performing his duties as Lord President of the Marches of Wales, in May 1573, it was to Lancashire that his servant was sent on two market days to buy 120 yards of linen of three different qualities, some at $7\frac{1}{2}d.$, some at $8d.$, and some at $8\frac{1}{2}d.$ a yard. (J. Thirsk, *English Peasant Farming* (London, 1957), 176; Kent Archives Office, U 1475, A 53 (iv).)

themselves were recruited.[32] When Richard Ligon wrote in 1657 advice to shopkeepers setting up business in Barbados, they were told that nails of all sorts, together with hooks, hinges, and iron cramps should be bought at Birmingham and in Staffordshire for they were much cheaper there than in London. Gloves of thin leather, supple and washable, that would not shrink—presumably for work purposes— could be bought at easy rates at Yeovil, Ilminster, and Ilchester, in Somerset. Shoes and boots should be bought at Northampton.[33]

The speed with which the new-style consumer goods penetrated the length and breadth of the kingdom should also be noticed, for markets quickly expanded by this means. At a time when courtiers relied on London for the latest haberdashery and fashion clothing, almost as much variety was being offered to the purchaser shopping in far distant counties. Take, for example, the use of silk. In 1570 Sir Henry Sidney, who was considered something of a dandy at court, was supplied with most of his personal clothing needs from London. In 1570 not even he wore any silk cloth on his person, only silk thread that was sold to his tailor by the ounce or skein, and was used to stitch on lace and some-times taffeta. In about 1573 Mistress Mary Sidney acquired, apparently for the first time, a scarf of green striped silk that cost 16s. But it was not until March 1575, and regularly thereafter, that Sir Henry bought any silk stockings.[34] Since they were supplied by a Mr. Thomas Thornes [sic] of London, and the Thorne family were notable merchants in the Spanish trade, it is likely that these silk wares came from Spain. Still we cannot be absolutely sure for Mistress Mountague had successfully knitted a pair of black silk stockings for Queen Elizabeth in 1560,[35] and who can say how many more pairs of hand-knitted silk stockings were on sale by 1575 to courtiers who could afford to pay, as did Sir Henry, 35s.,

---

[32] S. Kingsbury, *Records of the Virginia Company of London* Washington, 1906–35) iii: *1607–22*, 186, 390, 387, 392. It is not yet certain, however, that stocking knitting in the Winchcombe area started as early as this.

[33] Ligon, *History of Barbados*, 109–10.

[34] Kent Archives Office, U 1475–57, 56 (2), A 53 (iv), A 50, 12.

[35] Thirsk, 'Fantastical Folly', 54.

40s., 50s., 53s., 53s. 4d., and even £3 a pair?[36]

Suffice it to say that the use of silk in Sir Henry Sidney's household was confined to silk thread in 1570, and not until 1575 did he possess any silk stockings. We can be sure that the latest fashions were more accessible to Sir Henry than to most other people. It is remarkable, therefore, to find that a draper of Kirkby Lonsdale in Westmorland only three years later, in 1578, had a range of goods that cannot have fallen far short of the selection in London, and included a choice of three kinds of stitching silks—London silk, Spanish silk, and Scottish bobbin silk; admittedly, no silk stockings were to be found on his shelves, but he certainly stocked some silk hats.[37] As for prices, if the values in a probate inventory can be equated with retail prices, they were rather less than Sir Henry paid in London. James Backhouse stocked white thread at 10d. a pound (the cheapest thread used by Sir Henry cost 2s. a pound), green thread at 2s. 4d. a pound, black thread at 3s. 4d. a pound, and Coventry thread at 6s. a pound (Sir Henry paid 7s. for the same article). Some stitching silks, called London silk, and presumably English made, cost 10d. and 10½d. per ounce, while Spanish silk at 18d. and 20d. an ounce was perhaps comparable with the sewing silk bought by Sir Henry at 24d. 'Scottish bobbin silk', so called, suggests that Scotland had started to develop its own silk industry at this time. The same shop also had an impressive array of wool and linen cloth, both English and foreign, stockings of several different prices, hats not only of silk but of felt, lace of several kinds, including Norwich lace and Scottish lace, girdles and fringes, garters both English and French, Oxford gloves (perhaps from Woodstock?), plus all the other consumer goods that were so much deplored at the time because they mostly came from abroad: pins, needles, knives, daggers, silver and brass buttons, inkhorns, parchment, Turkey purses, playing-cards, and dice.

Surveying this remarkable display of wares in a shop in one of the poorest counties of England in 1578, we can see England's bullion reserves draining away, but the discerning

---

[36] Kent Archives Office, U 1475–59 (4), A 58 (i).
[37] J. Raine (ed.), *Wills and Inventories From...the Archdeaconry of Richmond*, Surtees Soc. xxvi (1853), 275–81.

eye will also see that the tide was turning. The Spanish silk and the French garters, perhaps all the inkhorns, the pins, needles, and some of the other items of haberdashery were of foreign make, but England's rural industries were already replacing other foreign goods. The gloves in Backhouse's shop were made in England, as were most of the New Draperies, the nails, the linen, and the sackcloth. It may be that we can also glimpse the difference in quality between urban and rural-based industries, though transport costs confuse the issue: Lancaster sackcloth was sold for 7*d*. a yard, whereas London sackcloth cost 10*d*. or even 14*d*. a yard. Among discriminating purchasers, no doubt, these two qualities served different uses, but the cheaper kind served the turn of Westmorland customers who could only have gazed at the expensive London kind and turned sorrowfully away.

Shops in English provincial towns became increasingly numerous in the seventeenth century, but they were not the only sellers of consumer goods, turned out in country workshops. Rural craftsmen had other loyal allies in pedlars and chapmen. Walking the length and breadth of the kingdom, selling their wares from door to door, they enlarged the market for country crafts to an unprecedented extent.

We have seen how the unwelcome attention of aulnagers obliged the makers of lace in Norwich to send their goods to London by secret means, avoiding the recognized carriers, or alternatively, to sell to chapmen who frequented the country fairs. This was only one of the many reasons why craftsmen found it advantageous to use the pedlars. They could find buyers for faulty wares; they could find their way into the darkest corners of the realm. Seventeenth-century commentators liked to say that the pedlars were mainly Scotsmen: 'all Scotchmen and other persons carrying packs', hawking goods for sale, was the description given them in the court records of Congleton borough, Cheshire, in 1642.[38] Some of the first pedlars had evidently sold Scotch cloth, a cheap linen (though in 1641, at least, it was not the very cheapest). They increased to a 'prodigious number'

---

[38]   Thirsk and Cooper, 359.

after the Civil War.[39] Through them a multitude of light-weight consumer goods were carried to customers in the smallest hamlets of the kingdom. The novelty of this situation is perhaps underlined by the fact that the stock-in-trade of pedlars in our fairy tales was standardized, and fossilized, as a list of fancy goods that were newly in vogue in the sixteenth and seventeenth centuries. As John Heywood described it, pedlars sold

> gloves, pins, combs, glasses unspotted,
> Pamades, hooks, and laces knotted;
> Brooches, rings, and all manner of beads;
> laces round and flat for women's heads;
> needles, thread, thimble, shears and all such knacks,
> Where lovers be, no such things lacks;
> Sipers, swathbands, ribbons, and sleeve laces,
> Girdles, knives, purses and pincases.[40]

But this was not all. Pamphleteers wrote of wandering glass-men, carrying glasses and earthenware, packed in straw on their backs. Robert Plot wrote of poor cratemen who carried Staffordshire pots round the country villages.[41]

By the later seventeenth century hawkers were considered to be a positive nuisance, taking away the business of traditional tradesmen of the town, the woollen draper, linen draper, mercer, and grocer.[42] Rarely were they now the makers of the goods as had often been the case before; rather they were wholesalers, intermediaries between maker and shopkeeper. They were 'women in London, in Exeter, and Manchester, who do not only proffer commodities at the shops and warehouses but also at inns to country chapmen'; or they were 'the Manchestermen, the Sherborne men and many others that do travel from one market town to another and there at some inn do proffer their wares to sell to the shopkeepers of the place'.[43]

A writer of a pamphlet in 1681 condemning the confusion

[39] Ibid. 418.
[40] John Heywood, 'The Four P.P.', in W.C. Hazlitt, *A Select Collection of Old English Plays* (London, 1874), i. 349–50. The earliest version of this play is dated *c.* 1540, the latest 1569.
[41] Thirsk and Cooper, 419; Plot, *Nat. Hist. of Staffs.* 124.
[42] Thirsk and Cooper, 389 ff.
[43] Ibid. 392–3.

in trade that resulted from these developments wanted buying and selling to return to the recognized markets. But he wasted his breath. Ten years later the pedlars were said to have increased greatly, so much so that they were employing servants, three or four apiece.[44] Not surprisingly, the shopkeepers in towns were a persistent pressure group behind the agitation against the pedlars outside and inside Parliament in the 1680s, but as a spokesman on behalf of hawkers and pedlars exclaimed with some vehemence in 1700, a great increase in consumption was achieved by hawking about the street, 'for without doubt importunity and opportunity do great things. . .I do think that a great trade is far better for any country than a little one; and I never yet met with the man that could pretend with any colour of reason that such doings caused a lesser consumption. I would fain have those that are against them [i.e. hawkers] consider what would become of our milk and mackerel, our other fish, oranges, and lemons, etc., if nobody could buy a single pennyworth unless they went to a market or a shop for them. Besides there are vast quantities of damaged goods that would never be sold if 'twere not for carrying to the mob in this manner.'[45] This defence of sellers of perishable and damaged goods was equally applicable to pedlars who sold the lowest grade of manufactured goods. As long as they were cheap, they were assured of a sale somewhere or other.

Even this was not the limit of the market, however. Innumerable merchants in overseas trade were constantly probing and prodding sales outlets abroad, attempting to supply the needs of another highly differentiated clientele, potentially embracing all classes, having even more varied likes and dislikes than the ones they knew at home. The complexities of this other world of potential customers with their fickle tastes also requires to be more carefully investigated, for in it we see reflected as in a mirror the boundlessly expanding horizons that opened up for the most successful rural industries.

But immediately we view these wider horizons, we are brought face to face with the question that has lurked in the

[44] Ibid. 417.   [45] Ibid. 428–9.

background throughout this discussion. Among what classes of customers did the consumer industries achieve their main successes? It has become a convention to treat the mass market for consumer goods as a product of the Industrial Revolution, insignificant before the later eighteenth century. It is then argued that demand built up first, and was met first, among the middle class, and gradually filtered down to the working class. But the seventeenth-century evidence for the production of such articles as knitted stockings, knitted caps, cheap earthenware, nails, tobacco pipes, lace, and ribbon proves the existence at a much earlier date of a mass market for consumer goods. And if we lengthen our perspective to accommodate it, we have to admit at once that the mass market did not always obediently follow the one-way traffic system that economic historians have prescribed for it. Reality was much more complex.

The stocking knitting industry, for example, was launched by the rich man's fashion for silk stockings, imported from Spain. But as soon as Italian fashions in knitted worsted stockings came in, they stimulated an occupation that already existed among poor people. Under Continental influences the knitting industry then improved its techniques to reach standards that, at their best, satisfied the middle and upper classes, but still catered for the labouring class. Then English stockings began to go overseas. They first appeared in vessels going to Ireland in the later 1570s from Chester.[46] Since they were carried in cargoes that also contained Kendal cottons and northern kerseys, we can reasonably guess that the stockings came from the nearby knitting district around Richmond in north Yorkshire; they were what Defoe later called 'very coarse and ordinary stockings'. The English soldiery were in Ireland in considerable numbers at this time, dealing with the Desmond rebellion, and it is fairly certain that they were the first customers for these stockings, just as their commanding officers were the recipients of the luxury goods,[47] such as the velvet caps and hats that were

[46] PRO E 190/1324/17. In 1577 cargoes frequently contained small packs of e.g. 3 doz. worsted stockings, 2 doz. woollen stockings, and 1 doz. women's hose.

[47] Barnaby Rich in 1610 declared that Dublin merchants found their customers for luxury goods among the English, not the Irish. Quoted in Longfield, *Anglo-Irish Trade* 149.

sent in March 1577 along with money for the Lord Deputy of Ireland. But English soldiers and civil servants spread the fashion to the native Irish, and a century later the Irish were such large customers for English knitted stockings that loud cries of dismay were raised in England when the Irish Cattle Act killed the trade dead. Demand in this case had spread from English soldiers and government officials (the middle and labouring classes in England) to the Irish peasantry (or those who were their social equivalents).[48]

When demand for English stockings built up on the Continent of Europe, revealing itself conspicuously in the portbooks by the 1590s, the quantity involved, the wide range of qualities of woollen stockings, *and* the diversity of markets suggest that purchasers were again found among the middle *and* lower classes. A portbook of 1598–9 shows large consignments of woollen and worsted stockings from many different manufacturing centres in England—Norwich and Yarmouth, Cornwall and Devon—going to France, Holland, and Germany, and displacing woven kersey stockings which had been the best-selling lines in English stockings on the Continent in the 1570s.[49] We must assume that the price of knitted woollen and woven kersey stockings now did not greatly differ. By 1609 exports of kersey stockings had fallen away, though a small demand for them persisted in Spain and Portugal, at Stade and Amsterdam. But woollen knitted stockings were rising rapidly in esteem, both for adults and children, while far above these in popularity, not only in Europe, but in Barbary too, were short worsted stockings, of which some cargoes destined for ports like Stade contained over 1,000, 2,000, and even over 2,500 pairs.[50] By 1641 kersey stockings had altogether disappeared from the cargoes taken on board in London, as knitted woollen and worsted stockings together held the mastery of fashion. They went in thousands and tens of thousands of pairs, to Spain, to France, and to Holland:

[48] Thirsk, 'Fantastical Folly', 67.

[49] Ibid. 66; PRO E 190/6/4. I owe the information from this list of London exports to Mr. K.G. Ponting and the Pasold Foundation. Between April and September 1576 the kersey stockings (which went mainly to Dordrecht) were far more numerous than the jersey, worsted, and woollen hose combined.

[50] PRO E 190/14/7. I owe this information to Mr. K.G. Ponting and the Pasold Foundation.

58,000 pairs of children's woollen stockings were shipped to St. Lucar and Malaga alone. But in addition to the seven ports in these three countries, forty more ports could be named as recipients of English stockings, including ports in Ireland, the Azores, Madeira, the Canaries, New England, Italy, Sweden, and Denmark.[51] Few countries in Europe were ignorant of what English knitted stockings looked like. Clearly, they were not rich men's wares, but the clothing of the common people. The market was lodged mainly at the lower end of the social scale.

If we turn to another successful project, the manufacture of knives and edge tools, we see an industry that started by catering for working people who needed knives for everyday purposes, and reached a discriminating and high-class foreign clientele at a late stage in the seventeenth century. In the *Discourse of the Commonweal* in 1549, the merchant in the dialogue had bemoaned the fact that iron and steel, knives and daggers, were all brought into England from abroad, and, moreover, were costing one-third more than they did in 1542. Foreign knives filled the windows of fashionable shops in the City, and even the poorest country folk insisted on buying foreign makes. Tools also seem to have been subsumed under the same heading, for the list of goods named in the *Discourse* that Englishmen should make for themselves ran to daggers, knives, hammers, saws, chisels, and axes.[52] Domestic manufacture of these goods became another serious project. When foreign immigrants were made welcome in England in the 1560s, the lord of the manor of Sheffield, where useful but not beautiful knives had been made since at least the mid-fourteenth century, interrogated foreigners carefully: 'Can you make anything in the iron and steel way?', he asked.[53] Stamford town council, in whose affairs Cecil took great interest, asked for foreign craftsmen who could make knives, as well as workers in steel and copper.[54] Improved techniques were being actively

---

[51] New England was alone in taking great quantities of Irish stockings and some Scottish mill stockings.

[52] *A Discourse of the Common Weal*, 16–17, 64, 125, 127.

[53] G.I.H. Lloyd, *The Cutlery Trades* (London, 1913), 101–2.

[54] Thirsk, 'Stamford in the Sixteenth and Seventeenth Centuries', 65.

sought. In 1565 Jacobus Acontius received a patent for a machine for grinding. In 1571 Richard Mathew received a patent for making knives and knife handles of Turkish design.[55] His efforts evidently bore fruit, for, according to Edmund Howes, in his revision of Stow's *Annals* in 1615, the same Richard Mathew at Fleet Bridge was the first Englishman to attain perfection in the making of knives and knife handles, having learned his art by travelling and residing abroad. Before that, for many hundred years, Howes explained, 'there were made in diverse parts of this kingdom many coarse and uncomely knives', whereas 'at this day the best and finest knives in the world are made in London'.[56] This advance in the reputation of English, or rather London, knives seems to have occurred in Elizabeth's reign and slowly received general acknowledgement. The Huguenot schoolmaster, however, who wrote a textbook of French conversation for his English pupils between 1566 and 1597, was a reluctant convert. He still believed in the superiority of Flemish knives. He included in his exercises in French translation a gibe at one of his Flemish pupils who had no knife, though he came from the country 'where the best knives are made'.[57]

Thus the knife and edge tool industry modernized itself not only in London, but in Sheffield and north Worcestershire. By 1622 foreign cutlers living in St. Martin's le Grand in London were a celebrated group of craftsmen who were said to have made the metropolis famous by their wares.[58] By the early eighteenth century the improvements achieved by the knife industry obliged Monsieur Misson, a very critical Frenchman, to admit (in 1719) that England made 'the best knives in the world'—though, in fairness, we must add his adverse criticism that England made the worst scissors in the world, and that the penknives were so large that you could 'scarce use anything but the points of 'em'.[59]

[55]   Hulme, LQR xlvi. 148; lxi. 45.
[56]   Stow, *Annales* (1615 edn.), 948.
[57]   Byrne, *The Elizabethan Home*, 10.
[58]   W. Durrant Cooper, *Lists of Foreign Protestants and Aliens resident in England, 1618–88*, Camden Soc. 82 (1862), Intro. iii.
[59]   M. Misson, *Memoirs and Observations in his Travels over England* (London, 1719), 171.

Edge tools may not have achieved the same reputation in Europe but they ceased to be imported into England from abroad. By the early seventeenth century they were on the shopping list of many colonists going to America, from which we must assume that they reached a standard that was satisfactory to middle- and working-class people, whose livelihood in their new country was going to depend on them.[60] Richard Ligon's list of wares for a shopkeeper to stock in Barbados and buy in England (1657) named whipsaws, two-handed saws, hand saws, files, axes for felling and hewing, hatchets for carpenters, joiners, and coopers, chisels, adzes, pickaxes, mattocks, hoes for weeding ground, planes, gouges, augurs, handbills for negroes to cut sugar canes, and drawing knives for joiners. Only mallets were better made in Barbados because the woods were harder than in England.[61] Ligon's advice was plainly not singular or eccentric. Ports on the western side of the country all carried regular consignments of tools to America and the West Indies.[62]

The knife and tool industry, then, must count as another of the projects, stimulated in the 1540s, which, with the help of foreign expertise, greatly enhanced its reputation in the seventeenth century, sufficiently, indeed, to command the American market for edge tools, and to make an impression on the luxury French market with its knives.[63] It had started as a service to working men and gradually raised its sights.

If space permitted, the success of projects, first in English, and then in European markets, could be demonstrated in the history of many other wares: felt hats, Caster hats, Monmouth caps, buttons, copper thread, tobacco pipes, girdles, gloves, glass, and earthenware. It must suffice to consider the growing overseas market for wares that *have* received attention. About 1679 a list was compiled of goods exported from London in the year Michaelmas 1662 to Michaelmas 1663.

[60]   Bristol portbooks, 1600–1, name knives, pocket knives, penknives, shoemakers' knives, hand saws, and files. (PRO E 190, 1132/11.)
[61]   Ligon, op. cit. 110.
[62]   e.g. Dartmouth in Devon in 1640–1. (PRO E 190/951/8.)
[63]   The portbook for Dover, 1697–8, lists various consignments of knives to Calais. (PRO E 190/675/2.)

It claimed to be an account of English manufactures, and to exclude re-exported goods. Being confined to London, it is only a rough-and-ready indicator of the way the new industries were competing overseas, but it is better than nothing.[64]

English alum now went (in order of value) to Holland, Germany, France, Spain, Portugal, the American Plantations, East Indies, Scotland, and Ireland. Aqua vitae went to the Plantations, Russia, the East Indies, Africa, and Portugal. Strong waters went to Africa, Spain, Germany, Portugal, France, Scotland, and Italy. Copperas went to Holland, Germany, France, and Spain. Leather gloves went in large quantities to Germany, Holland, and Sweden, and in lesser quantities to five other European countries as well as to the Plantations, Scotland, and Ireland. Gold and silver lace went to Portugal in quantity, less to Italy and Spain, to the Plantations, and to Scotland. English wrought silk went to Spain, Portugal (4,105 lb) the Plantations (3,427 lb), France (2,346 lb), Holland, Italy, Scotland, Germany, Ireland, Flanders, Africa, and Denmark (amounts ranging from 200 to 2,000 lb). English thrown silk went to Germany, Portugal, and Scotland (over 1,000 lb apiece), and in small quantities to Denmark and the Plantations.[65] Every single country in this list invites us to investigate the manufacturing centres in England of these commodities, and the quality of the wares that yielded them such a market overseas. Gold and silver lace was being sold in Italy, whence the manufacture had first infiltrated into England. Wrought silk was being sold in Spain, whence the first silk stockings had come to England. Alum was sent to Spain, whence it had been imported in the sixteenth century. How had quality and price been upturned in the interval?

Differentiation plainly deserves attention as a positive force in expanding consumption. It is a subject that is generally

[64] London was certainly not always a reliable guide to the national market in goods sold or in goods bought. For example, in September 1596 an account of customs and subsidies paid in the Port of London declared that far greater sums were paid in the outports for imported cambrics and lawns. (CSPD 1595–7, 287); a trade balance, compiled for 1612-14, shows that goods imported into London were little more than one-third of those delivered to the outports. (Thirsk and Cooper, 455.)

[65] BL Add. MS. 36785. For a partial summary, see Appendix II.

ignored in studies of long-term economic development, even though it may contain the most valuable clue to the vitality or decay of particular regions in England, each having its own peculiar mixture of industrial specialities, employing large populations. Phelps Brown and Hopkins, for example, could only assess the cost of living over six centuries by ignoring the changes in the quality of the goods they were costing. This was, of course, justified by the end they had in view, to show the long-term trend. But to use this graph as a guide to the purchasing power of all classes, and hence as a guide, at one remove, to the demand for consumer goods, is to show concern for one factor only in a highly complex process of decision-making. It screens from sight many other factors that made or marred the consumer industries. None was based on a single centre, rather each had many centres, whose survival depended on the relationship of each centre with its competitors in other parts of the kingdom, and in other countries; some served only one class of society, whose fickleness was notorious; others served several classes. So a perpetual restructuring of the consumer industries was forced upon them from without.[66] In addition, it was likely to be generated from within, for the discrimination and satisfaction of buyers intensified specialization, it encouraged producers in each branch of the same industry to strive for higher standards. This not surprisingly sometimes raised prices, and might in the end price wares out of the old markets. When industries found new clients who were as satisfactory to them as the old, their former purchasers had to seek further afield for another source of cheap wares. Some such process may lie behind the growing market for Irish linen in England, which in the 1670s began to compete with English and Scottish linen. In the early seventeenth century Scottish linen was among the cheapest; by 1641 it was no longer so. The same process of 'improvement' is hinted at in the history of the lace industry. Who, it may

[66] Restructuring is implied by Penelope Corfield in her description of the market for the worsted cloth of Norwich in the seventeenth century. It was mainly exported in the early seventeenth century, sold mainly on the home market in the later seventeenth century, and mostly exported in the mid-eighteenth century. (P. Corfield, 'A Provincial Capital in the late 17th Century: the Case of Norwich', in Clark and Slack, *Crisis and Order in English Towns* 279–80.)

be asked, were the customers of the lace makers of Bedford-shire and Buckinghamshire at the end of the seventeenth century? At one time they produced the cheap lace, but they now claimed to be making something that was up to the standard of Flemish lace.[67] Once it had cost 8s. per yard. Now it cost 30s. per yard. Where did servants now find cheap lace for their aprons?

Such questions direct attention at the need for more careful analysis of the internal structure of domestic in-dustries, for every single one was made up of many parts. But a further question concerns their standing in relation to their European counterparts. In a discerning book in 1958 on *The Cultural Foundations of Industrial Civilization*, Professor Nef made the distinction between the industries of the Continent, especially Holland and France, which concentrated on artistic wares in the sixteenth and seventeenth centuries, and Great Britain (and Sweden) which produced a flood of cheap wares. For England we begin to measure the full truth of this generalization. English industries selling overseas for the most part succeeded best with cheap consumer wares. There were some exceptions, of course: some English knives achieved a high reputation abroad, but the craftsmanship in that case seems to have been of London not of the rural areas. The truth touched some writers with melancholy. One wrote in 1662 sadly reporting how the Dutch commanded the quality market for cloth in France, Poland, the East Indies, Scotland, Ireland, even England itself, leaving England to 'become the poor man's clothier'.[68] Seen by those who wanted England to have the prestige of making the best of everything, it was, indeed, a sad business. But seen from the point of view of the large rural populations at home, more fully employed in the seventeenth century than at any earlier time, it was a matter for congratulation not lamentation. It was the political economists who first recognized in the success of the new consumer industries a changed situation that they could contemplate with satisfaction, not with dismay.

[67] Victoria and Albert Museum Library, 43 A 2h: *Case of the Lacemakers in Relation to the Importation of Foreign Bone Lace* (1698). I owe this reference to Dr. Roger Richardson.
[68] Bodleian Library, Clarendon MS. 77, fo. 171.

VI. PROJECTS AND POLITICAL ECONOMY

Political economists formulate their theories late in the day when the changing realities of life have become inescapably obvious. They are not the pioneers of economic change, but follow in its wake, interpreting it and generalizing from it. Thus any policy which they formulate for the future reflects past experience. Having reviewed some of the many sixteenth- and seventeenth-century projects, we are now in a position to trace in the writings of political economists attitudes and advice that reflect that experience.

Although many economic projects were instigated, in one way or another, by the government, they flourished best when they had passed beyond the pioneer phase, and had entered the deep interstices of the economy, establishing themselves in places that were out of sight of authority and government. No searchlights any longer gleamed upon the proceedings; no loud trumpets drew attention to what was going on. Even the journalists took time to appreciate what was happening. When Walter Blith wrote his textbook of husbandry in 1649, seeking to enlighten his readers upon six measures of agricultural improvement that they might adopt, they promptly drew his attention to six 'newer pieces of improvement' which he had completely overlooked. He duly incorporated these into the next edition of his book in 1652. 'I fear men's spirits are strangely private that have made excellent experiments and yet will not communicate', he remarked petulantly.[1] He had travelled widely in England and yet all this had escaped his notice because he had not pried sufficiently in the dark corners of the realm.

As with novel agricultural crops, so with the new consumer industries. They installed themselves unobtrusively in many scattered centres, frequently in hamlets and cottages that were out of sight of interfering lords, and often enough safe from judicial authority. Some of the new and expanding labourers' and squatters' settlements in the seventeenth

---

[1] Blith, *The English Improver Improved* (London, 1652 edn.), 224–5.

century were deliberately located on the boundaries of parishes, hundreds, or counties, where jurisdiction was disputed, for in such places escape from the law was relatively easy.

In these circumstances, it was not surprising that the political economists only slowly grasped the significance of these unobtrusive but influential features appearing on the English industrial scene. At the beginning of the seventeenth century their basic article of faith was summed up in the title of Thomas Mun's famous essay, written in the early 1620s, on 'England's Treasure by Foreign Trade'. England's treasure *was* her foreign trade, or, as the sub-title expressed it, 'the balance of our foreign trade is the rule of our treasure'. The writer's attention was riveted on England's overseas trade, and especially on the cloth industry as the main export. This had to pay, and more than pay, the cost of imports, if England's wealth was to be increased. 'The ordinary means therefore to increase our wealth and treasure is by foreign trade, wherein we must ever observe this rule: to sell more to strangers yearly than we consume of theirs in value,'[2] To obtain this surplus, two alternative or complementary courses were open: Englishmen must reduce their consumption of foreign goods, or sell more of their native products overseas. It was anathema to Mun to observe in the frequent changes of fashion in food and clothing—many of them imported from France, Italy, and Spain—the signs of a developing home market in consumer goods. He would have had laws curbing such excesses. As for his second objective, to promote the sale of English goods overseas, he agreed that every effort had to be made to suit our wares to the foreigners' taste and purse.[3] He did not seem to see the irrationality of his double standard.

Common sense prevented Mun from judging *all* manufactures by their contribution to foreign trade. The luxury needs of the English nobility and gentry created work for the poor, he conceded, and this was beneficial to the commonwealth. But better by far to engage in activities that enriched

---

[2] J.R. McCulloch (ed.), *Early English Tracts on Commerce* (Cambridge, 1952), 125.

[3] Ibid. 127, 180, 128.

the whole kingdom, including the King. This was achieved only by exports. These secured a favourable balance of trade, gave a living to labourers, manufacturers, and merchants, *and* brought in customs revenue to the Crown. As McCulloch graphically phrased it, when reviewing the theory in 1856, the balance of trade was thus erected into a 'gilded image of clay and mud' standing for more than a century as 'an object of slavish adoration'.[4]

The tricky arithmetic necessary then, as now, to arrive at a final account of the overseas trade balance need not concern us. Built upon shaky foundations, a seemingly firm figure was somehow arrived at. In 1612-14 it seemed that England had a favourable balance of trade. In 1616 it was pronounced unfavourable, and it was still deemed so in 1622-3, when a serious economic crisis provoked a long and deep inquiry into its causes. This was wholly concerned with the terms of overseas trade and the exchange rate.[5] The solution to the depression seemed to lie in exporting every more competitively, ever more cheaply.

In fact, as we have seen, the influence of this way of thinking was an obstacle to industrial advance along the lines now being charted by projectors. The campaign waged at this time to improve the quality of English cloth (the main export) insisted on uniform lengths and widths. It was contrary to the wishes of the English consumer who rejoiced in the variety of price and quality that was available; for him, the more variety, the better. But since it was the merchant who held the balance of trade in his hand, and was responsible for tilting it one way or the other, the merchant's word carried most weight. He wanted uniformity and this therefore became government policy. Fortunately, it proved impossible to put this policy effectively into practice. Variety rather than uniformity continued to sustain the domestic market. It was even encouraged by foreign demand. According to William Temple, writing in 1668, foreigners found cheap English manufactures as useful as did their English customers. The Dutch made a good bargain out of selling

[4] Ibid. vii.
[5] Thirsk and Cooper, 457, 461, 473-4; Thomas Mun, 'England's Treasure by Foreign Trade' in McCulloch, op. cit. 117 ff.

their own fine-quality cloth to France and buying the coarse
cloth of England for their own wear. They sent their best
butter abroad, and bought for their own use the cheap butter
made in Ireland and in northern England.[6] In this casual
remark from a contemporary. we solve the mystery of why
northern English butter became an export from Northumberland and Durham in the second half of the seventeenth
century.[7] Its quality is the vital clue that explains its success
as a new export. It was cheap, and Holland's own butter was
now in the luxury class, too expensive for ordinary Dutchmen to put on their own tables.

Thus, while Thomas Mun and Edward Misselden concentrated their attention in the early 1620s on the problems of
overseas trade, the world around them was being shaped in a
new image. Industrial and agricultural producers were toppling
the gilded image of clay and mud from its pedestal by producing goods, many of them cheap and cheerful, for the
home market; if they attracted purchasers from abroad so
much the better but that was incidental. We may remind
ourselves by a few random illustrations of the projects that
were well under way or were being initiated in these same
years in villages scattered all over the kingdom. Already in
1608 men confidently claimed that English manufacturers
had triumphed over foreign competitors in the making of
fustians, cards, silk laces, ribbons, points, silk garters, girdles,
bewpers, bolsters, and knives. In 1620 John Stratford, who
had once traded as a merchant buying undressed flax from
Holland, started to grow flax at Winchcombe in Gloucestershire. The same John Stratford had launched the earlier
venture of tobacco growing in 1619, that had been brought
to an end by government edict. But as a *peasant activity*,
tobacco growing forged ahead in the 1620s and was destined
to enjoy a long, though illicit career in twenty-two counties,
likewise supplying the home market.[8] In Somerset flax

---

[6] William Temple, *Observations upon the United Provinces of the Netherlands* (London, 1673), 208.

[7] P. Brassley, 'The Agricultural Economy of Northumberland and Durham in
the period 1640–1750', Univ. of Oxford B.Litt. thesis (1974), 148. I wish to
thank Mr. Brassley for allowing me to quote from his unpublished thesis.

[8] BL Lansdowne MS. 152, fos. 324, 329; Thirsk, 'Projects for Gentlemen'
160–2; *idem*, 'New Crops and their Diffusion', *passim*.

growing was being assiduously promoted in 1625 by various
local gentry who invited Christopher Cockerell of Elham in
Kent to go to Glastonbury to improve local skills in growing
flax and dressing it for the spinner. Cockerell remained in
the Somerset Levels for more than thirteen years, demon-
strating his way with flax as an *agricultural* crop in newly
drained fen, and *industrially* as an employer of poor spinners.[9]
Even while he promoted this project, stocking knitting and
the spinning of wool for the knitters were already keeping
many others occupied in Glastonbury.[10] In these same years,
Anthony Cope of Hanwell was growing woad in Spalding,
Lincolnshire, and despite the gloomy tales that some men
circulated in the 1580s about the inferior quality of English
woad, it nevertheless built up a solid reputation as a profitable
crop in the course of the seventeenth century.[11] Men came
to terms with its cultivation and recognized that it could not
be grown on half-acres and small quillets of land. It had to
be a well-organized enterprise, backed by men with enough
capital to own a woad mill and keep it busy, but when these
requirements were met, as Walter Blith affirmed, it made a
fortune for many a Midland landowner in the mid-seventeenth
century, and gave plenty of work to labourers.[12] In Northamptonshire it remained a favourite crop well into the eighteenth
century. 'Of all the Midland counties', wrote John Morton
in the *Natural History of Northamptonshire* in 1712, 'this
I am pretty sure is, or has been, woaded most'.[13] Among yet
more successes in this period, trials with rapeseed oil for
cloth making were brought to fruition by Benedict Webb in
Gloucestershire shortly before 1620. In 1625 he grew 550
acres of rape in the Forest of Dean, while others in the East
Anglian fens grew hundreds of acres more.[14] From a Scots-
man travelling south to congratulate George I on his accession
to the English throne in 1714, we catch a glimpse of the
quiet diffusion of this innovation. At Easingwold in Yorkshire

---

9   HMC 7th Report (Taunton Records), 694.
10   Corporation of London Record Office, GCE Estates, Rentals 4.7. I am
grateful to Professor Maurice Beresford for this reference.
11   See above, p. 22.
12   Blith, op. cit. (1653 edn.), 229, 234.
13   John Morton, *Natural History of Northamptonshire* (London, 1712), 17.
14   Thirsk and Cooper, 220–2; Brace, *History of Seed Crushing* 22.

James Hart reported seeing fields of 20 to 30 acres, all sown
with rapeseed, destined to be crushed for oil to serve the
clothiers.[15] The crop yielded a very satisfactory profit to the
farmer of £10 an acre, and even served overseas as well as
domestic demand. Some was shipped from London, but the
trade had greater proportionate importance in lesser places:
a petition to the House of Commons in 1719 described the
shipping of a thousand tons annually from the little port
of Wisbech.[16]

These are but a few of the industrial and agricultural
occupations that transformed the pattern of employment in
the seventeenth century. They serve as a reminder that
important initiatives were being taken in the 1620s, at the
very moment when Mun and Misselden tendered their advice
in quite other terms in an effort to ameliorate the trade
depression. Political economists did not then appreciate
the role of consumer industries and of the expansive home
market, and it was not for another twenty years, not until
the Civil War, that fresh experience drove home the lesson.
The Civil War was indeed a landmark in developing a new
economic policy out of the history of projects, simply
because it gave influential writers and politicians a deeper
knowledge of the variety of local economies than they
could ever have acquired in peacetime.

Men moved around the country more than was their wont.
Some were men of influence on the Parliamentary side,
serving on Parliamentary committees as sequestration commissioners, militia commissioners, surveyors, and so on. They
carried with them on their journeys political and social
ideals and a practical concern for economic progress. The
urgency of measures to revive the economy was impressed
upon them by the severe depression, which began in 1646,
deepened in 1649 with the execution of the King, and
plumbed the depths between 1649 and 1651. The new
republic had to revive confidence and infuse fresh economic
energy by a programme that made the new Commonwealth
more than just a new name. Pamphlets enumerating the great
economic possibilities that lay ahead clearly reflected the

[15] *The Journal of Mr. James Hart* (Edinburgh, 1832), 9.
[16] Brace, op. cit. 27.

lessons which their authors had learned in their perambulations of the kingdom. Their first concern was to mitigate poverty and unemployment that had been grievously aggravated by the war. They placed their strongest hopes, not unnaturally, on agricultural improvement, especially on the improvement of wastes, forests, and parks which might be made into smallholdings for cottagers and farms for husbandmen. The confiscation of Crown, Church, and royalist lands made this an immediately attainable goal. The second theme in their campaign was the economic value of vegetables, fruit, and industrial crops. These demanded intensive labour but yielded a large profit. Their third recommendation was for industrial work to employ the poor, and in pamphlets on this subject an appreciation of the role of rural industries was clearly discernible.[17] It was clearest of all in Henry Robinson's wide programme of economic reforms, which gave prominence to the value of the home market. Even though it was still regarded as the handmaid of overseas trade, it was deemed indispensable in that role, for what else was overseas trade but 'exportation of the overplus of all such commodities as the inland trade hath produced more than are sufficient for service of the nation'.?[18]

Henry Robinson was groping his way only slowly towards an understanding of the economic potential of rural industries. In 1641 he had written a brief essay suggesting that improved river navigation would assist inland trade, a matter on which England, he thought, was backward compared with Germany and Italy. In a new survey in 1649 Robinson wrestled with a related problem—the difficulties created by the existence of scattered populations, all having to be supplied with the raw materials of manufacture. The straggling sprawl of hamlets and villages greatly increased the costs of transport and put up the prices of manufactured goods. These passed back and forth too many times between the markets and the craftsmen who specialized in different operations. He proposed to tidy up the time-wasting pattern of dispersed settlement by grouping tenements into villages

---

[17] See e.g. William Goffe, 'How to Advance the Trade of the Nation and Employ the Poor', *Harleian Miscellany*, iv, 366 ff.

[18] Thirsk and Cooper, 53.

and establishing cities near rivers. The solution was unrealistic, and we can imagine what his critics said to him in private. His scheme finally appeared in a much more acceptable guise in his third essay, written in 1652, urging that all rivers be made navigable, and canals be built to towns lacking rivers.[19] This was a suggestion that bore a rich harvest. Rural industries continued in the same locations, but the improvement of navigable rivers became one of the most impressive achievements of the second half of the seventeenth century.

In some ways it is surprising that the theoretical insights of men like Henry Robinson, whose ideas, we may reasonably assume, were discussed with his contemporaries before they appeared in print, and reflected more than one man's individual and eccentric opinions, did not result in another outburst of projects initiated by a fresh generation of projectors with strong Parliamentarian sympathies. It would not have been unreasonable to expect more projects, similar in purpose to those of the period 1540–1630, started this time by Commonwealthmen as courageous and public-spirited as those of the Elizabethan age. In fact, the evidence points rather to projects of a more personal kind at a more experimental stage. The experiments of John Beale with ciders that would sell in wider markets, the experiments of Sir Richard Weston with clover on the sandy heaths of his own estate in Surrey, the trials of flax growing by Parson Giles Moore of Horsted Keynes in Sussex, the collecting and publicizing of new varieties of vegetables and trees, were all intended to improve employment prospects in the long run.[20] Men, in the Hartlib circle especially, were planning economic growth in many different directions, confidently predicting that each scheme would greatly increase employment for the poor. But the schemes were in their initial

[19] Henry Robinson, *England's Safety in Trades' Encrease, 1641*, BL Thomason E167 (5); *Briefe Considerations concerning the Advancement of Trade and Navigation*, 1649, BL Thomason E589 (6). This is reprinted in its entirety in Thirsk and Cooper, 52–7; *Certain Proposals in order to the People's Freedom* (London, 1652), 9.

[20] John Beale, *Herefordshire Orchards* (1657); Sir Richard Weston, *A Discours of Husbandrie used in Brabant and Flanders* (2nd edn., London, 1652); R. Bird (ed.), 'The Journal of Giles Moore', *Sussex Record Soc.* 68 (1971), 113.

stages, and consisted in individual experiments in the private houses, gardens, and fields of gentlemen and parsons.

One is driven to the conclusion that men were now more cautious, partly because the economic and political climate was different, and the future still uncertain, but also because, for other reasons, men were less sure of themselves. They were not now copying foreign models, of whose success they could be confident. They were venturing upon newer and less well charted paths.

At a lower level of society, however, the industries launched earlier were forging ahead under their own momentum. Poor men, and the not so poor, were pursuing their own solutions without assistance from above. The history of tobacco growing is the superb, and unusually well documented, illustration of a new enterprise that had cost its pioneer hundreds, even thousands, of pounds in 1619. But two years were enough to set it going among humbler men. It became an occupation that employed hundreds of poor by the 1640s and 1650s.[21]

The full strength of the many novel industrial undercurrents in the economy was fully recognized at last in the 1670s when a new depression deepened and pamphleteers took up their pens again in an effort to alleviate 'the fall of rents and the decay of trade'. Much the most discerning writer of the new generation was Carew Reynel, a Hampshire country gentleman, educated at Oxford and the Inns of Court, who made his only appearance on the political stage when he took part in Penruddock's Rising in 1655, and was charitably pardoned on account of his extreme youth.[22] His later years were spent in economic studies that were presented in his book, *The True English Interest*, published in 1674. Who would have expected that this man, seemingly with the conventional upbringing of an English landed gentleman, would so eloquently urge the expansion of domestic industries, even shaking himself free from the most deep-rooted prejudices against forbidden occupations such as tobacco growing?

[21] Thirsk, 'New Crops and their Diffusion', *passim*.

[22] These details are taken from the DNB. But remarkably little is known of the influences that shaped Reynel's views, though it is believed that he went abroad when released from Exeter gaol in 1655.

He had listened to government propaganda over several decades proclaiming that tobacco growing injured the health of Englishmen. Yet he boldly dedicated a chapter of his book to this topic, advocating tobacco as a crop that improved the rent of land extremely, 'as well as employing great numbers of people...Land otherwise worth 10s. an acre was worth £3 p.a. under tobacco (and hence was highly satisfactory to the landlord), while the tenant could make a profit of £30 and £40 an acre, all charges paid...All the objections that are against it cannot vie with the advantages that it produces', he asserted, in defiance of all received doctrine. Even the argument that English tobacco was inferior to foreign was summarily dispatched. 'If people will take it as they do, and it will go off, what matter is it?...Others say 'tis *better* than any foreign tobacco, especially for English bodies.' In fact, it was a common practice to mix English tobacco with foreign, and when this was done, it passed for foreign tobacco, commanding the higher price.[23]

Carew Reynel was clearly an original mind, and offered a remarkably penetrating commentary on the English economy and the way forward. To encourage England's wealth and prosperity, he held it necessary to encourage home trade rather than foreign. His message was now much clearer and more positive than Henry Robinson's had been. 'Trade is to be advanced every way at home and abroad, but especially the home as being of more consequence than the foreign...Foreign trade is a secondary help, home trade is our primary advantage.'[24] To encourage home trade, river transport must be improved; even now two new engines were being offered as a method of cutting rivers at an easy rate. Turning to agriculture and measures to employ the population on the land, he favoured small farms rather than large: 'the smaller estates the land is divided into, the better for the nation; the more people are maintained, and the land better husbanded'. Here was another original and unfamiliar argument reflecting accurate observations on the success of intensive cultivation—of vegetables, and industrial crops like dyes, hemp, and flax, as well as tobacco. Reynel came from

[23] Reynel, *The True English Interest* (London, 1674), 32–3.
[24] Ibid. 7.

Hampshire, be it noted, the first home of woad growing in its new phase, launched under the projectors' stimulus in the sixteenth century. As for industrial occupations, he handed out warm praise for rural industries that employed a large labour force—lace making in Manchester, band-string making at Blandford, Dorset, knives at Sheffield, fustians in Lancashire, sail making in Ipswich ('the best sails that ever were made', he claimed), liquorice at Worksop, hops at Farnham, saffron at Saffron Walden, tobacco at Winchcombe, stuffs, silks, satins, and velvets at Norwich, Canterbury, Colchester, Spitalfields, and in the London suburbs, thread making at Maidstone (where they sold a thousand pounds' worth a week), and serges at Exeter.[25] What were these but sixteenth-century projects—new industries, and old ones that had been transformed by new techniques into a virtually new occupation? Only saffron at Saffron Walden looks like a survival from a medieval past, though, for all we yet know, the method of cultivating saffron may well have been improved by Dutch expertise, renowned in Holland, in the later sixteenth century. Reynel associated all these new occupations with towns, for towns were the collecting centres and markets, but much of the labour force, as we have seen, was mixed, partly of the town, and partly of the countryside, where a duality of occupation still held sway.

Another list of trades compiled by Reynel offered occupations that in his view gave scope for yet further improvement. These also were projects carried over from the sixteenth and early seventeenth centuries: linen, silk, tapestry, cider making, tobacco growing, vine growing, mining, salt making, the manufacture of brass goods, and paper making.[26] With their achievements so far Reynel was dissatisfied. But it would be an error to dismiss them as insignificant simply because Reynel expressed a hope of better things. Every one of these occupations was being actively pursued in special localities. Every one would repay investigation by a local historian who could define the places and the circumstances in which each provided employment, even perhaps measuring the scale of that employment, as it has proved possible to

---

[25] Ibid. 20, 53–4.   [26] Ibid. 22 ff.

do with woad growing. Silk, salt, brass, paper, and cider spring immediately to mind as industries having clearly defined local centres in the later seventeenth century. Their role as employers of *local* labour and suppliers of *local* markets was, in some cases, already substantial. In one case, that of the linen industry, we can set Reynel's exhortations for the future against what had already been achieved. In northern England the scale of the linen industry is only now being investigated by local historians. Their findings do not support Reynel's gloomy strictures. 'Now we make not so much as the sheets to our beds or shirts to our backs', he complained.[27] Was it that he wanted to see *finer-quality* linen produced? Was it that he hoped to see flax and hemp growing everywhere he went? Since the soils were not everywhere suitable, this was impossible. The truth is that in 1673 hemp and flax were being grown in many scattered but well-defined regions, notably in the fens and marshlands of eastern England and in certain districts of the West Midlands and the south-west. More than this, increasing quantities of yarn were being imported for the benefit of English linen weavers from the Baltic and Ireland.[28] The weavers did not attempt to compete in the making of fine linen like that for which Holland and Silesia were renowned, but instead they met a demand for coarse linen. Perhaps this was what caused Carew Reynel's dissatisfaction.[29]

A glimpse of the local significance of the linen industry is given in two local studies of regional economies in Nidderdale, Yorkshire, and in Lancashire: in both places it was a substantial employer of labour. The people of Nidderdale had earned their living in the sixteenth century as stock farmers with a subsidiary interest in wool cloth making. But the market for their cloth was at Leeds, a distant centre, that placed the dalesmen at some disadvantage. From the 1560s onwards Hull imported increasing quantities of flax from the Baltic. York merchants, moreover, took Nidderdale's

[27] Ibid. 24.
[28] On Baltic imports of flax, see B. Jennings (ed.), *A History of Nidderdale* (Huddersfield, 1967), 176; on imports from Ireland, see Lowe, *Lancashire Textile Industry in the Sixteenth Century*, 11.
[29] Houghton, *A Collection of Letters for the Improvement of Husbandry and Trade* (London, 1681), 114–15.

lead to Danzig and also returned with cargoes of flax, finding it a convenient journey to bring the flax to Boroughbridge, the very entrance to the dale. Nidderdale's economy was transformed in the late sixteenth and seventeenth centuries. Its population increased, land was found for larger numbers of people by reducing the size of individual holdings, and a linen industry became ever more widely dispersed through the valley. The characteristic farmer-clothweaver of the sixteenth century with one woollen loom in his house, gave way to a much larger population of linen weavers with two linen looms and a smallholding. Coarse linen manufacture became one of the twin pillars of Nidderdale's economy.[30]

On the Lancashire side of the Pennines, the linen weavers depended not on Baltic, but on Irish yarn to support their labours. Norman Lowe's account takes the story only to the end of the sixteenth century, but it presents in sharp relief the familiar features of all rural industries. Irish yarn was imported in increasing quantities until even the Irish themselves grew alarmed and in 1569 laid a heavy tariff on exports. This failed to check the trade, and in 1593–4 Liverpool's imports of Irish yarn reached new and unprecedented heights. In this decade too, Lancashire linen—a coarse cloth for sacking and similar rough uses—was selling in Warwickshire, Northamptonshire, Bedfordshire, Cambridgeshire, Suffolk, Berkshire, and Wales.[31] And if linen weavers seemed to lack the ambition to see their cloth going overseas, perhaps they were better off for that very reason. Their home market was more secure, as experience in the 1580s and 1590s taught them. When interruptions to trade overseas became almost continuous after 1585, the Lancashire makers of woollen cloth—Manchester cottons, as they were called—who set their sights on foreign markets, were glad to turn to the home market to rescue their industry from collapse. To do so, they had to change their style, and make cottons in a sober grey colour that sold best at home, as opposed to the highly coloured varieties that found favour abroad. As things turned out, the foreign, and especially the French, market revived again,

---

[30] Jennings, op. cit. 171–6.
[31] Lowe, op. cit. 43 ff., esp. 58.

and Manchester cottons resumed their gay colours and were again dispatched overseas.[32] Meanwhile the linen industry proceeded on its way, unruffled by foreign turmoil so long as its supplies of linen yarn came through safely. In the words of Negley Harte, who plans a full study of English linen in the seventeenth and eighteenth centuries, it was a substantial industry, strangely neglected by historians hitherto, presumably because it supplied only the home market, perhaps also because hindsight tells us that Ireland and Scotland had a greater future in the business than England.[33] But even in 1756 England produced 26 million yards of linen, compared with at most 25 million yards imported from Scotland and Ireland.[34]

As Carew Reynel stressed in 1673 past achievements and the future potential of many new industries, he went out of his way to proclaim the benefits of diversity. 'It is an advantage to have variety of manufactures',[35] he argued. The more numerous they were the better. Unconsciously, he echoed the words of Lord Burghley whose interest in projects in the Elizabethan period had had the same end in view. Studying the new industrial pattern, contemporaries grasped another truth that found its way with increasing frequency into economic treatises: occupations which passed work through many hands benefited the nation more than those which involved one process only and passed directly from producer to consumer. In the sixteenth century men had held the opposite view. They had favoured as much direct contact as possible between producer and consumer, and in rural areas where markets were distant, and pedlars and chapmen found a niche for themselves as middlemen, they legislated strenuously to eliminate these parasites. The success of the new industries taught another philosophy which was eloquently expressed by John Corbet, chaplain to the Gloucester garrison in 1647. It was appropriate that he should write in this vein of a county where many different

---

[32] Ibid. 96–7.

[33] N.B. Harte, 'The Rise of Protection and the English Linen Trade, 1690–1790', in Harte and Ponting (eds.), *Textile History and Economic History*, 74.

[34] Ibid. 107, 93. The figure for Ireland and Scotland is for 1760. In 1750 it was 18½ million yards.

[35] Reynel, op. cit. 19.

rural industries were flourishing in a pastoral setting: wool cloth making, silk weaving, pin and nail making, wiredrawing, card making, edge tool making, mining, wood trencher making, bottle making, and cider making, not to mention tobacco and woad growing.[36] He viewed with sympathy and approval the rural society of Gloucestershire, unencumbered by lords, and composed rather of yeomen, farmers, and petty freeholders, and 'such as use manufactures that enrich the country and pass through the hands of a multitude'.[37] Defoe writing in 1725 preached the same argument when applied to commerce. Describing with pride the organization of the corn trade and the hierarchy of dealers in corn from corn factors and mealmen, to maltsters and carriers, he declared it to be a wholesome rule of commerce 'that trade ought to pass through as many hands as it can'.[38] The many labour-intensive consumer industries of the seventeenth century surely passed this test with flying colours.

As the employment of labour now ranked high as a criterion for judging the merits of new industries and agricultural occupations, a quiet revolution occurred in attitudes towards arable and pastoral husbandry. It had been axiomatic in the sixteenth century that tillage should hold first place in farming. Cereals were the staff of life and ploughmen formed the backbone of the nation. But seventeenth-century experience taught that pastoral products like cattle hides, sheepskins, wool, and timber in the long run created more employment than cereals since they provided raw materials that then passed through the hands of a multitude on their way to becoming ready-made goods.

This novel argument in favour of pastoral as against arable farming first occurred in Sir Richard Weston's writings in the 1640s, and reflected his experience in France, Holland, and Flanders where he noted that the pastoral regions were the most populous. Dairy farms of 100 acres, he claimed, employed many more hands than 100 acres of corn; sheep-

---

[36] See the occupations in John Smith, *Men and Armour for Gloucestershire in 1608* (London, 1902), *passim*.

[37] *Somers Tracts* (London, 1811), v. 303.

[38] A.E. Bland, P.A. Brown, and R.H. Tawney, *English Economic History. Select Documents* (London, 1914), 487–8.

keeping gave more work than corn growing, if you included
the spinning and weaving of wool, and the manufacture of
sheepskins.[39] The argument subsequently became a commonplace. It was advanced by Samuel Fortrey in *England's
Interest and Improvement* in 1663.[40] It was restated by
John Houghton in 1692, and rephrased by Charles Davenant
in 1699, when he claimed that pasture farming was more in
the national interest than corn growing.[41] Thus the plough-
man was dethroned. It had been an article of faith with Mr.
Secretary Cecil in 1601 that 'whosoever doth not maintain
the plough destroys this kingdom'.[42] The new rural economy
of pastoral England with its combination of farming and
industry taught another point of view.

To sum up, the new consumer industries and the success
of industrial occupations combined with farming in rural
areas introduced new propositions that displaced some
long-established tenets of the old political economy. These
were, firstly, that the home trade was as advantageous to the
nation as foreign trade, if not more so, 'the people of Great
Britain being the best customers to the manufacturers and
traders of Great Britain', as David Macpherson roundly put it
in 1760.[43] Secondly, the more variety of these manufactures,
the better; thirdly, the most beneficial manufacturing
industries were those that passed through the hands of a
multitude; fourthly, pasture farming benefited the nation
more than corn growing. The old theories of how to increase
the wealth of a nation were accommodating themselves to
the new facts. The way was being paved for Adam Smith
who would fundamentally and heroically revise the whole
theory.

Professor Seligmann, the editor of one of the most used
editions of the *Wealth of Nations* describes Adam Smith as

[39] J. Thirsk, 'Seventeenth-Century Agriculture and Social Change', in *Land,
Church and People. Essays presented to Prof. H.P.R. Finberg*, ed. J. Thirsk, Agric.
Hist. Rev. Supp. XVIII (1970), 174–5.

[40] Samuel Fortrey, 'England's Interest and Improvement', in McCulloch
(ed.), *Early English Tracts on Commerce*, 227.

[41] J. Houghton, *A Collection for the Improvement of Husbandry and Trade*,
ed. R. Bradley (London, 1727), i. 49; Thirsk and Cooper, 815.

[42] Bland, Brown, and Tawney, op. cit. 274–5.

[43] Cited in W.E. Minchinton (ed.), *The Growth of English Overseas Trade
in the Seventeenth and Eighteenth Centuries* (London, 1969), 38.

'the first great theorist of that stage of capitalist enterprise which we call the domestic system'.[44] And certainly the domestic system shines through every page of his text in which he analysed the elements in industrial production. The pin industry gave him his first example of the economic advantages of the division of labour; other examples were drawn from the linen industry, the wool cloth industry, nail making, and button making. To illustrate further the division of labour and the market in everyday consumer goods, so necessary to ordinary men and women, he pointed to the clothing industries, making linen shirts and shoes (not stockings in this particular passage, though such a reference occurs later), the metalworking industries, supplying kitchen grates, knives, forks, and working tools of all kinds, the pottery industry making everyday earthenware plates, the tin industry that made pewter, and the glass industry that made window glass. Smith was erecting a new theory of wealth on the basis of an economic system whose remarkably expansive development we have traced through one and a half centuries between 1540 and 1700. But so far the term 'domestic system' has not been used because it has connotations that need to be dispelled. Its first historians were inclined to portray life under the domestic system as a poor makeshift, to which miserable men resorted for want of anything better. Emphasis was laid on the workers' industrial income, which was invariably assumed to be very low, and the working conditions of his cottage, which was invariably assumed to be dark and dingy. The agricultural holding that secured food for his family and gave work out of doors that compensated for the stuffy hours spent inside was quietly passed over. Life under the domestic system cut across neat categories of economic activity; it was neither completely industrial nor completely agricultural, and, being a half-breed, it had to be viewed in a sombre half-light. But its duality was its great advantage. It gave independence and often greater economic security than the living of many a single-minded artisan or farmer, and the routine of life was varied. The case for such duality of work can be argued, and,

[44] A. Smith, *The Wealth of Nations*, ed. E.R.A. Seligman (London, 1910), i, p. xi.

indeed, it is being argued in some quarters nowadays, as a solution to the problems of dreary working routines that destroy the human spirit in industrial societies. If we admit the term 'domestic system' into our discussions, then, we must attempt to shed the prejudices that usually attach to it.

Smith's theories on the role of industrial production were shaped by his view of the world that existed all around him, and which included numerous examples of the domestic system. But the grandeur of his total theoretical structure is the most impressive part of his achievement, not the detail of its component parts. Examination of the detail reveals that Smith's propagandist purposes could only be achieved by simplification, sometimes almost at the expense of historical truth. Hence Smith presented the domestic system through a spotted mirror that reflected things clearly at one moment while distorting them at another. The best explanation seems to be that conditions in the 1770s justified the ambivalence of Smith's attitudes. The domestic system was about to crumble, just at the moment when Adam Smith constructed his economic theory, and since he saw himself not merely as a commentator on the existing economy but also as a theorist looking to the future and persuading men to take action and change their course, he accepted that the domestic system necessarily had to be dismantled. Thus he presented a simplified, and occasionally harsh, view of the domestic system in order to persuade the government to adopt the policy that seemed to him to be necessary for the future. His was a partial view of the domestic system, for his purpose did not require him to analyse its qualities as the historian would wish. Smith's ideas, says Professor Seligman, were formed on the very threshold of the Industrial Revolution.[45] If we recognize that they were intended to press that revolution more rapidly ahead, at the risk of diminishing the role of existing institutions, we can better understand his equivocal comments on the domestic system. In the first place, it was while assessing workers under this system, notably the pin makers, that the values of the division of labour presented themselves to Smith. The logic of his arguments in its favour necessarily

[45] Ibid. xii.

compelled him to condemn those who followed more than one type of employment. He therefore condemned in no uncertain terms the weaver/smallholder who worked his loom *and* cultivated his land.

The country weaver who cultivates a small farm must lose a good deal of time in passing from his loom to the field and from the field to his loom. When the two trades can be carried on in the same workhouse, the loss of time is no doubt much less. It is even in this case, however, very considerable. A man commonly saunters a little in turning his hand from one sort of employment to another.[46]

It would be anachronistic to utter regrets that no industrial psychologist stood at Smith's elbow moderating this condemnation of the domestic system. At that stage in the organization of industry, men could justly express concern at time wasted. But even without the advantages of hindsight, no intelligent reader of his words could fail to see the gross exaggerations in Smith's following sentences:

The habit of sauntering and of indolent careless application, which is naturally or rather necessarily acquired by every country workman who is obliged to change his work and his tools every half hour, and to apply his hand in twenty different ways almost every day of his life, renders him almost always slothful and lazy, and incapable of any vigorous application, even on the most pressing occasions.[47]

This is not the impression conveyed by such diaries of peasant workers as have come down to us from the eighteenth and nineteenth centuries. Nor is it in the nature of men with a modicum of intelligence to dissipate their energies so carelessly by changing their work and their tools every half hour. Smith had already admitted in other passages on the division of labour that most industries had already embarked on some division of labour in an intelligent and rational manner. Spinning was done in a separate household from weaving; and even within the individual cloth working family, which did not appear to specialize, its members engaged in division of labour. In short, Smith's portrait of the weaver-farmer was a grotesque caricature necessary to make his point effective, but it would not pass the scrutiny of the historian.[48]

---

[46] Ibid. 8.
[47] Ibid.
[48] Strong criticism of this passage was made at the time by J.S. Mill in *Principles of Political Economy*, Bk I, Ch. VIII (Toronto, 1963) ii, 126–8. 'This is surely a most exaggerated description of the inefficiency of country labour', he wrote. I wish to thank Dr. Maxine Berg for this reference.

In this instance, however, as in the whole of his work, Smith was assuming the posture of an accountant employed to draw up a balance-sheet of the nation's resources. He was not concerned with the personal lives led by individuals, and could only achieve the superb clarity of his exposition by detaching his theory from any sensitive consideration of the human beings whose labours created the wealth of the nation. Yet at every turn their lives obtruded themselves, insisting on inserting question marks at the end of his confident propositions. For example, he had to explain inequalities in the wages of labour and among his examples he recognized the people who derived their substance from more than one employment. As an illustration he chose the poor cottagers in Scotland, who were employed as casual labourers by landlords and farmers, and who supplemented their wages with food from a small herb garden, with grassland that fed a cow, and 'perhaps an acre or two of bad arable land'. Prejudices were built into the example: the arable land was bad; having two occupations, he reminded his readers, was a common phenomenon 'in countries ill cultivated and worse inhabited'.[49] Even then the gloomy picture could not be consistently maintained. Under another domestic system in Scotland, Smith explained how stockings were knitted that were sold much more cheaply than any that were wrought on a frame. The knitters were servants and labourers in Shetland, and they exported to Scotland annually more than a thousand pairs of stockings at 5d. and 7d. a pair. Without their land they could not have sold their labour so cheaply, he argued.[50] But was this really the full explanation for the cheap labour? In the next sentence he admitted that some of Shetland's knitted worsted stockings were sold for a guinea a pair and upwards. Should not such a fact have prompted further investigation of the quality of goods made under the domestic system, in relation to their price, since these fine but costly worsted stockings were also produced under the same system?

In another passage he reiterated the view that instances of people living by one employment and at the same time deriving 'some *little* advantage [my italics] from another occur chiefly in poor countries'. Yet in the next sentence he allowed that 'something of the same kind was to be found in the capital of a very rich one', namely in London, where shopkeepers gained an extra source of income from letting lodgings, in consequence of which lodgings were much cheaper in London than in Edinburgh.[51]

The truth is that the domestic system could not be summarily condemned by a succession of damaging adjectives and biased examples. It required careful analysis of its merits and demerits in differing economic and social conditions. Smith did not attempt to weigh its *advantages*—the fact that these people produced most of their own food, for example—against its disadvantages, because this would have cut across the argument he was building up in favour of specialization. It would have delayed his progress, and complicated his argument. So he averted his eyes and preferred to see, *and promote*, the sharp distinction between the economic activities of town and country, in a way that reflected past and future, rather than present realities. Industry was the business of the towns, and agriculture 'the industry' of the countryside, he declared. Even then the recent origins of industry in the countryside did not escape him, and he had to allow for the rise of towns such as Leeds, Halifax, Sheffield, Birmingham, and Wolverhampton from these beginnings.[52]

But Smith's work is best remembered for its condemnation of the mercantile system. He saw rich manufacturers using their power and influence over governments to shape policy in ways that suited their interests, and these were plainly at variance with the interests of small manufacturers working under the domestic system. At times he seemed concerned to protect them. Thus he explained how all involved in the manufacture of linen cloth would benefit if foreign undressed flax were made exempt from customs duties, since in this way raw materials would reach England as cheaply as possible. But rich manufacturers had importuned the government, and secured the import of dressed flax in order to cheapen their costs, with complete disregard for Englishmen who had

[51] Ibid. 106–7.   [52] Ibid. 3, 113–14, 336, 361.

formerly dressed the flax and were now put out of work. A multitude of other examples came to Smith's pen of restrictions on inland and overseas commerce in the interests of rich and powerful manufacturers at the expense of the small manufacturers and the artisans. 'It is the industry which is carried on for the benefit of the rich and powerful that is principally encouraged by our mercantile system', he concluded. 'That which is carried on for the benefit of the poor and the indigent is too often either neglected or oppressed'.[53] He seemed to be on the brink of defending the domestic worker against rich merchants. But no, he turned the evidence to support a different argument.

In a longer historical perspective, however, the other faces of mercantilism must be brought into view. Smith was criticizing the debasement of mercantilism, its manipulation by 'the rich and powerful'. But that same system, building up national self-sufficiency, had in its earlier phase permitted many new industries to establish themselves in the deep interstices of the economy. They proved to be the mainstay of men who would otherwise have lived in indigence. It was under the mercantile system that this class of small producers had come into being, and had been allowed to flourish without too much damaging interference. Destructive influences had been exerted upon their development between 1580 and 1624, but, thereafter, they had quietly resumed their course. In the later seventeenth century and still in the early eighteenth century, in the time of Defoe, rural industries as by-employments presented themselves to some observers in bright colours, that reflected the pride and quiet prosperity of many independent workers.

By the time that Adam Smith viewed the national scene, however, a qualitative change was taking place. Within the framework of the same mercantile system that had first encouraged rural industries to proliferate, the consistent pursuit of mercantilist objectives had begun to undermine the livelihood of peasant workers. Smith saw these men in their small workshops constantly affronted and injured. Indignation flowed from his pen as he condemned an economic

[53] Ibid. ii, 137 ff., esp. 139.

policy which hurt one order of citizens for no other purpose than to promote the interests of another.[54] But while his attack upon mercantilism paid due attention to the injuries inflicted by great merchants and manufacturers on the small, he offered no advice to save the latter. Instead, under the influence of the French physiocrats, we are told, he turned to defend another and larger group, also injured by the power of the master manufacturers, namely the consumers. 'In the mercantile system the interest of the consumer is almost constantly sacrificed to that of the producer.'[55] The influence of the new consumer society was thus recognized, but no prominent role was given to the men and women who had been for a time such faithful servants of that society. The interests of consumers now dominated Smith's argument, though we may reasonably speculate how far the physiocrats were indeed responsible, and how much Adam Smith had learned from observing the world around him.

A last word must be devoted to the longer perspective in which we should view dual occupations in economic development. In the sixteenth century the system offended deeply: the belief was strongly rooted that no one man should gather divers men's livings into his hands.[56] Yet men defied the government and increasingly gathered two and even three men's livings into their hands. In the difficult economic conditions of the seventeenth century, this proved to be the salvation of townsmen, like the back-street starch makers-cum-pig keepers, and of many rural communities who were able to support not only themselves but a steady inflow of immigrants from other parts of the country. Such communities plainly enjoyed a measure of freedom denied to labourers who were tied to one calling only. In the course of the seventeenth century the opposition of the government died away.

The system of dual occupations enjoyed its heyday in the seventeenth century and was most colourfully and optimistically described in Defoe's writings in the 1720s as he toured the clothing country of Somerset, Gloucestershire, and

---

[54] Ibid. 148.
[55] Ibid. i, p. x; ii, 155.
[56] TED i. 353 (Memo on the Statute of Artificers).

Wiltshire, heard the whirring of the looms in Halifax, and was invited into the home of a lead-miner with a small-holding in the Derbyshire Peak. The system ran into trouble in the eighteenth century as handicraftsmen found themselves trying to compete with factory production. The equilibrium between the demands of agriculture and of industry had been held for a while, but inevitably the success of the rural industries drove men to devise more intensive and more labour-saving methods of industrial production in factories that doomed the domestic worker to extinction. It was this stage in its development that inspired the tales of sweated labour for long hours for a pittance. Opinion turned against the domestic system.

In Adam Smith's writings this feeling was expressed in terms of relatively mild disapprobation. In the nineteenth century much stronger condemnation came from the pen of none other than J.R. McCulloch, editor of a principal text, much used nowadays by economic historians, of *Early English Tracts on Commerce*. This work includes Thomas Mun's essay on 'England's Treasure by Foreign Trade', and other seventeenth-century treatises by Samuel Fortrey, Sir Dudley North, and others. In 1825 McCulloch gave evidence to the Select Committee on Ireland: 'I consider the combination of manufacturing and agricultural pursuits to be a proof of the barbarism of every country in which it exists.' he declared, 'and so far from its being advantageous to the country, I think it decidedly the reverse.'[57]

But this is not the final verdict on dual occupations. Conveyor-belt production in the twentieth century has carried the industrial revolution on to a new plane, treating men as machines and degrading them to the point where they rebel. A 'new' point of view, though the historian will smile for it seems far from new to him, was presented in a headline in *The Times* on 30 March 1974:

'Two jobs may be better than one for keeping workers happy', it proclaimed.

---

[57] Cited in D.P. O'Brien, *J.R. McCulloch. A Study in Classical Economics* (London, 1970), 283 from BPP *Select Committee on Ireland, 1825* (129), viii, 812. I wish to thank Professor P. Mathias for this reference.

Too many jobs give little or no satisfaction. The solution is for man to diversify. Variety is a prime need for a healthy balanced life at work as well as at home. Everybody should have at least two jobs on the go at once, spending part of the week on each and mixing employments to suit his individual taste...If part time work were readily available to all who wanted it at all levels of status and skill the benefits in personal satisfaction and economic stability could be enormous.[58]

A twentieth-century judgement, couched in such cogent terms, sheds a fresh light on the projects which enabled such doctrines to be practised in the sixteenth and seventeenth centuries. At that stage in English economic development, however, the practice had a different purpose, not to mitigate the boredom of one occupation, but to fill days and weeks when otherwise men and women would not have had enough to do, would not have earned enough, and hence would not have had enough to eat. Vagrants and landless people without any means of livelihood produced the first and most convinced advocates of projects in provincial communities. And their most fervent spokesman? Surely, it was the surveyor, Matthew Bedell, who inspected many different manorial estates in 1628, and pronounced these words on two of them. After visiting Rothwell in the West Riding of Yorkshire, he wrote:

In this town the inhabitants make great store of bone lace, whereby their poor are employed and themselves much enriched. They make a quick return of this commodity for it is fetched and carried away from their doors by chapmen continually resorting thither.

After visiting Glastonbury in Somerset, he wrote more eloquently still:

There are very many poor people in the said town and yet by reason of their large commons and benefit of turves, they make good shift to live, employing themselves in spinning and knitting of worsted stockings, by means whereof they keep themselves from begging, for although I was there about twelve days and in that time was in every house that belonged to the manor, yet there was not one, either old or young, that did beg for anything.[59]

[58] Patrick Goldring, writing on his newly published book, *Multi-Purpose Man.*
[59] Corporation of London Record Office, GCE Estates, Rentals, 6.16; 4.7. I wish to thank Professor M. Beresford for this reference.

VII. CONCLUSION

Throughout the seventeenth century the production of new consumer goods absorbed an increasing quantity of the nation's economic resources. By way of conclusion, we must consider this development in a wider context, in order to indicate the source of these new-found resources, and the way in which the new productive effort was integrated with other sectors of the national economy. The discussion of these matters must inevitably be tentative, since the quantitative contribution of the new industries and of new crops in agriculture and horticulture cannot be precisely measured. But the same difficulties of accurate measurement apply to the products of traditional agriculture (cereals, meat, and dairy produce), and of traditional industries (minerals and textiles). All statistical estimates of production in the sixteenth and seventeenth centuries are the roughest approximations, and no one should think them more reliable than the impressionist observations of contemporaries, who drew on wide personal knowledge, culled in many geographically scattered areas of the kingdom. Some non-statistical, contemporary judgements on the economy (as we have seen) were sensitive and shrewd, going beyond the compilation of mass figures to make perceptive, qualitative assertions. Since it is easier to pass correct judgements of a qualitative kind than to count a nation's total output, the former are usually more trustworthy than the latter. However, it is instructive to consider the two in combination, remembering that all generalizations about the state of the economy at this time were carefully read and discussed by contemporaries, and wild statements, whether statistical or impressionistic, did not pass unchallenged.

The first and principal resource used by the new consumer industries and occupations was labour. Overwhelming evidence was offered on this score by contemporaries not only in England but on the Continent, particularly in Holland and

France, where the same activities prospered similarly. Pin making, stocking knitting, lace making, vegetable, hemp, flax, and woad growing employed the poor on an unprecedented scale. It is not difficult to identify the source of all this labour. It was made available by the great increase of population between 1500 and 1700. In the early 1520s the total population of England was approximately 2¼ million. In 1603 it stood at 3½ million. The rate of growth slowed down after 1640 and in 1688 the population was estimated by Gregory King at 5½ million.[1] The most rapid rise had taken place between 1520 and 1640, years in which the most successful projects of seventeenth-century England had been initiated, and had become established on the industrial scene.

The employment of all these additional workers cannot, however, be separated from the problems of feeding, clothing, and housing them. These, indeed, were the matters that first evoked anxious, urgent concern. Extra hands were capable of increasing production *if employed*, but people noticed first of all how extra mouths consumed precious resources that were becoming scarce. Even before 1520 public attention was drawn to shortages that were reflected in the scarcity of farms for husbandmen, the poverty of the labouring man, and the inflation of prices. More's *Utopia* expressed concern for all these matters in trenchant terms, and it was written in 1515–16: the productive capacity of labour was not yet being absorbed.

In the 1520s and 1530s the incipient economic problems, perceptively observed by More, found no solution. They rather deepened as Henry VIII prosecuted his war against France at heavy expense, called for subsidies and a forced loan from his better-off subjects, and dissolved the monasteries in 1536–9. This last action did not affect all communities equally. But it aggravated the poverty of all who had lived in the shadow of a monastic house, and who had depended heavily on the work it afforded and on its charity. The distress of the landless and unemployed worsened in the 1540s when Henry launched a third campaign against France

[1] Julian Cornwall, 'English Population in the early Sixteenth Century', EcHR 2nd Ser. xxiii (1970), 44; Thirsk and Cooper, 772.

in 1542, and at the same time harassed Scotland by burning and pillaging its towns, and debased the coinage to pay for these adventures. He made the substantial profit from debasement that he had hoped for, but he impoverished all his subjects. Prices rose alarmingly: in 1508 the price index of a group of essential foodstuffs, textiles, and fuel had stood at 100. It reached 191 in 1545, and in one dramatic leap rose to 248 in 1546. The purchasing power of a building labourer's wage in 1508 had been halved by 1546.[2]

With the accession of Edward VI, Protector Somerset launched another harsh military campaign in Scotland and war with France broke out afresh; both called for even larger expenditure than that of Henry VIII. A fresh debasement of the coinage was followed by a succession of three bad harvests in 1549, 1550, and 1551, which launched prices into another inflationary spiral. The price index which stood at 248 in 1546 stood at 285 in 1551.[3]

These circumstances account for the eloquence and determination of the Commonwealthmen in Edward VI's reign to launch fresh policies to assist the poor. They account also for the government's action against greedy farmers who engrossed land (since rising prices had spurred farmers to enlarge their enterprises), and against those who converted arable land to pasture (whereby they earned profits from wool and meat but reduced employment for labourers).

Rising population and price inflation were linked developments lying at the base of the economic crisis. But even while they left the labouring classes without adequate means of livelihood, forced to live from hand to mouth, begging, borrowing, stealing, they thrust opportunities into the hands of substantial men. The history of projects and projectors mirrors the undertakings of business men whose energies were stimulated by inflation; out of their adventures flowed the beneficial consequences of work for the poor. Gradually,

---

[2] W.G. Hoskins, *The Age of Plunder. The England of Henry VIII, 1500–47* (London, 1976), 209–10; E.H. Phelps Brown and Sheila V. Hopkins, 'Seven Centuries of the Prices of Consumables, compared with Builders' Wage Rates', in P.H. Ramsey, *The Price Revolution in Sixteenth-Century England* (London, 1971), 39.

[3] Ramsey, op. cit. 39; Bush, *Government Policy of Protector Somerset*, Chs. 2 and 3.

foreign imports of consumer goods were curtailed as the same articles were manufactured or grown at home. New work was created for women and children, as well as men, and family incomes rose, enabling industrial workers in their turn to become spenders.

Before we attempt to measure the absorption of labour by the new industries, it is necessary to consider the response of the agricultural sector of the economy to increased demand and increasing food prices. For every two mouths to be fed in 1500 there were five in 1700. Yet whereas grain had been imported in many scarce years in the early sixteenth century, when the population was only beginning its upward trend, by 1621, when the population had risen by over a half, Members of Parliament were expressing concern about the abundance of corn and its low price. Increased production had been achieved by the more intensive cultivation of land in the best corn-growing areas (the result, in part, of heavier manuring with more animals), and by the conversion of some selected grasslands to corn—most successfully in drained fens and marshlands, but also in some forests and vales. As the seventeenth century wore on, the corn growers' continuing efforts even caused embarassment. They had succeeded in producing more than enough grain to meet home needs; prices sagged in consequence, and men complained that there was not enough profit in it. Yet the government clung to the view that the corn grower must be encouraged at all costs for he was 'the staple man of the kingdom', as Mr. Johnson, M.P., had expressed it in the House of Commons in 1601. To encourage corngrowing, bounties were paid from 1673 onwards to farmers who exported grain. Such exports were especially high in 1675–7, and continuously so after 1700. During the first half of the eighteenth century the export of corn, measured by official values, was the fastest-growing component of all English domestic exports. Production was efficient enough for English corn to compete in price with Baltic grain.[4]

[4]   Thirsk, 'Seventeenth-Century Agriculture and Social Change', 148; Bland, Brown, and Tawney, *English Economic History. Select Documents,* 274; A.H. John, 'English Agricultural Improvement and Grain Exports, 1660–1765', in *Trade, Government and Economy in pre-industrial England, Essays presented to F.J. Fisher,* ed. D.C. Coleman and A.H. John (London, 1976), 48, 51, 59.

Yet it is far from certain that the total manpower employed in corn production increased in the course of the seventeenth and early eighteenth centuries. In some areas the acreage under corn was extended, and must have employed more labour. But considered nationally, corn growing became a more concentrated activity in the most efficient and productive regions, and this specialization went hand in hand with measures for increasing yields and economizing in labour (with the use of improved implements for sowing, weeding, and harvesting).[5] Seasonal surges in the demand for labour could then be met by the casual employment of labourers from neighbouring pastoral areas, as Henry Best, in the Vale of Pickering, used the 'moorfolks' to bring in his grain harvest in the 1640s.[6]

To measure with any exactitude changes in the manpower employed in grain production between 1540 and 1740 is impossible. But some indication of the more economical use of labour may be gauged from the generally observed tendency for husbandmen's farms in arable areas to diminish in number, while large farms grew larger, but not noticeably more numerous. Since the larger farms deployed their labour more rationally, and complaints about the depopulation of corn areas persisted into the 1650s in the East Midlands, and in the Act of Settlement (by implication) until at least 1662, it would be rash to assume an increase in the labour employed in corn growing.[7] Two Cambridgeshire parishes examined in detail by Dr. Spufford provide supporting illustrations of this general proposition. These examples may well prove to be typical of corn growing communities, though it would be premature now to judge them so. In Chippenham, on the corn growing chalklands of this East Anglian county, the population remained relatively stable between 1544 and 1664 (250–300 people in 1544, 310–80 in 1664). But the number of landholders fell from 45 (excluding the lord) in 1544 to 18 in 1712. The rest of the

---

[5] These general remarks will be substantiated in the next volume of *The Agrarian History of England and Wales*, v: *1640–1760*.
[6] AHEW 434.
[7] See e.g. Thirsk and Cooper, 147–50; Bland, Brown, and Tawney, op. cit. 647–9.

population consisted of landless households, but these only
rose in number from 15 in 1544 to 26–31 in 1712. Considerable changes in the occupation of land had not enlarged
the opportunities for agricultural work, and so people had
been forced to emigrate. In a similar study of Orwell, Cambridgeshire, on the corn growing clays, where the documents
are somewhat less abundant, Dr. Spufford again concluded
that large farms increased in size in the shorter period,
1600–30, while cottagers increased in number. But the
natural increase of population from 1570 to 1650 was not
absorbed by the parish; the community remained of the
same size, and its surplus members migrated elsewhere.[8]

The only arable areas in which it can confidently be said
that a larger labour force was employed in the seventeenth
century were those in which specialized crops like vegetables,
saffron, and hops were being developed. Gregory King
estimated the annual value of home-produced fruit and
vegetables in 1695 at £1,200,000.[9] If only a quarter of this
amount represented the wages of labour (a reasonable but
conservative estimate), then, at the average labourer's wage of
£15 per annum, this represented the full-time employment of
20,000 men, or 2.6 per cent of that large class of labouring
people, outservants, cottagers, and paupers, whom Gregory
King estimated at 764,000 families.[10]

The contribution of pastoral regions to the food supply,
and to the employment of the growing labour force, reflects
a more complex response to more complex economic
pressures. Pasture farming is far more economical in the use
of labour than cereal growing. When some pastoral regions in
the seventeenth century ceased to grow even a modest quota

[8] Margaret Spufford, *Contrasting Communities. English Villagers in the
Sixteenth and Seventeenth Centuries* (Cambridge 1974), 61–2, 90, 118; *idem, A
Cambridgeshire Community. Chippenham from Settlement to Enclosure* (Leicester
Univ. Press, Occasional Paper, no. 20, Dept. of English Local History, 1965), 39,
48.

[9] G. Chalmers, *An Estimate of the Comparative Strength of Great Britain...*
(London, 1804), 67.

[10] This calculation is based on the estimate that £15 was the average annual
earnings of labouring people and outservants, as suggested by Gregory King
(Thirsk and Cooper, 781), that these households numbered 364,000, and that
cottagers and paupers numbered 400,000 (total: 764,000). Any of these might
have been employed in market gardening.

of cereals for their own support, and depended increasingly on grain supplied from the arable zones, they aggravated their own latent problem of underemployment or unemployment. An account of the pastoral vale of Tewkesbury at the beginning of the seventeenth century crisply described a condition typical of many other pastoral areas: 'there being no kind of trade to employ men, and very small tillage, necessity compelled poor men to. . .stealing of sheep and other cattle, breaking of hedges, robbing of orchards, and what not; insomuch that the place became famous for rogues. . .and Bridewell was erected there to be a terror to idle persons.'[11]

The underemployment of labour was an inherent weakness of pastoral country, which might have reached the dimensions of a major crisis in the seventeenth century when the natural increase of population, experienced by the kingdom as a whole, was combined with the migration of landless people into these districts from arable areas. As enclosure, the engrossing of farms, and the rationalization of corn growing in arable country diminished the demand for labour, people were driven to places where they could still find generous commons on which to squat and common grazings to feed their animals. The rapidly growing populations of pastoral districts were reflected in the vehement complaints of squatting and of despoliation of the commons from areas as far apart as the Forest of Dean, Rossendale Forest, and the Kentish Weald;[12] in more general terms, the Act of Settlement in 1662 bemoaned the fact that people were moving from parish to parish 'to settle themselves where there is the best stock, the largest commons or wastes to build cottages, and the most woods for them to burn and destroy'.[13]

In the event, this development was far from being economically destructive. Landless families, arriving in this underdeveloped countryside, quickly built a roof over their heads, and were at hand to exploit many fresh ways of earning a living. Landlords and projectors were being exhorted at the

[11] Thirsk, 'Projects for Gentlemen' 49.
[12] AHEW 410–12.
[13] Bland, Brown, and Tawney, op. cit. 648.

same time to turn derelict pastures to more productive use. They responded with the same optimistic Puritan enthusiasm that infused the activities of industrial projectors. Much energy was poured into the improvement of fens, forests, and chases. In the course of the seventeenth century the fens were transformed into cornlands, and other grasslands were turned into more productive grazing grounds for the rearing and feeding of livestock for meat.[14]

Systems of animal production in consequence became more efficiently integrated between regions, so that specialized rearing took place in one area, feeding in another, and fattening in another. Pasture farmers had the incentive of stable, or even rising, prices in the seventeenth century. Demand was upheld by more people, especially more townsmen and more industrial workers in areas like Tyneside and the Black Country. Even in Elizabeth's reign Englishmen were deemed by foreigners great eaters of meat and dairy products, but their capacity to consume was far from sated even then, as the increase in dairying and the rise of cattle imports from Ireland, especially after 1620, bear witness. Figures calculated from Irish customs yields suggest that 34,000 cattle were imported into England *circa* 1631, 46,000 cattle and 35,000 sheep in 1640–1, and 58,000 cattle and nearly 100,000 sheep in 1664–5.[15] Yet demand was sufficiently buoyant in England for these imports to take place without effectively lowering meat prices. When the Irish Cattle Act of 1667 put a stop to the trade, it gave to English stock breeders in the highland zone of England the greatest financial incentive ever to rear more young stock. Indeed, prices of store stock immediately after 1667 were so high that stock fatteners in the Home Counties were at first panic-stricken, seeing little hope of profit for their efforts.[16] The prices of pastoral products in the second half of the seventeenth century, however, suggest that supply never exceeded demand. Pasture farming was generally considered to be more profitable than corn growing. 'It seems more to

[14] Thirsk, 'Seventeenth-Century Agriculture and Social Change', 167–70.
[15] D. Woodward, 'The Anglo-Irish Livestock Trade in the Seventeenth Century', *Irish Hist. Studies*, xviii, no. 72 (1973), 493–4.
[16] Roger Coke, *A Discourse of Trade*, 33; Thirsk and Cooper, 85.

the national interest of England to employ its land to the
breeding and feeding of cattle than to the produce of corn',
wrote Charles Davenant in 1699.[17]

Meat production, however, was not the only branch of
livestock husbandry to prosper in the seventeenth century.
Even more impressive was the expansion of cheese production,
which was far more labour intensive than stock keeping.
Cheese making became a specialized activity in many new
districts of England, expanding conspicuously in the West
Midlands, whence it was able to supply the growing industrial
population around Birmingham (as well as London and the
south-east) with cheap and nourishing protein.[18] This fact
has to be set against Gregory King's estimate that $1\frac{3}{4}$ million
people ate meat on only two days in seven, and another
$1\frac{1}{3}$ million, who received alms, ate meat only once a week.[19]
The labouring poor were eating a great deal more cheese.

In the light of abundant contemporary evidence on the
improvement of run-down land in pastoral zones in the
seventeenth century, it must be assumed that more labour
was employed in livestock husbandry than under the old
extensive systems of pasture farming. Grasslands were drained,
fertilized, and cleared of molehills; woodlands and scrub were
turned into pastures; hedges were planted to make warm,
enclosed grazing grounds. In the expansion of dairying, we
can confidently see a large increase in the labour employed,
for this occupation was built upon the efforts of family
farmers. Dairying maintained, and in some areas increased,
the number of smallholdings. And while some work hitherto
given to cereal growing was no doubt lost by more intense
specialization on cheese and butter production, against
that may be set agricultural improvements in other patches
of old pastoral country where men turned from grass to
intensive grain production. The Forest of Arden in Warwickshire, for example, was described *circa* 1540 as 'much enclosed,

[17]   A.H. John, 'The Course of Agricultural Change, 1660–1760', in *Essays in
Agrarian History*, i, ed. W.E. Minchinton (Newton Abbot, 1968), 239–43, 247,
249; Thirsk 'Seventeenth-Century Agriculture and Social Change', 150–1, 174.
[18]   This is indicated in Defoe's description of England. It will be substantiated
in *The Agrarian History of England and Wales*, v: *1640–1750*, especially in David
Hey's account of the economy of the North-West Midlands.
[19]   Thirsk and Cooper, 784.

plentiful of grass, but no great plenty of corn'. By the end of the seventeenth century, in contrast, 'so much of wood and heathland [had been turned] into tillage and pasture that they produce corn, cattle, cheese, and butter enough not only for their own use, but also to furnish other counties; whereas within the memory of man, they were supplied with corn, etc., from the Feldon'.[20]

Pastoral country successfully absorbed much additional labour into farming. But more important still was its integration of these pursuits with industrial by-employments. These had been a feature of many pastoral economies since the Middle Ages, but their growth in number, and their wider geographical dispersal in the seventeenth century, wrought a qualitative change in the content of the pastoral economy. Not all the consumer industries, described in these pages, found their home in rural areas; some, such as starch making and vinegar making, afforded new occupations for townsmen. But the majority found their first and most congenial environment among pasture farmers, as by-employments in the households of some yeomen, and many smallholders. On this basis the industries expanded for many decades, recruiting more workers without creating a large army of landless. It was not until after 1700—in the case of the metalworkers of south Staffordshire and north Worcestershire, for example, after 1720—that the *landless* industrial worker began to form a considerable proportion of the workforce in consumer industries.[21]

We cannot measure on a national scale the numbers so employed, but we can give some orders of magnitude. In one new industry—stocking knitting—100,000 knitters were needed to make two pairs a week for 50 weeks a year, in order to satisfy the demand of the home market for 10 million pairs. This work called for a knitter from 13 per cent of all labouring and poor households in the kingdom. In

[20] V.H.T. Skipp, 'Economic and Social Change in the Forest of Arden, 1530–1649', in *Land, Church, and People*, 91.

[21] M.B. Rowlands, *Masters and Men in the West Midlands Metalware Trades before the Industrial Revolution* (Manchester, 1975), 42–3; D. Hey, writing on the economy of the North-West Midlands in the forthcoming *Agrarian History of England and Wales*, v: *1640–1750*.

addition, to knit the 143,823 dozen pairs of stockings
(1¾ million pairs) that were exported from England overseas
in one year between 1697 and 1698 required 17,258 knitters,
or one member from 2·3 per cent of labouring and poor
households.[22] Altogether, to satisfy the home and foreign
demand for stockings in the 1690s, 15·3 per cent of labouring
and pauper families could have supplemented their living
by knitting as a by-employment. If knitters knitted for only
30 weeks in the year, and this is, perhaps, a more realistic
estimate, then one person would have been needed from
every fourth labouring household.

Yet knitting was only one out of a hundred new occupations
making consumer wares. Their variety introduced into single
communities many alternative sources of work. This is well
illustrated by local examples. The parish of Winchcombe in
Gloucestershire was described in Elizabeth's reign as a borough
'fallen into so great ruin and decay that its inhabitants were
not able to support and repair it for the great poverty that
reigned amongst them'. It remained a poor town throughout
the seventeenth century, but its poverty was relieved by
several new occupations: a short-lived attempt at woad
growing was succeeded by tobacco growing in 1619, which
then persisted among small growers of an acre or two until
the later 1680s; flax growing, flax dressing, and, experi-
mentally, linen weaving were introduced *circa* 1620 and
continued at least until the mid-1630s; stocking knitting had
arrived on the scene by the 1660s.[23] Turning to a larger tract
of country, Staffordshire was a county brimming with rural
industries. 'Only a small central zone of the county does
not appear to have pursued industries in conjunction with
farming.' Wood turning, carpentry, and tanning gave work
in Needwood Forest; south Staffordshire produced coal,
and iron and metal goods in everyday use, such as locks, door
and window handles, buttons, metal fittings for saddles and
harness, spurs, stirrups, snaffles and buckles, and nails by the
tens of thousands. Colliers and ironstone miners found a
living in Cannock Chase. Kinver Forest in the south-west
of the county harboured scythesmiths, and makers of edge

[22] See above, pp. 5–6.
[23] Thirsk, 'Projects for Gentlemen' 149.

tools, while glassworkers were settled on the Staffordshire–
Worcestershire border at Stourbridge. The pottery industry
was growing around Burslem in the north-west; lead and ironstone mining occupied the north-east; leather working and
textile weaving in hemp and flax, as well as wool, were
scattered throughout the county.[24]

Consumer industries in the sixteenth and seventeenth
centuries exploited hitherto underused labour in rural areas
as well as absorbing a large share of the extra manpower
made available by population increase and immigration.
How, it must now be asked, was the capital found to sustain
this enterprise? Fixed capital costs in most of the consumer
industries were tiny. Stocking knitters needed no more than
a pair of needles, lace makers a crochet hook, pins, and a
cushion. The sheds needed by starch makers and nailers were
flimsy wooden structures that were not built to last a
generation, merely to serve anticipated needs for two or
three years ahead. In market gardening it is true that if early
vegetables were to catch the highest market prices, they
required cloches and bell glasses, but less ambitious gardeners
could manage without these aids. Handtools cost a shilling
or two, and seeds not more than a few pence a pound.[25]
In all trades and occupations it was possible to spend more
on capital equipment, but perfectly possible to manage
with little.

The largest expense in virtually all the new consumer
occupations was the cost of labour, but this lagged well
behind prices throughout the sixteenth century; and the gap
only slowly narrowed in the seventeenth. Those enterprises
which had to meet large expenses over a short period—for
example, to pay many day labourers in high summer—tended
to be the concern of landed gentlemen and substantial
merchants. The woad growing enterprise at Milcote, near
Stratford on Avon, Warwickshire, in 1626, for example,
cost its owner on average £3. 15s. daily in the wages of
casual labourers during the high summer season.[26] But the

---

[24] J. Thirsk, 'Horn and Thorn in Staffordshire: the Economy of a Pastoral
County', *North Staffs. Jnl. of Field Studies*, 9 (1969), 8–10.
[25] For the tools of metalware tradesmen, see Rowlands, *Masters and Men*
27–34, 39–40.
[26] Kent Archives Office, U269 A415.

contractual arrangements in such cases nearly always spread risk and expense between several parties, namely merchants, landlords, and farmers (or craftsmen) as well as relations and friends. Tobacco growing was managed on this basis, and not only in England. Merchants, landlords, and farmers shared the costs and the profits, and, at any one moment, all would be bearing a part of the production costs before the final balance-sheet was prepared. The documents do not always reveal the full extent of these ramified partnerships. In the case of the tobacco growing experiment at Winchcombe in 1619 a partnership was formed between two men only, John Stratford (the merchant) and Henry Somerscales (the skilled cultivator). When they leased a piece of land for tobacco, they took the owner of the land into partnership for that particular enterprise, sharing the costs and the profits. To all appearances, there were only three partners. Yet a later legal dispute brings to light the fact that John Stratford's third share was in fact subdivided into eight parts among his friends and relations. One partner with an eighth share was a friend who had negotiated with the owner of the land, another was Stratford's brother-in-law. In her recent study of glass making in England between 1560 and 1640 Mrs. Eleanor Godfrey has offered similar, instructive examples of such partnerships.[27]

In consumer occupations, where the workforce was the family labouring at home, each household purchased its own raw materials (or secured small quantities on credit) and worked them up. Not until they sold their finished goods to the chapman could they start afresh.[28] Credit facilities thus consisted in a long chain of dependence that involved the poor in small debts, the roving chapman in medium debts, the merchant in the local market in a slightly larger debt, and the London merchant in the largest debt of all. This long chain of indebtedness sufficed to keep consumer industries functioning smoothly, but every link in this long chain was in fact supported by a network of credit, consisting of small loans and debts raised by small producers

[27] Thirsk, 'New Crops and their Diffusion' 82; PRO C24/498/22; E.S. Godfrey, *The Development of English Glassmaking, 1560–1640* (Oxford, 1975), 169–72.
[28] See above, pp. 111–112.

among their neighbours and kinsmen in village and town. Even the larger ventures calling for more substantial capital investment survived on the same hand-to-mouth basis. George Mynne, a London dyer and projector, initiated a madder growing project in 1621, but it was his employee, George Bedford, who had to finance it for long periods before his accounts were settled by Mynne. While learning how to cultivate the crop in Holland, Bedford was continually shifting and scraping for a few shillings, going without meals, walking from town to town to save expense. Back in England, and growing madder on his own in Kent, he knew that he had to wait three years before he could gather his first crop, yet this was no deterrent. He went ahead, still begging for £2 here, £5 there, to tide him over, raising a loan at one moment from his stepfather, at others from different men in his home town of Salisbury.[29]

The carefully planned financial organization of industry that we take for granted in the nineteenth century was rudimentary in the seventeenth. Industrial enterprises were launched without great expectations of their long-term survival and without calling for investment in expensive fixed equipment. Makeshifts were just as serviceable. Men and women might in the end continue in the same occupation for forty years as did Ursula Hicks, the stocking knitter of Richmond, but they did not plan on this basis.[30] Rather their careers suggest a more flexible, even casual, attitude to the choice of an occupation. This explains why new ventures could be launched quickly and spread without much preparation or fuss. Woad growing could appear as a new crop in a community one year and disappear the next.[31] The sheds that were used to dry and ball the woad leaves one year would serve to dry tobacco in the following year. To dry madder, it was perfectly satisfactory to use a malt or hop drying kiln. In Holland they built expensive houses for pounding madder, but, in fact, any common building would serve.[32] A woad

---

[29] Hants. R.O., 44M69, xxxiii.
[30] See above, p. 63.
[31] Thirsk, 'Projects for Gentlemen' 158.
[32] Philip Miller, *The Method of Cultivating Madder* (London, 1758), 19, 21.

mill might represent £20 of capital expenditure,[33] but it was a demountable building that was easily moved from one place to another between seasons.

Other factors of production were also made available at short notice. Judging by John Stratford's account of tobacco growing in Winchcombe, his negotiations with local landlords and farmers did not begin until January in the year 1619 in which he grew his first tobacco crop. He needed land and labour quickly yet it was all found in good time. Jobs came and went unceremoniously and did not call for deep-laid plans.[34] This was as true for entrepreneurs as for day-labourers. John Stratford's many occupations in the course of his life in London and Winchcombe have already been listed. His partner, Henry Somerscales, who had the knowledge of cultivating tobacco, arrived in Winchcombe having spent some time previously in Amsterdam trading in timber from Norway to London.[35] Reflecting the same outlook poorer men had two and three occupations at once. Licensed alehouse keepers in Staffordshire, for example, were also tailors or weavers, shearmen or wheelwrights, husbandmen, shoe makers, dyers, or joiners.[36] We have already encountered starch makers who were also pig fatteners.[37] Most of the consumer occupations, in short, were started on a shoe-string. They grew rapidly because they quickly attracted many individual undertakers, operating independently and at their own risk. Each household enterprise subsisted on a precarious base, and might not continue in existence for any long period, but it was the multitude of household undertakings that ensured the survival of the occupation.[38] Only after many decades of

---

[33] The cost of a woad mill in Elizabeth's reign is indicated in the statement that a house called Bellhouse, built in Claxby, Lincs., by Robert Thorpe in preparation for woad growing, cost £16 'without chambering', and about £20 'with chambering'. (PRO E134, 39 Eliz., Hil. 27.)

[34] Thirsk, 'New Crops and their Diffusion' 83–4.

[35] Amsterdam Archives, Not. arch., no. 198, fo. 576, nots. J.F. Bruyningh, 7 Apr. 1616. This information was supplied to me by Dr. H.K. Roessingh, of the Department of Rural History at the Landbouwhogeschool, Wageningen, to whom I am indebted for much suggestive comparative material on tobacco growing in Holland. See his *Inlandse Tabak* (Wageningen, 1976), *passim*.

[36] Thirsk, 'Horn and Thorn in Staffordshire' 11.

[37] See above, p. 91.

[38] For the same conclusion in the metalware trades, see Rowlands, op. cit. 40.

domestic enterprise did larger, more capital-intensive undertakings emerge from among the more successful operators.

The consumer industries were launched with modest
capital resources and a plentiful labour supply, but whence
came the demand for their products? We have seen that
consumer wares were not uniform articles that sold at one
price only; they were made in a wide range of qualities. No
gilds supervised standards in rural areas, and even in the
towns (apart from London) most new industries refrained
from setting up gild organizations. The geographical scatter-
ing and unregulated internal structure of the industries
enabled their goods to be made in an infinite variety of
designs and qualities, and at many different prices. Nevertheless, since country-based households, with a stake in the
land as well as in industrial employment, were in the majority,
the average standard of craftsmanship was low, and the
average goods cheap. Most country wares were made for the
common people. How did they afford to buy them?

Throughout the sixteenth century wages lagged behind
prices, and the labouring family's demand for non-essential
consumer goods was negligible. The fancy clothing of young
apprentices and servants in London drew tart comment
from their elders, but the bulk of the population had nothing
to spare for such purchases. In the seventeenth century the
incomes of the lower classes improved. Projectors, who
cited 4d. a day as an average wage in the 1580s, quoted 8d.
in the 1620s. It is true that the index of wage rates for
London building workers does not reflect this improvement
clearly until the 1650s, though a move in that direction
is measurable from the first decade of the seventeenth
century. But working conditions in London were untypical,
for the rate of immigration into the capital was abnormally
high.[39] Moreover, the wage rates of men alone tell us nothing
about the earnings of families. It was the wages earned
by wives and children, added to that of their husbands,
which most impressed economic writers and prompted

[39] E.A. Wrigley, 'A Simple Model of London's Importance in changing English
Society and Economy, 1650-1750', *Past and Present*, 37 (1967), 47.

their praise for new consumer occupations.[40]

The cash benefits derived from rising *family* incomes have already been indicated in contemporary commentaries. They are implied in the steady movement of the labouring population from arable to pastoral-industrial regions from the mid-sixteenth century onwards.[41] Perhaps they are hinted at in Gregory King's estimates of annual agricultural production, though we have no comparative figures for an earlier period. From arable land he valued production at £10 million per annum; from pastures and woodlands £12 million.[42] At all events, King's estimate implies that more agricultural wealth was being created in pastoral than in arable country, though it might not be equitably distributed between the classes. But since a more egalitarian social structure was evident in pastoral than in corn growing regions, we may hazard the guess that agricultural incomes were in fact more evenly distributed between the classes. At the same time, consumer industries were multiplying in pastoral areas, and dispersing extra cash among wage labourers, cottagers, and smallholders, their wives and their children. Purchasing power and productive capacity were thus mutually sustaining. Moreover, the pastoral areas which relied on corn produced elsewhere benefited from the fact that grain growers were feeding larger populations at lower cost. Thus new industrial work and a sustained demand for the products of pasture farming (which kept their price throughout the seventeenth century) brought security and some degree of quiet, unobtrusive prosperity to pastoral regions in the course of the seventeenth century. It makes sense of the sardonic comment of the Grand Jury to the J.P.s of Worcestershire in 1661 that it was becoming difficult to distinguish between master and servants 'except it be because

[40] This factor has recently been underlined by Neil McKendrick in 'Home Demand and Economic Growth: a New View of the Role of Women and Children in the Industrial Revolution', in *idem* (ed.), *Historical Perspectives: Studies in English Thought and Society in honour of J.H. Plumb* (London, 1974), 171–3.

[41] It is worth adding to the seventeenth-century evidence, cited above, p. 164, the similar observation of Phyllis Deane and W.A. Cole, in *British Economic Growth, 1688–1959* (Cambridge, 1962), 75, that in the first fifty years of the eighteenth century the increase in numbers of those engaged in agriculture was concentrated in seven industrial (i.e. pastoral) counties.

[42] Thirsk and Cooper, 782–3.

the servant wears better clothes than his master'.[43]

How the mass of the population fared in arable country is less certain. Yeomen farmers were engrossers of land at this period and their larger undertakings often gave them the means to become consumers of luxury wares, as inventories of their goods bear witness. But Richard Baxter's emotional appeal to landlords in 1691 suggests that smaller farmers—his 'poor husbandmen'—were hard pressed to make ends meet, and had little cash to spend on anything beyond essential household needs. In his opinion, labourers and servants fared better, for at least they were housed, fed, and clothed.[44] The steady migration of young people from arable areas mirrored the same conviction that economic prospects at home were poor, and a better living could be got elsewhere, in pastoral-industrial country or in neighbouring towns. Many market towns were growing in size in the later seventeenth century, and were assuming a grander role as centres of social and cultural life, as well as trade. The lively demand for consumer goods that was maintained there was fuelled by the purchasing power of yeomen and gentry from a wide rural area. And some of the goods they bought were doubtless made and sold by young men and women who could find no work labouring in their fields.

If we cannot speak with certainty of rising *per capita* incomes throughout the population in the seventeenth century, we can point to numerous communities in the kingdom, especially in towns and in pastoral-industrial areas, where the labouring classes found cash to spare for consumer goods in 1700 that had no place in their budgets in 1550—brass cooking pots, iron frying pans, earthenware dishes, knitted stockings, even a lace frill for a cap or apron. In the home of one lead-mining family at Wirksworth in the Derbyshire Peak, visited by Defoe about 1720, we catch a glimpse of some of the consumer goods bought out of a cash income of 5*d*. a day for the husband and an occasional 3*d*. a day for the wife. The couple lived in a cave in the hillside and were rearing five 'plump and fat, ruddy and wholesome children'.

[43] Bland, Brown, and Tawney, op. cit. 361.
[44] *The Rev. Richard Baxter's Last Treatise*, ed. F.J. Powicke (Manchester, 1926), 22–6.

Their bread was made from barley growing in a close at the door, meat was got from several pigs, reared with a sow, and milk came from a little lean cow. Cash had bought them earthenware, pewter, and brass to put on their shelves.[45]

At the national level we may glimpse consumers' purchasing power in Gregory King's estimate of 'the annual consumption of apparel' in 1688. His calculations suggest that nearly 10s. per year were spent per head of population on items of clothing that represented new, but far from luxury, consumer industries: 10 million pairs of stockings were bought per year (approximately 2 pairs per person), 8 million pairs of gloves and mittens, 6 million shoe-strings and buckles, 4,910,000 hats and caps of all sorts (almost 1 per person), 4 million bands and cravats, both plain and fancy, and 2 million neckerchiefs and tuckers, laced and plain. All these represented a total expenditure of £2,302,375. The sizes of King's estimates tell us which items he expected to be bought by the different classes. In suggesting consumption of 5 to 10 million for some articles, he did not have in mind a home market for clothing that served only the middle and upper classes. Over and above the demand for basic items of clothing such as shirts, skirts, breeches, coats, doublets, and shoes, King envisaged virtually the whole population as purchasers of stockings, gloves, shoe-strings and buckles, hats and caps, bands and cravats, neckerchiefs and tuckers. Another £400,000 he reckoned would be spent on decorative ribbons, fringes, gold, silver, and worsted lace, embroidery, and thread, Some of the cash for these items, particularly for the ribbons and lace, would have been drawn from the pockets of yeomen and craftsmen, but only a small fraction could have been spent by husbandmen and artisans. The articles which he confined to the wardrobes of the upper-middle and gentry classes were plainly the 100,000 belts and girdles, 200,000 sleeves and ruffles, 100,000 girdles and sashes, 50,000 muffs, and 200,000 fans and busks, whose value amounted to only £55,000.[46]

[45] D. Defoe, *A Tour through England and Wales* (Everyman edn.), II. 161–3.
[46] Greater London Council RO, Burns Journal, fo. 203. I owe this material to Mr. N.B. Harte.

Estimates of gross national production have been made for the eighteenth century, which ideally should be set beside their counterpart in the seventeenth. The theme of this book would be satisfyingly rounded off, if it were possible to measure the value of the contribution made by new consumer industries and new crops to the total production of the nation. In fact, it is only possible to offer estimates for a small fraction of this effort. At the end of the seventeenth century Gregory King compiled with considerable care some such calculations. Grain output per annum he valued at £10,000,000; pastoral and woodland products at £12,000,000; industrial crops like dyes, hemp, and flax at £1,000,000; fruits, vegetables, and 'garden stuff' at £1,200,000.[47] Thus we are told by a contemporary that the new industrial crops, plus fruit and vegetables, added £2,200,000 to traditional agricultural output, itself valued at £22 million. These additions represented 9 per cent of total agricultural production, and since almost nothing of this was being grown in 1540, reflected, virtually in its entirety, the success of agricultural projects to reduce imports and provide work for the poor.

The production of industrial goods for the home market, however, defies all attempts at measurement in monetary terms. Their growing contribution can only be deduced from the steady geographical dispersal of home industries into more and more villages around existing centres and further afield in entirely fresh places. The dispersal of the hand knitting, framework knitting, silk ribbon, lace, and pin making industries are but a few examples. In general, we can speak confidently of the multiplication of centres of manufacture as a conspicuous feature of the seventeenth century. Not until the second half of the eighteenth century, when competition sharpened, were manufacturing centres reduced in number and more geographically concentrated.

None of this material is precise enough to bear comparison with the statistical evidence offered in the current debate on economic growth in the eighteenth century.

---

[47] Thirsk and Cooper, 782–3; G. Chalmers, *An Estimate of the Comparative Strength of Great Britain*... (London, 1804), 67.

Nevertheless, a review of its main components in the seventeenth century suggests grave weaknesses in the analysis
of the eighteenth-century English economy. Deane and Cole's
estimates of agricultural production, for example, are based
on grain output alone, and assume constant consumption per
head.[48] No estimate for livestock and woodland products
is attempted. Yet these represented a higher total value in
Gregory King's calculations, and we have seen reason to
suspect that output under this heading increased at a much
faster rate than that of grain. The rapid spread of the dairying
industry certainly hints at such a possibility. In addition,
fruit and vegetables are omitted from the eighteenth-century
calculation, yet they constituted 5 per cent of produce from
the land. And since they took the edge off the appetite for
grain, they left more cereals for export, enhancing the
value of foreign trade. Finally, there is no reason to think
that the output of industrial crops, valued by King at one
million pounds in 1688, declined in the eighteenth century.

Furthermore, the variety of consumer goods manufactured
for the home market is far from sufficiently appreciated and
weighted in Deane and Cole's balance-sheet. Miscellaneous
wares are represented only by beer, leather, candles, and
soap.[49] Some of the 'minor home industries' (unnamed) are
admitted to have doubled or even trebled their output in the
first half of the eighteenth century, but since the leather and
brewing industries barely kept pace with the growth of population, theirs is judged to be the trend of home manufacture as
a whole. Yet beer, leather, candles, and soap represent only
four out of a hundred home industries. If their output could be
quantified, and if they all measured up to the rate of growth
indicated, say, by the stocking knitting industry, could we be
so certain that 'industries which were mainly dependent on
the home economy, both for their supplies of raw materials
and for a market for their products, tended in general to
expand much less rapidly than the major export industries'?[50]

[48]   Deane and Cole, op. cit. 74.
[49]   Ibid. 76.
[50]   Ibid. 61. Table 19, p. 78, reckons the contribution of home industries to
real output in 1700 at 12 per cent, that of export industries at 18 per cent, and
agriculture at 43 per cent.

The role of the home market in stimulating the production of consumer goods in the period 1700 to 1760 has been cogently argued by Professor John, and by Professor Eversley for the period from 1750 to 1780.[51] The evidence adduced here identifies the roots of this development in the first half of the sixteenth century, when a deliberate policy decision was taken to encourage consumer industries, in order to reduce imports, and to give more work to the poor. By the end of the sixteenth century goods that had been deemed rich men's luxuries in 1540 were being made in so many different qualities and at such varied prices that they came within the reach of everyman. In the course of the seventeenth century deflation was not accompanied by any slowing-down of agricultural and industrial production,[52] and although inequalities in the distribution of this enhanced wealth remained, a conspicuous redistribution had taken place that was partly geographical and partly social. The result was that home demand for cheap goods was as stimulating and expansive as the demand for expensive quality wares, probably even more so. This truth was understood by contemporaries who in the later seventeenth century sought for ways to increase the manpower of the kingdom. In 1609 Robert Gray had written in melancholy mood about the economic prospects in England for its surplus men and women, and urged them to seek their fortune in Virginia. 'Our land hath brought forth, but it hath not milk sufficient in the breast thereof to nourish all those children which it hath brought forth. It affordeth neither employment nor preferment for those that depend upon it.' In contrast Carew Reynel, writing in 1674, at a moment when trade was depressed and population growth was slowing down, expressed a view formed out of his different experience of industrial and agricultural production

[51] A.H. John, 'Agricultural Productivity and Economic Growth in England, 1700–1760', *Jnl. Econ. Hist.* xxv (1965), 19 ff.; D.E.C. Eversley, 'The Home Market and Economic Growth in England, 1750–1780', in *Land, Labour, and Population in the Industrial Revolution*, ed. E.L. Jones and G.E. Mingay (London, 1967), 206–59.

[52] For possibly similar circumstances in the period 1700–40, see N.F.R. Crafts, 'English Economic Growth in the Eighteenth Century: a Re-examination of Deane and Cole's Estimates', EcHR 2nd Ser. xxix. 2 (1976), 226-35.

in the course of the seventeenth century. 'If we had but a
million more of people than now, we should quickly see how
trade and the vend of things would alter for the better.'[53]
Fear that another million mouths could not be fed no longer
haunted men like a spectre. They saw rather a million pairs
of productive, busy hands.

[53] Thirsk and Cooper, 758, 759.

APPENDIX I.   FOREIGN WARES IMPORTED INTO
LONDON IN 1559 and 1564–1565

Two separate lists of imports into London are united in this appendix. The first, dated 1559, is entitled 'The Particular Value of certain necessary and unnecessary Wares brought into the Port of London in the second year of the Queen Majesty's reign, the overquantity whereof most lamentably spoileth the realm yearly'. It listed the majority of, but evidently not all imports, for in summing up their total value it declared the total of the listed items to be worth £643,319.18s. while 'the sum of the residue inwards' was £49,480.16s.6d. (PRO SP 12/8, no. 31). It plainly reflected official government determination, at the beginning of Elizabeth's reign, to reduce unnecessary imports.

The second list, dated 1565, is entitled 'An Account of the Wares or Merchandise brought from abroad to the Port of London from Michaelmas 1564–65' (BL Lansdowne MS. 8/17).

Substantially different sums were spent on certain items in these two years, but the significance of this should not be hastily interpreted. Either or both years 1559 and 1565 may not have been typical. Indeed, the second list of 1565 followed a two-year trade stoppage with the Netherlands. It is noticeable that much larger sums were spent in 1565 than in 1559 on mockado, sarcenet, steel, taffeta, and wire. But some items appear in the first list and not in the second (for example, babies i.e. dolls, and tennis balls), probably at the whim of the clerk compiling the list. It is impossible to believe, for example, that woad which cost the kingdom £33,431 in 1559 had disappeared from London's imports in 1565.[1]

---

[1]   For a discussion of these two documents, with particular reference to the balance of trade, see L. Stone, 'Elizabethan Overseas Trade', EcHR, 2nd Ser. ii (1949), 36–57. In the second document (1565) certain wares are listed (e.g. anchovies, hose of silk, etc.) but no figures are set beside them. These are omitted from this list. Not all the items are readily explicable. Buds are possibly the same as cloves; they appear in the separate lists but not together. (I owe this suggestion to Mrs. Carolina Lane.) Chambletts or camlets were fabrics of silk, wool, cotton, or linen, originally from the east, but subsequently copied in Europe. Crewell was a thin, worsted yarn for making fringes, lace, and stockings, and for tapestry and embroidery. Gawles were oakgalls or galls from other trees, used in dyeing and medicine. Incle was linen tape or the thread from which it was made. Dornix, mockado, sarcenet, and satins were New Draperies. Wormseed meant any of various plants used for curing intestinal worms, but its secondary meaning was eggs of the silkworm moth. Silkworms were being kept with enthusiasm in the early seventeenth century, and it is not impossible that earlier experiments are indicated by the entry in 1565 of wormseed imports, valued at £192.

	1559			1565
	£	s,	d.	£
Alum	7151	13	4	
Almonds	912	0	0	
Aniseed	520	6	8	500
Apples	876	3	4	260
Ashes, soap	4665	0	0	2600
Babies	178	3	4	
Balls for tennis	1699	0	0	
Baskets voc. sports	247	0	0	
Battery	6078	15	0	3600
Bayeburyes	109	4	0	
Bells for hawking	112	18	8	159
Blankets	368	0	0	
Books unbound	813	6	8	
Bottles	237	13	4	52
Bowtell	1161	16	8	1180
Brushes	757	18	8	365
Buckram	2885	3	4	2569
Buds				1688
Buttons	108	10	0	
Cabbages and turnips	157	16	8	
Canvas	39 072	10	0	32 124
Canvas for doublets	685	0	0	
Canvas, striped				600
Cards for playing	2837	10	0	2800
Carpets				887
Carpets, bankers, and				
cushion cloths	6620	0	0	
Chambletts	3627	16	8	9268
Cheese of Holland	2482	13	4	
Chests and coffers	578	0	0	
Cinnamon	2333	0	0	
Cloves	892	0	0	
Combs				169
Crewell	3038	0	0	
Currants	2848	0	0	
Damask	1269	0	0	375
Dates	610	0	0	
Drapery				475
Draper and damask work	875	0	0	
Dornix				500
Eels	1580	13	4	329
Feathers	1863	0	0	
Figs	5517	0	0	2823
Fish, salt	7996	0	0	1462
Flax	16 852	10	0	13 217

	1559			1565
	£	s.	d.	£
Fustian	23 349	10	0	27 254
Gawles	3611	0	0	
Ginger	1115	0	0	3000
Gingerbread	165	0	0	
Girdles	998	10	0	
Glasses:				
Looking	667	0	0	⎰1662
Drinking	663	10	0	⎱
Gloves	2636	10	0	
Grenes for women's apernes				
(aprons?)	3967	0	0	
Hats	7915	10	0	
Hatbands	109	13	4	269
Hemp	3288	10	0	4038
Herring				227
Herrings, white	1797	0	0	
Hops	16 925	0	0	? [2]
Inkhorns				154
Incle	8812	10	0	1860
Iron	19 559	10	0	6394
Iron, wrought				519
Knives	1558	0	0	362
Laces of all sorts	775	6	8	
Lemons and oranges	1756	0	0	
Linen cloth	61 673	13	4	86 250
Lings	3176	0	0	
Madder	11 135	0	0	12 133
Mares	930	0	0	
Marmalade	337	0	0	
Matches	466	13	4	
Meal	1340	0	0	
Mockado	3087	10	0	6400
Nails	5636	0	0	5730
Needles	471	10	0	
Nuts	58	0	0	
Nutmegs	677	16	8	1300
Oats	2121	0	0	
Onions	1489	10	0	523
Onion seed				770
Oil	38 020	13	4	39 377
Panyles	1648	0	0	
Paper	3304	0	0	3000
Pepper	11 852	0	0	27 000

[2] The figure beside hops is faded and illegible.

	1559			1565
	£	s.	d.	£
Pins	3297	0	0	4274[3]
Pitch and tar	3300	0	0	
Pots	627	13	4	316
Points of thread	234	0	0	400
Prunes	9405	15	0	4500
Raisins	9135	15	0	7325
Rings for children				60
Rods				258
Rods for baskets	129	13	4	
Ropes				2759
Ropes and cables	2303	10	0	
Rye	2728	0	0	
Sackcloth of thread	717	15	0	1600
Salmon	1387	0	0	
Salt	2943	0	0	3325
Sarcenet	1903	0	0	9934
Satins	3436	0	0	3264
Saws				259
Says	3630	0	0	
Sewing silk	7130	0	0	8004
Sipers	780			1672
Spanish skins and stanneys				3691
Skins	4838			
Skins of sable				800
Sables and other furs	3793			
Soap	9725	10	0	4422
Steel	2920	0	0	5007
Stockfish	2605	0	0	
Sugar	18 237	0	0	18 000
Taffeta	1632	16	8	3452
Tapestry	5405	16	8	5588
Thread	13 671	13	4	15 745
Ticks (for beds)	5939	0	0	4955
Trenchers				146
Velvet	8614	0	0	1292
Vinegar				1000
Wheat	9285	0	0	
Wines:				48 634
Gascoyne, French, Rochelle	36 210	0	0	
Malmsey and Muskadell	4905	0	0	
Rhenish	4340	0	0	
Sack	21 742	0	0	
Bastard	1257	10	0	
Wire	1375	0	0	2197

[3] The figure for pins is indistinct, and could be £4 374.

	1559			1565
	£	s.	d.	£
Woad	33 431	0	0	
Worsteds				18 374
Wormseed				192
Wool, Estrige wool voc. cotton wool, Spanish wool	5683	0	0	
Wool for hats				7469
Yarn				627

APPENDIX II. MISCELLANEOUS GOODS EXPORTED FROM LONDON, MICHAELMAS 1662 TO MICHAELMAS 1663

The list of exports given below has been compiled from that part of BM Add. MS. 36785, which is entitled 'An Accompt of the Several Goods and Merchandises of the Growth and Manufacture of England exported out of the City of London from Michaelmas 1662 to Michaelmas 1663'. Only miscellaneous wares, mostly manufactures, have been selected in order to illustrate the kind of goods that were being exported by the later seventeenth century. The list does not give an accurate idea of quantities, since some goods were exported in far greater quantity from the outports than from London, for example, horses.

Items in the original document, which are not noted in this list, include Old and New Draperies, leather skins of all kinds, lead, alabaster, coal, cereals, books, etc.

	Quantity		Value			
			£.	s.	d.	
Alum	1032	tons	19 842	0	0[1]	
Aqua vitae	8118	galls	2435	8	0	
(see also) +	204	tons	8160	0	0	} 10 615 8 0
strong waters) +	2	hogsheads	20	0	0	
Bandaleers[2]	155	hundred	775	0	0	
Barrel hoops	2273	thousand	1929	3	0	
Beer	568	tons	2272	0	0	
Bellows	60	doz.	45	0	0	
Birdlime	4	cwt.	13	0	0	
Brass, wrought	613	cwt.	55 455	0	0	
Bridles	138	doz.	207	0	0	
Butter	21 006	firkins	18 953	4	0	
Buttons	740	gross	111	0	0	
Hairbuttons	12	gross	1	16	0	
Candles	693	doz.	155	18	6	
Caps, Monmouth	3619	doz.	4343	9	0	
Cards, Wool	1325	doz.	1560	16	0	
Tow	92	doz.	138	0	0	
Cheese	378	cwt.	460	0	0	
Cloth, lists[3]	26 500	cwt.	3312	0	0	
purls[4]	310	doz.	46	10	0	
shreds[5]	18 086	lbs.	3165	1	0	

[1] This figure should almost certainly be £20 640. The value of alum sent to Scotland is underrated, if the quantity is correctly stated: 42 tons should have been valued at £840, not £42.

[2] Broad belts worn across the chest, originally to support a musket or cartridges.

[3] Edging strips or borders of cloth.

[4] Threads of gold or silver for decorative edgings or the edgings themselves.

[5] Fragments of cloth, probably tailors' and dressmakers' pieces.

	Quantity		Value £ s. d.						
Coaches	2		80	0	0				
Copper, wrought	2637	cwt.	25 051	10	0				
Copperas	247	tons	1784	0	0				
Cordage	1743	cwt.	2614	10	0				
Cushions	3	doz.	3	0	0				
Earthenware	1400	doz.	175	0	0	⎱	360	19	0
(see also sub glass)	+ 17 850	pieces	185	19	0	⎰			
Girdles, leather	856	gross	2568	0	0				
Glass and	3806	cwt.	3806	0	0	⎱	8481	0	0
earthenware	+ 36 700	doz.	4675	0	0	⎰			
Glass	57	chests	199	10	0				
Glass, window	47	chests	164	10	0				
Gloves, fringed	14	doz.	42	0	0				
leather	6747	doz.	3373	10	0				
wool	329	doz.	164	10	0				
worsted	80	doz.	60	0	0				
Glovers' clippings	4	maund	3	8	0				
Glue	172	cwt.	387	0	0				
Goose quills	10	thousand	3	6	0				
Grindstones	6	chald.	12	0	0				
Gunpowder	757	cwt.	2271	0	0	⎱	19 980	0	0
+	590	barrels	17 709	0	0	⎰			
Haberdashery	827	cwt.	24 760	0	0				
Harness, coach	63	sets	252	0	0				
Hats, beaver	97	doz.	2328	0	0				
castor[6]	844	doz.	6076	16	0				
felt	1565	doz.	5634	0	0				
Hops	395	cwt.	8382	10	0				
Horse collars	50		15	0	0				
Horses	37[7]		600	0	0				
Iron, wrought	3967	cwt.	5950	10	0				
Lace, gold and silver	1033	lbs.	3099	0	0				
Lampus	278	thousand	83	8	0				
Lanthorn leaves	1866	thousand	3265	10	0				
Lead, black	20	cwt.	15	0	0				
red and white	2806	cwt.	2104	0	0				
Leather, wrought	110	doz.	231	0	0				
+	1140	lbs.	200	0	0				
Linens, English	775	pieces	1937	10	0				
Linseed	65	qtrs.	211	5	0				
Morkins[8]	4078	cwt.	10 234	10	0				
Molasses	7	tons	105	0	0				
Nails	1234	cwt.	2468	0	0				
Oil	3	tons	96	0	0				
Oxbones	79	thousand	19	14	0				

[6] Originally of beaver, later of rabbit fur.
[7] This figure gives a totally false impression of the scale of horse exports. Many were shipped from outports like Dover and Sandwich.
[8] Carcasses of beasts dying by disease or accident.

	Quantity		Value		
			£	s.	d.
Oxcutts	105	barrels	157	10	0
Pewter	11 204	cwt.	4045	0	0
Paper	57	reams	28	10	0
Points, leather[9]	1309	gross	201	7	0
Rapecakes	2015	thousand	806	0	0
Saddles	522		399	15	0
Shoes[10]	4250	lbs.	10 187	12	0
	2250	doz.	1350	0	0
Shovels	86	doz.	77	8	0
Silk, thrown	3397	lbs.	3227	3	0
wrought	23 670	lbs.	53 256	15	0
Soap	89	cwt.	133	10	0
Socks, woollen	24	doz.	12	0	0
Starch	155	cwt.	193	15	0
Stockings:					
Children's woollen	11 897	doz.	7128	4	0
Children's worsted	4184	doz.	4184	0	0
Irish	303	doz.	227	5	0
Men's woollen	12 842	doz.	15 410	8	0
Men's worsted	23 351	doz.	48 552	10	0
Thread	127	doz.	190	10	0
Steel	12	cwt.	21	12	0
Strong waters	3605	galls.	1080	10	0
Sugar, refined	856	cwt.	4280	0	0
Thread, copper	3596	mark	359	12	0
Tin	3076	cwt.	11 535	0	0
Tobacco pipes	902	gross	67	13	0
Wax, bees	830	cwt.	5187	10	0
hard	10 693	lbs.	1688	7	6
Woad	172	cwt.	136	0	0

[9] Cords or laces.
[10] These were described as old shoes, and were being shipped to France.

INDEX